New York University Studies
in Near Eastern Civilization
Number XV

General Editor
Peter Chelkowski

ALSO IN THIS SERIES

Number I: F. E. Peters, *Aristotle and the Arabs*

Number II: Jacob M. Landau, *Jews in Nineteenth-Century Egypt*

Number III: Lois Anita Giffen, *Theory of Profane Love Among the Arabs: The Development of the Genre*

Number IV: Lewis V. Thomas, *A Study of Naima*, Norman Itkowitz, editor

Number V: Carl Max Kortepeter, *Ottoman Imperialism During the Reformation: Europe and the Caucasus*

Number VI: Linda Fish Compton, *Andalusian Lyrical Poetry and Old Spanish Love Songs: The Muwashshah and Its Kharja*

Number VII: Peter J. Chelkowski, *Ta'ziyeh: Ritual and Drama in Iran*

Number VIII: Arthur N. Young, *Saudi Arabia: The Making of a Financial Giant*

Number IX: Donald Quataert, *Social Disintegration and Popular Resistance in the Ottoman Empire, 1881–1908: Reactions to European Economic Penetration*

Number X: Tawfiq Al-Hakim, *The Return of Consciousness*, Bayly Winder, translator

Number XI: F. E. Peters, *Jerusalem and Mecca: The Typology of the Holy City in the Near East*

Number XII: Bruce Masters, *The Origins of Western Economic Dominance in the Middle East: Mercantilism and the Islamic Economy in Aleppo, 1600–1750*

Number XIII: Julian Baldick, *Mystical Islam: An Introduction to Sufism*

Number XIV: Martin Camaj, *Selected Poetry*, Leonard Fox, translator

New York University Studies in Near Eastern Civilization

The participation of the New York University Press in the University's commitment to Near Eastern Studies provides the American and international public with a greater diversity of exposure to professional perceptions of the Near East. Focusing on those various peoples, religions, arts, and cultures of the Near East who throughout the centuries have profoundly influenced and given form to mankind's most fundamental concepts and whose economic and political spheres have been wide reaching, this series, New York University Studies in Near Eastern Civilization, seeks, solicits, and publishes significant research in this ever vital area. The concept embraces many facets of the Near East, welcomes varied and even disparate interpretations as well as concentration on specific historical periods, including the whole spectrum of social scientific approaches. It is, moreover, particularly sensitive to work in two aspects of the area as a whole that reflect the University's expertise and concern, and that have perhaps received less attention than their excellence merits. These are literature and art. Again with the intention of widening the impact of New York University Press publications, the series welcomes translations of significant Near Eastern literature, as an integral part of its attempt to deepen and enrich the experience of Near Eastern thought, prose, and poetry, for an audience unacquainted with the original languages.

Peter Chelkowski
General Editor

Divorce in the Libyan Family

A study based on the *sijill*s of the *sharīʿa* courts of Ajdābiyya and Kufra

AHARON LAYISH

Foreword by
Norman Anderson

New York University Press, New York and London
The Magnes Press, The Hebrew University, Jerusalem

First Published in the U.S.A. by

NEW YORK UNIVERSITY PRESS,

Washington Square,

New York, NY 10003

Library of Congress Cataloging-in-Publication Data

Layish, Aharon, 1933-

Divorce in the Libyan Family: a study based on the sijills of the sharīʿa courts of Ajdābiyya and Kufra / Aharon Layish; Foreword by Norman Anderson.

p. cm. — (New York University Studies in Near Eastern civilization; no. 15)

Includes bibliographical references and index.

ISBN 0-8147-5053-2 (cloth)

1. Divorce (Islamic law)—Libya. 2. Customary Law—Libya.

I. Title. II. Series.

LAW

346.61201'66—dc20 90-19364

[346.1206166] CIP

Manufactured in Israel

In memoriam
Professor Noel J. Coulson

Contents

Foreword

I warmly welcome this careful, detailed and perceptive study of the way in which two *sharīʿa* courts in Libya deal with questions of divorce in an almost exclusively tribal, and still largely nomadic, environment. Professor Aharon Layish is uniquely qualified, by his previous studies and publications, to unravel and record the complex interplay of Islamic law and tribal customs in such areas.

In 1950 and 1951 I myself spent three months in East Africa, followed by three months in West Africa, doing a survey of the application of Islamic law in what were at that time British dependencies in Africa and in the Colony and Protectorate of Aden. This involved visits to what were then the administrations of Tanganyika, Zanzibar, Kenya, Uganda, Nyasaland, Somaliland and Aden in the east, and to Nigeria, the Gambia, the Gold Coast and Sierra Leone in the west. Several of these countries have, of course, changed their names since attaining independence; but when the survey (with the short title of *Islamic Law in Africa*) was reprinted in 1970, the original text was almost exclusively retained, together with its appendices on the then Anglo-Egyptian Sudan and on Immigrant Muslim Communities, etc.

In each of these territories there were, inevitably, distinctive blends of statutory, Islamic and customary law. A matter of particular interest to me was what the Qāḍīs, Liwalis and Alkalai—most of whom, fortunately, were able to converse with me in Arabic—told me about their work. But I also learnt a lot from British judges and administrative officers, from tribal heads (including some of the Emirs of Nigeria, whose courts had very extensive jurisdiction), from reported cases and from other documentary material. Most interesting of all, in the context of Professor Layish's book, were the conversations I had with some of the Alkalai of Nigeria—where, as in Libya, the Mālikī school of Islamic law prevails.

When questioned about the law relevant to a series of putative cases on which I consulted them, the Alkalai usually replied initially in terms of what I knew to be the dominant Mālikī doctrine; but when I pressed them about whether this was really the way in which they would, in practice, decide such a case, they sometimes told me a rather different story. This proved to be either a variant (and technically "weaker") opinion in the Mālikī school, which represented the practice (*ʿamal*) of *sharīʿa* courts in that region or, more simply, what was in reality a compromise between Islamic law and local customary law.

More relevant still to Professor Layish's book is the fact that the vast majority of divorces in Nigeria are at the instance of the wife. Those at the instance of the husband do not, of course, normally come to court; and where husbands do, in fact, desire a divorce, they commonly try to provoke their wives into taking action. A discontented wife in northern Nigeria can almost always get release from an unhappy marriage if she can provide suitable financial compensation, since a husband whose wife runs away and cannot be brought back by compulsion will normally agree to release her for a sum that would enable him to replace her. Sometimes a wife will be able to provide this from her own resources; but more often it will be supplied either by her guardian—who will hope for reimbursement out of the dower for another marriage he arranges for her, or (secretly) by another man who wants to marry her.

Cases like this, which are very common in Nigeria, were helped rather than caused by the British refusal to countenance the forcible return of runaway wives to their husbands; for it represents, in fact, an outstanding example of the triumph of customary law—under which a marriage can almost always be dissolved if the "bride-price" is returned—over the *sharīʿa*. It is also helped by the fact that Mālikī law, alone in Sunnī Islam, allows for compulsory *khulʿ* (release of the wife in consideration of a money payment), but only after two family arbitrators appointed by the court have recommended this solution.

Now, however, Professor Aharon Layish has investigated all the varieties of dissolution of marriage recorded in the *sijillāt* of the *sharīʿa* courts of Ajdābiyya and Kufra and has analyzed the part played, respectively, by *sharīʿa* law, customary law and some compromise between the two. He has done this, moreover, in such a comprehensive manner as to provide hard evidence on one point after another. And the value of this study is that its principles are by no means confined to the localities on which he has concentrated in such meticulous detail, for it throws much light on the way in which the authority of *sharīʿa* law habitually tends to impinge on tribal or local customs in such areas, on the one hand, and how Muslim courts, on the other hand, try to adapt the principles of the *sharīʿa* to the exigencies of the local situation.

Norman Anderson
O.B.E., Q.C., LL.D., F.B.A.

Acknowledgments

This book was begun in late 1986, when I spent my sabbatical at Eliot College, University of Kent at Canterbury, and was completed in Jerusalem. It could not have been achieved without the strenuous efforts of the anthropologist Professor John Davis, who took photographs of tens of thousands of legal documents from the archives of the *sharīʿa* courts of Ajdābiyya and Kufra and stored them in his study at Eliot College. I learned of the existence of those documents through a note in BBRISMES.[1] When I expressed interest, Davis invited me to work on them, and he willingly and unreservedly placed them at my disposal—although we had not known each other previously. I wish to thank him most heartily for this rare generosity. Davis has been researching Libyan society for years, and his professional advice and guidance have been freely given at every stage of my work, for which, too, thanks are due. It is to be hoped that our common interest in the subject will lead to further fruitful cooperation. A selection we have prepared of some 160 documents from the archives of the two courts, in Arabic, has already appeared; it is intended for advanced students in various fields.[2] The next step will be the publication of an English translation of several dozen documents out of that selection, with notes relating to the legal and social aspects.

It was Professor Barry Hooker, a specialist in the Islamic law of South East Asia, who encouraged me to come to Canterbury and placed his study, with its large library, at my disposal for the duration of his stay abroad. On his return, Hooker helped me clarify various legal problems. For all this, I am most grateful.

D. Morgan, dean of the Faculty of Social Sciences, Dr. Shirley A. Barlow, master of Eliot College, and Dr. C. W. Watson of the Centre of South-East

1. Davis, *Note.*
2. Layish & Davis.

Asian Studies jointly invited me to be a visiting professor and a member of Eliot College, which enabled me to concentrate undisturbed on my research, far from the Middle Eastern turmoil. The secretarial staff of the college—the secretarial supervisor Yvonne Latham, as well as Linda Williams and Jo Snow—were very courteous and efficient in providing technical aid. The library of the University of Kent and particularly its Inter-Library Loan Department greatly assisted me in obtaining the necessary specialized literature. To all these, I am much indebted.

After my return to Jerusalem, my research was supported by the Fund for Basic Research administered by the Israel Academy of Sciences and Humanities, which support I am very pleased to acknowledge. Thanks are also due to the Hebrew University of Jerusalem as well as to the Hagop Kevorkian Center for Near Eastern Studies, New York University, for their financial help in the publication of this book.

My student Ron Shaham, who is preparing a doctoral dissertation based on the Egyptian *sijill*s, has greatly helped me at various stages of the work. Isaac Hollander, another student, has been of great help in preparing the Index and the Glossary of Arabic Legal and Technical Terms. Sara Modena, a law student at the Hebrew University, has ably assisted me by translating, from the Italian, legal literature relating to Libya. I owe sincere thanks to all of them.

The books and articles of Professor Sir Norman Anderson were an endless source of inspiration and provided me with a valuable basis for making comparisons. His *Islamic Law in Africa* contains information that is both qualitatively and quantitatively impressive on the confrontation between the various schools of the *sharīʿa*, and custom in some African countries when under British rule. I was privileged to hear his lectures while a research student at the School of Oriental and African Studies of the University of London, and he kindly took time off to join me in wrestling with methodological problems involved in research on the *sijill* and to write a foreword to this book.

My friend and colleague Professor Frank H. Stewart of the Jacob Blaustein Institute for Desert Research at the Ben-Gurion University of the Negev, an anthropologist who works on Beduin customary law, has stood by me for about ten years now in all my researches relating to that subject. His uncompromising strictness and precision have restrained, sometimes ruthlessly, any tendency on my part to be led to intuitive but unwarranted conclusions. He has helped me not only by his invaluable advice but also by supplying me with literature on tribal law in North Africa and the Middle East from his copious private library. Moreover, he read the manuscript of this book and made valuable comments. For all this, he deserves my profound gratitude. However, it goes without saying that I alone am responsible for any errors that may have remained.

My thanks go also to my teacher and colleague Pessah Shinar, Emeritus Professor of Islamic Civilization at the Hebrew University, a world-renowned authority on contemporary Maghribī Islam, who has been most helpful with bibliographical hints and in other ways. His *Islam maghrébin contemporain: Bibliographie annotée* (Paris, 1983) is an indispensable tool for any student of present-day North African Islam.

Special thanks are due also to Dr. Menahem Eichelberg. In this instance, as well as on earlier occasions, he has with devotion and diligence translated my work, contributing to the elucidation of complex matters and to their presentation in simple, easily intelligible form. He has worked with me for about twenty years now, and this seems an opportune moment to thank him for his unfailing cooperation.

I am most grateful to Professor Peter Chelkowski, director of the Hagop Kevorkian Center for Near Eastern Studies, for including this book in the Series "New York University Studies in Near Eastern Civilization" and for his untiring efforts to bring about its publication jointly by the Magnes Press of Jerusalem and New York University Press.

Evelyn Katrak has painstakingly edited the manuscript of this book and improved it in many respects, for which I am profoundly grateful. Sincere thanks are due also to the Magnes Press, and particularly to director Dan Benovici, for his invaluable help and advice. The printers, Kesset Ltd., assigned Sami A. Salman to this book, and he has done a very competent job. Grateful mention should also be made of Shira Twersky-Cassel, who so conscientiously typed the material.

Lastly, it remains for me to thank my wife, Bilha, who typed the first draft and continually encouraged me to persevere and bring the work to its conclusion.

This book is dedicated to the late Professor Noel Coulson, holder of the Chair of Oriental Laws, who in the last few years before his untimely death in August 1986 was head of the Department of Law at the School of Oriental and African Studies, and dean of the Faculty of Laws of the University of London. Originally an Orientalist, Coulson took up law for purposes of research. This combination accounts for his professional legal approach together with his openness to historical and social aspects. In fact the unique virtue of his handling of Islamic law lies in his attempt to bridge the gap between two schools, the Orientalist and the legal. The former treats law as a medium to explore the spirit of Islamic civilization, seeing law as a series of formal patterns reflecting cultural and social norms in their historical development. The latter treats Islamic law as a self-contained entity, seeking to study it as an operative system applied in everyday life throughout the Muslim world. Coulson's books are an instructive effort to synthesize the two schools; historical analysis is combined with illustrations from the various departments of law at a very high professional-technical level. Already in his lifetime, Coulson's books became standard works and a constant source of inspiration to scholars in various fields, as well as for legal practitioners.

The passing, while still in his prime, of one of the great present-day experts in Islamic law is a universal loss.[3] For me it is also a personal loss. I took my first steps in the tangle of Islamic law under the guidance of Noel Coulson and was encouraged by him in my studies in innumerable ways. This book is inscribed to the memory of a devoted teacher and faithful friend.

Jerusalem, August 1990 | Aharon Layish

3. See obituary by I. Edge in *BSOAS*, vol. 50, pt. 3 (1987): 532–35.

Preface

Research into modern Libyan society is mainly anthropological. Evans-Pritchard's excellent work has revealed to the Western reader the social organization of the Sanūsī revivalist movement, out of which modern Libya has emerged. Further social studies have appeared in its wake, each of which has made an important contribution to the elucidation of some aspect of Libyan society.[1] No systematic, comprehensive research has so far been carried out on the basis of the *sijill*s of the *sharīʿa* courts, although the *sijill*s have in some places been preserved for centuries past (e.g., in Tripoli since the seventeenth century);[2] the reasons for this are both objective (difficulty of access by Western scholars) and subjective (the need for Islamistic and legal training).

It is unnecessary to dwell at length on the importance of the *sijill* as a source for research. It is sufficient to note Milliot's impressive discovery of the Mālikī *ʿamal* (judicial practice) reflected in the decisions of the *sharīʿa* courts of the late Middle Ages.[3] The *sijill* is a first-rate source also of social information on the family and other spheres under the jurisdiction of the *sharīʿa* courts, because of the readiness of the parties to expose themselves without inhibition to the homely *sharʿī* authority even as regards the most intimate matters. The *qāḍī*s record the social data in their decisions candidly, without considering that the *sijill* may some day be used for purposes of research; candor is of course essential to the credibility of the information, and it is not always possible to obtain it through other methods of research. In fact, in the past generation there has been a revolutionary breakthrough in the utilization of the *sijill*, as far as it has been preserved in various Middle Eastern countries, for purposes of

1. See "Secondary Sources."
2. Abou El-Haj, pp. 309–10.
3. Berque and the sources indicated there.

historical, social, and legal research; and it seems that the process is only just beginning. Awareness of the importance of the *sijill* exists, and all that is required is to equip researchers with the necessary linguistic and disciplinary tools so as to enable them to cope successfully with the documentary material.[4]

The purpose of this book is to describe and analyze, from the angle of the *sharīʿa* court, divorce in a tribal society in process of sedentarization, against the background of the contest between *sharīʿa* and custom. Divorce according to the Mālikī school has special characteristics that distinguish it from divorce according to other schools existing in the Middle East, and in view of the quality and quantity of the material in the Cyrenaican *sijill*s, it deserves a separate study. Unfortunately, the material at my disposal on other subjects of personal status and succession is not sufficient to permit extending the scope of the present study in this direction.

John Davis, who has collected the documentary material from the Cyrenaican *sijill*s, intends to computerize the social data on marriage and divorce contained in marriage contracts and divorce certificates, for the purpose of quantitatively processing and analyzing correlations between the different variables with the tools of the anthropological method in which he specializes. His research will draw on the rich experience he gained through field work in Libya. I am certain that Davis will make a very important contribution to the knowledge of various aspects of the Libyan family. Cyrenaican society is in a period of transition: the sedentarization of the Beduin, the development of a new economic and class differentiation, and the abolition of the Sanūsī order are lessening the individual's dependence on the tribe and on the Sanūsī religious brotherhood, which were interlocked. However, in the nature of things, the normative values rooted in the traditional loyalties change more slowly and are preserved in new social frameworks.

The *sharīʿa* court is the foremost meeting-place between normative Islam, represented by the *qāḍī*, and the social reality reflecting norms of tribal customary law. The contest between the two norms, the *sharʿī* and the customary, is the essence of this book. The divorce theme is not only an end in itself but also a means to assess the interaction between the *sharīʿa* in its Mālikī version and the customs of a tribal society in process of sedentarization. I am of course aware that the *sijill* does not reflect social

4. Mandaville, *Jerusalem*; Mandaville, *Syria & Jordan*; Layish, *Sijill*; Doumani.

reality in full. Thus, for example, the determination, by a succession order of the court, of a woman's *sharʿī* rights in an estate is not in itself evidence that she realizes her rights; for in everyday reality there are many ways of circumventing the *sharʿī* law of succession, either in or out of court.[5] As we shall see, even a study based on the *sijill* is not free from methodological problems.[6] Nevertheless, it is difficult to imagine a better source than the *sijill* for the subject of our study. The *qāḍī*, more than any other religious-legal functionary, is in daily confrontation with a population nurtured on custom, and it is he who actually determines the scheme of relations between the *sharīʿa*, with the application of which he is charged, and custom, which is supported by those resorting to his jurisdiction. The *muftī*, on the other hand, is entrenched in his ivory tower; he does not interfere in the matter of relations between *sharīʿa* and custom unless a litigant or the *qāḍī* requests him to give an opinion on a controversial subject. In any case his opinion binds no one; the *qāḍī*'s judgment alone is binding. Nor does juristic literature, based mainly on casuistic reasoning, necessarily reflect social reality.

Experience gained by research during the past twenty years has greatly helped me to cope with the complex subject of this book. My studies on the *sijill*s of the *sharīʿa* and Druze courts in Israel deal quite particularly with the interrelation between religious and customary law in the fields of personal status and succession. My research, for about ten years now, on legal documents of the Beduin in the Judean Desert, covering a wide range of subjects besides personal status and succession, focuses almost exclusively on this aspect. Study of the Cyrenaican *sijill* may add a new regional dimension to my experience and deepen my acquaintance with the Mālikī school, which in the Middle East is mainly reflected through the prism of legal reform in matters of personal status in the modern era. I have already had a fascinating opportunity—in my reliance on selected documents from the *sijill* of Tangier—to study the Mālikī school when carrying out research on the family *waqf* as a means to circumvent the law of succession.[7]

The methodological peculiarity of the present work lies in the attempt to utilize the plentiful material contained in the decisions of the *sharīʿa* courts

5. E.g., Layish, *Women*, pp. 290ff.; Layish, *Druze*, pp. 337ff.
6. See below, Introduction, pp. 1–4.
7. Layish, *Mālikī waqf*.

for the purposes of sociolegal analysis. This book is largely structured on the pattern of my earlier books, with a view to facilitating occasional comparisons with regard to various subjects. The Introduction deals with the conceptual framework, with methodological problems involved in research of this kind, and with the changes undergone by the *sharʿī* judicial system as to jurisdiction and material law, from the late Ottoman era via the periods of Italian rule and the independent Sanūsī state until the abolition of the *sharīʿa* courts by Qadhdhāfī's revolutionary regime. The reform in matters of personal status was modest and was carried out only in the early 1970s; in any event, it is not reflected in the decisions of the courts until their abolition. The Introduction also contains basic data on social conditions in Ajdābiyya and Kufra.

The present volume consists of two unequal parts: a systematic sociolegal description of divorce in its various aspects (chapters I–VI) and an integrative analysis of the findings in the context of the interaction between *sharīʿa* and custom (chapter VII). The first part deals with the causes of divorce; unilateral divorce; divorce by consent; judicial divorce on *sharʿī* grounds, which is peculiar to the Mālikī school; and the legal and financial consequences of divorce. Chapter VI, the final chapter of the first part, deals with the attitude of the *qāḍī*s toward each of the subtopics discussed in the preceding chapters. Each chapter opens with a short introduction, intended to clarify the legal terms and institutions relevant to the subject at hand. These introductions serve the purposes of the subsequent social analysis. Anyone wishing to inquire more thoroughly into the legal aspect of the issue involved will do well to turn to the sources indicated in the Notes and especially to Linant de Bellefonds' excellent comparative study of the law of the different schools.[8]

The analysis of the social findings is qualitative, not quantitative; however, with regard to some essential subjects, I have permitted myself to make quantitative assessments on the basis of the cumulative impression gained from the findings. A minute analysis of the findings will, as stated, be made by John Davis after he has computerized them. The selected documents from the *sijill*s of the *sharīʿa* courts cover a period of some forty years, until the early 1970s. Although during that long time some changes may have occurred in Kufra and Ajdābiyya as to various aspects of divorce, I have found no indication of them in the *sijill*s. This may be due to the fact

8. Linant, *Traité*.

that the *qāḍīs* in their decisions tend to blur custom in its various manifestations and to couch it in *sharʿī* terms.[9] Under these circumstances, the picture arising from the *sijill*s is static, not subject to the time factor.

The second part of the book (chapter VII) attempts to survey the interaction between *sharīʿa* and custom integratively and to analyze its significance in assessing the status of normative Islam in a tribal society in process of sedentarization. This part deals successively with instances of the supremacy of custom outside the control of the *sharīʿa*, the impact of the *sharīʿa* on the Beduin in process of sedentarization, and the role of the *qāḍīs* in the Islamization of a tribal society in process of sedentarization. The last involves a wide scale of grades: from compromise with custom, to assimilation of custom with the *sharīʿa*, to adjustment of the *sharīʿa* with social reality, to absolute rejection of custom and attempts to enforce the *sharīʿa*.

The book seeks to maintain a suitable balance between legal discussion and social analysis so as to bring it close to readers from different fields: Orientalists, Islamists, social scientists, and lawyers interested in Islamic and comparative law.

The Notes give only abbreviated titles of the sources adduced in the book. A list of the full titles of the archival sources and another of the full titles of the books and articles used as secondary sources (alphabetized according to authors' names) appear in the Bibliography.

Arabic technical and legal terms are given in exact scientific transliteration (except for the forms *walī* and *waṣī*) to facilitate their location in dictionaries and professional literature. They are explained on their first occurrence in the relevant chapters. Reference should also be made in this connection to the Index and the Glossary of Arabic Legal Terms at the end of the book.

9. See below, Introduction, pp. 2–3.

Introduction

a. Conceptual Framework and Methodological Problems

This study does not deal with the theory of Islamic law but with its practical application or, more exactly, with the encounter of *sharīʿa* and custom. The media for this purpose are the *sijill*s of the *sharīʿa* courts. The Libyan *sijill*s are unique in that the *sharīʿa* court in that country is the meeting-place *par excellence* of the *sharīʿa* in its Mālikī version, on the one hand, and the custom of a tribal society with remnants of the Sanūsī order, on the other. The Mālikī school, dominant in North Africa, shows special characteristics in matters of divorce (and succession), which are tantamount to a complete departure from the legal systems of other Sunnī schools. Moreover, the Mālikī school, probably because of its tribal background in Medina, where it grew and consolidated, tends more than any other school to compromise with custom and has developed sophisticated mechanisms for this purpose, the most important of which is *maṣlaḥa*, the public interest. There is, of course, a close connection between social custom and the public interest.

John Davis photographed tens of thousands of legal documents from the *sijill*s of the *sharīʿa* courts of Kufra and Ajdābiyya. The documents cover, though not completely, a period extending from 1932 in the case of Kufra and from 1942 in the case of Ajdābiyya until the abolition of the *sharīʿa* courts in 1973 (until the late 1970s as regards marriage contracts).[1] They deal mostly with matters of marriage and divorce and to a lesser extent with succession, civil claims, contracts, and property.[2] The documents from the period of Italian rule are in Maghribī Arabic. The writing in some documents is blurred or obliterated owing to wear and tear or from other causes; because of various constraints, not all the documents have been

1. For more details see Davis, *Note*; Davis, *Koufra*, p. 563.
2. For specimens of these documents see Layish & Davis.

photographed, and in some instances documents are partly missing or have not been photographed in their entirety. The *sharīʿa* court issues documents of various kinds: judgments (as in matters of maintenance and divorce); orders (succession and guardianship); minutes (*maḥḍar*), which are a kind of abstract, arranged in columns, of the findings and the judgment (a kind of certificate of divorce);[3] and statements—based on "transfer of testimony" (*shahādat naql*) concerning a factual situation—as to financial and other rights. The *qāḍī* "allows" (*ajāza*) the testimony after a particular procedure aimed at the *sharʿī* identification of the witnesses and the ascertainment of their credibility to his satisfaction.[4] The documents are usually short, couched in stereotyped phraseology; reasons for the decisions are not stated, and there are almost no references to *sharʿī* literature.

It goes without saying that the *sijill*s of those two courts do not reflect the reality of the whole of Libya; nor are they—owing to the location of the two towns, especially Kufra, in remote districts, far from the administrative centers—representative of the whole of Cyrenaica as to the type of settlement or in other respects. To complete the picture, albeit fragmentarily, the author has made use of a study based on the decisions of the Sharīʿa Supreme Court in Tripoli, the highest appellate court in Libya. The appeals are from judgments rendered by *sharīʿa* courts in various towns of the Province of Tripoli in the period of Italian rule.[5]

However, the most serious difficulty facing the author was a methodological one: how to distinguish, in the court documents, between *sharīʿa* and custom. The main problem is that the legal terms in the two systems are fairly similar, especially in the fields of personal status, succession, and homicide and assault (which are conceived of as falling under the law of torts). Customary law was adopted into Islam in the formative period, moderated by religious-ethical norms. In modern times, the interaction is in the opposite direction: Islamic legal terms and institutions penetrate into customary law when Beduin settle down.[6]

3. E.g., KD59–73, K47: p. 42 no. 77 22 Oct. 65.
4. E.g., A:E102, p. 27 no. 52 8 Sep. 51; A:E104, p. 230 no. 380 23 July 53; AP:E3, p. 340 no. 589 5 July 54; AP:E3, p. 342 no. 581 6 July 54.
5. d'Emilia, p. 15 n. 1, p. 16; Abou El-Haj, pp. 309–10.
6. Schacht, *Introduction*, pp. 77, 186; Coulson, *History*, pp. 9–10, 15–16, 23; Layish, *Judaean Desert*; Layish, *Challenges*, pp. 212ff.; Layish, *Islamization*, pp. 43ff.; Layish & Shmueli; pp. 41ff.

The *sharʿī qāḍī* is not helpful here; on the contrary, he aggravates the situation in that his smooth formulations tend to blur the customary origin of everyday practice. From earlier research, the author knows that the parties to a dispute are inspired by custom and that their knowledge of and familiarity with Islamic law are extremely limited. They formulate their arguments in simple language, in colloquial Arabic, without order or method; they usually employ no advocates; if there is a representative acting on their behalf, he is mostly an agnate without any legal education or training. The *qāḍī* sums up the arguments of the parties and the factual findings, using *sharʿī* technical terms that, in the nature of things, blur or obliterate the customary norms. In this sense the *sijill*s do not reflect the actual position. Charnay, whose study on Algeria is based on decisions of French courts of cassation in appeals from judgments of *sharīʿa* courts, notes that the social data are not an end in themselves but are designed to serve the legal process. The present author is unfortunately not able to grapple with this problem by attending court sessions or questioning *qāḍī*s, orally or in writing, to clarify the position (as he was wont to do in similar circumstances in earlier research). However, this problem is not strange to the scholar dealing with documentary material of past periods, which does not permit contacting by conventional means the originators of the documents. To all this must be added a further difficulty, which has been observed by Milliot in North Africa—namely, identification of the customary norm where it is different from region to region, fluid, changing, not finally molded. There are no collections of customary laws for this area in Arabic. The author had a similar difficulty in identifying some customary norms peculiar to the Druze community and in distinguishing them from religious-legal norms, which in turn are esoteric. The Druze *qāḍī*s, in their decisions, make a special effort to render the distinction more difficult, probably for reasons of *taqiyya*.[7]

The method proposed by the author for the distinction between *sharīʿa* and custom in the Libyan *sijill*s may be described as sociolegal. According to that method, which has been intensively applied in a study on legal documents of arbitrators in the Judean Desert, a legal term appearing in a document does not in itself indicate its identity and origin. Its connotations should be very carefully examined, having regard to its social content,

7. Charnay, pp. 9, 13; Milliot, pp. 159–160; Colucci, *Tribù*, pp. 24–25; Layish, *Druze*, pp. xx–xxi, 376ff., 383; Layish *Taqiyya*, pp. 257ff.

which in some essential respects is quite different in the two systems, the *sharʿī* and the customary. Thus, for instance, the terms *ṣadāq* and *mahr* mean dower in both systems; in fact, they passed into the *sharīʿa* from custom. Now in a marriage under customary law, the bride is not a party to the contract and the dower is, accordingly, the property of her guardian, an agnate; but under the *sharīʿa* the woman is a party to the marriage contract and the dower is, therefore, *her* property—a kind of consideration for the lawful maintenance of marital relations. In other words, when meeting the term "dower" in the *sijill*s, we must, in order to establish its *sharʿī* or customary identity, examine who is entitled to the dower or, more exactly, who actually receives it. Anderson, whose book on Islamic law in Africa was a source of inspiration in the writing of this study, confirms the validity of this method in his reliance on his scholarly experience of the encounter of *sharīʿa* and custom throughout Africa.[8]

b. Legal Background

(1) **The judicial system.** In the last third of the nineteenth century, following the establishment of direct Ottoman rule in Cyrenaica and the proclamation of that region as a separate sanjak controlled directly from Istanbul, the judicial system was reorganized. The judicial and the executive authority were separated, and a dual—secular and religious—system was set up. Courts for civil and criminal matters were established by the side of the *sharīʿa* courts. The *sharīʿa* courts had jurisdiction in matters of personal status, succession, and *waqf*. The courts were organized at two levels: first instance and appeals.[9]

On the conquest of Libya from the Ottoman Empire, the Italians declared that they would maintain the *sharīʿa* courts and the Islamic law applied in them. In the Lausanne Treaty of 1912 it was agreed between the parties to grant a special status to Libya, combining recognition of the Italian sovereign with recognition of the Ottoman sultan as the spiritual-religious caliph of the Muslim community (although the sultan was not, of course, a *sharʿī* authority). The sultan appointed a representative (*nāʾib al-sulṭān*), whose task was to watch over the application of the *sharīʿa* in matters of worship, personal status, and *waqf*. The sultan assumed the title of "religious head" and wished to retain the power to appoint *qāḍī*s

8. Interview with Prof. Anderson at Cambridge on 21 August 1987; Anderson, *Africa*.
9. Anderson, L., pp. 327, 330–31.

throughout Libya. Although the peace treaty provided that an Ottoman *qāḍī* should be appointed, the Italians, for political reasons, did not allow his appointment; they explained their refusal, *inter alia*, by pointing out that the Ottoman candidate belonged to the Ḥanafī school while most of the population were adherents of the Mālikī. The Ottomans, in accordance with their practice in other parts of the empire, conceded that the Ḥanafī *qāḍī* should have Mālikī deputies familiar with local custom. The London Treaty of 1915 abrogated the post of *nā'ib* and all the privileges of the sultan. In 1924 the caliphate was abolished in Turkey, so the question of its status in Libya ceased to be relevant.[10]

The Italian regime wished to acquire the image of a "defender of Islam"; it built mosques, restored the tombs of saints (while prohibiting manifestations of extreme asceticism on the part of religious orders) as well as *zāwiya*s (except those of the Sanūsī order), established a religious college in Tripoli, permitted the *ḥajj*, and even forbade the sale of alcohol in the month of Ramaḍān. Evans-Pritchard estimates that the Italians wished to combine political rule with social justice, avoiding both the British system of a colonial ruling class shunning all contact with the natives and the French system aimed at cultural assimilation and social and political equality with the *évolués*; the Italian system was somewhere in the middle; it was careful on the one hand not to interfere with either Islamic or tribal law and on the other sought to mitigate and refine them by European legal-ethical norms. The Italians preserved that dual judicial system (religious and secular) and maintained the judicial and organizational autonomy of the *sharī'a* courts; but at the same time they sought to retain a certain measure of control over the decisions of the *qāḍī*s and some ingredients of sovereignty. The validity of the *qāḍī*s' judgments was conditional on the exequatur of the president of the Italian court, whose supervisory power was however confined to ensuring that the *qāḍī* did not exceed his jurisdiction and that the judgment was not contrary to public policy.[11] In actual fact the *sharī'a* courts wielded very wide powers; besides matters of personal status, succession, and *waqf*, the *sijill* comprises judgments and orders dealing with civil claims, contracts and property, "criminal" matters (homicide, assault), and so on—matters that theoretically were at

10. Cicchitti, pp. 482ff.; Simon, pp. 80, 83–84.

11. Evans-Pritchard, pp. 203–4, 208ff.; Bousquet, *Islamic & Customary Law*, p. 63 n. 8; Nelsen, p. 193.

the time amenable to the civil courts. This may have been a carryover from the period of Ottoman rule at a time when the reforms of the judicial system had not yet been put into practice. It should further be noted that the civil courts were authorized to refer civil claims of Libyan nationals to the *sharīʿa* courts. Davis says that in Kufra it was not unusual for civil claims to be brought before the *sharīʿa* court because the civil courts system was not fixed and institutionalized.[12] Anyhow under the Italian administration, and probably owing to its supervision, the *sharīʿa* courts came to deal only with personal status, succession, and *waqf*, which alone were in their jurisdiction.

Regard for public policy means normative supervision in accordance with Western standards. For instance, judgments of *sharīʿa* courts recognizing an extended period of pregnancy (anchored in the Mālikī school) and fixing the paternity of an illegitimate child were for reasons of public policy not carried out, just as judgments concerning purchases and sales were not carried out because obligations were outside the jurisdiction of the *sharīʿa* courts.[13] Judgments of the court of Kufra of the early 1930s contain a rather detailed abstract of the judgment, in Italian, followed by the remark "Seen. To be carried out!" and the signature of "the Military Governor of the Kufra Areas"—indicating that there was no normative or other obstacle to the execution of the judgment. The principle of public policy was already established in Italian legislation of 1882 that enjoined respect for all religious beliefs and rites, provided they did not conflict with universal morality and public policy. That principle also guided the League of Nations when entrusting mandates for certain countries to various powers.[14] The *sharīʿa* court was accustomed—and probably instructed—to demonstrate recognition of the Italian sovereign by prefacing documents with the formula "In the time of His Majesty King Victor Emmanuel III, may God long protect him and strengthen him by perpetual victory."[15] In the early 1930s a "deputy" (*nāʾib al-qāḍī*) carried out judicial functions in the *sharʿī* system, besides the *qāḍī*.[16] This too seems to have been a carryover from Ottoman days, when "deputies" of the Turkish *qāḍī* were appointed

12. Cicchitti, p. 485; Davis, *Koufra*, p. 558.
13. d'Emilia, p. 16 n. 2, p. 17. On *ḥaml nāʾim* see below, p. 112, 161, 187.
14. E.g., B2:KM38-43:EA, K4a: no. 7 5 Aug. 32, no. 8 6 Aug. 32, no. 9 [?] Aug. 32, no. 11 17 Sep. 32, no. 12 19 Sep. 32; Cicchitti, pp. 475–78.
15. E.g., KAMD, p. 29 no. 11 16 Feb. 34.
16. E.g., B2:KM38-43:EA, K4a: no. 1 4 July 32.

from among the local population. The judge is sometimes called "Inspector" (*mufattish*)[17] or a "responsible person" (*mas'ūl*)[18]—which seems to refer to the head of the *sharʿī* division of the summary court of Kufra. The marriage solemnizer in Kufra also had certain judicial powers, *inter alia* in divorce matters; but his judgments required the approval of the *mufattish* or *qāḍī*.[19]

In the reign of King Idrīs, which began with independence in 1952, Libya had a dual (civil plus *sharʿī*) judicial system. The *sharīʿa* courts retained sole jurisdiction in matters of personal status, succession, and *waqf*. In 1954 the *sharīʿa* courts were incorporated into the civil courts system. This move was inspired by ʿAbd al-Razzāq al-Sanhūrī, the architect of the civil code in Egypt and other Arab countries. It was expected that the *sharʿī qāḍī*s would take the place of the foreign judges and become the dominant factor in the civil courts system. However, in view of strong public criticism the former position was restored in 1958. In November 1973 the *sharīʿa* courts system was again abolished and its powers were transferred to the civil courts system, which was patterned on the Western model. The court of first instance, consisting of three judges, was empowered to deal with matters that were previously under the jurisdiction of the *sharīʿa* courts. *Sharʿī qāḍī*s who in the past had served on the Sharīʿa Court of Appeal were now to sit on the ordinary courts of appeal, and judgments concerning personal status, succession, or *waqf* were now appealable to one of the five chambers (with benches of five) of the Supreme Court, whose seat is in Tripoli. To justify this reform, the government argued that a dual courts system was inappropriate, since the law in Libya was in any case based on the *sharīʿa*.[20] As will become evident, this argument, seemingly based on the reinstatement of Islamic law in Libya, does not reflect the real facts. The Libyan government seems to have expected that the civil judges, trained in Western law, would apply Islamic law according to the principles familiar to them. The source of inspiration for the reform seems to have been Egypt, which a few years after the military coup abolished the *sharīʿa* courts and transferred their powers to the national courts, which were to apply Islamic substantive law by the side of civil rules of evidence and

17. E.g., KD59–73, K47: p. 41 no. 78 9 May 60; KM63DP:EP, p. 50 no. 95 6 July 60.
18. E.g., KD59–73, K50: p. 131 no. 270 11 July 62; p. 48 no. 90 12 Dec. 65.
19. E.g., KD59–73, K44: p. 1 no. 1 7 June 59, K48: p. 7 no. 14 28 July 59, K45: p. 79 no. 154 11 March 61, K48: p. 85 no. 166 25 April 61, K50: p. 90 no. 175 18 May 61.
20. Nelsen, pp. 193–94; Qasem, pp. 135–36; Mayer, *Resurgence*, p. 198; Mayer, *Criminal law*, p. 21 and the source indicated in n. 30; Mayer, *Livre vert*, p. 7; Harris, pp. 16, 20 n. 6.

procedure. The Egyptian government expected the burden of introducing reforms in matters of personal status to be shifted from the legislators to the national courts.[21] In any case, this study is based solely on decisions of the *sharīʿa* courts.

Evans-Pritchard notes that under Italian rule the Beduin resorted to the *sharīʿa* courts to only a very limited extent, as they preferred to settle their affairs according to tribal custom. In the early 1970s they still resorted to the *sharīʿa* courts and the tribal courts concurrently. Davis notes that the *sharīʿa* courts were preferred especially by people whose position in traditional society was weak and who therefore could not realize their rights under the tribal customary system. Thus the *sharīʿa* courts were resorted to by divorced women who had been denied their financial rights or by heirs who regarded themselves as deprived of their rightful share in the estate. They expected the *sharīʿa* courts to determine their rights by judgment or by enforceable orders.[22] In fact the matter of enforcement is strongly emphasized in the judgments of the *sharīʿa* courts. Thus in judgments for divorce, the *qāḍī* orders the husband to pay what is due to the wife and winds up with the words: "[Given as] a *sharʿī* judgment including immediate enforcement (*nafādh muʿajjal*) and coercion (*ilzām*) of the defendant [husband]." Charnay stresses that, unlike the French judge, the *qāḍī* is an agent charged with the enforcement of *sharʿī* judgments and his status is similar to that of a notary.[23]

The importance of court documents in the eyes of the Beduin becomes apparent in cases in which a civil claim was settled by the *sharīʿa* court and the *qāḍī* determined the rights involved, winding up saying: "For this purpose [the decision] has been written down and registered" (*fali-ajlihi ṣāra taḥrīruhu wa-tasjīluhu*). A similar formula occurs in documents of Beduin of the Judean Desert written by tribal arbitrators under similar circumstances. Written documents intended to establish the responsibility of the "vengeance group" to practice blood vengeance are common among the Awlād ʿAlī.[24] Tribal arbitrators were resorted to concurrently with the

21. Mayer, *Criminal law*, p. 23; Schacht & Layish, pp. 24–25; Layish, *Contribution*, pp. 271ff.

22. Evans-Pritchard, p. 204; Davis, *Politics*, p. 223. On resort to the *sharīʿa* court in matters of divorce see below, III7, IV3.

23. E.g., KD59–73, p. 123 no. 261 23 June 62, K44: p. [131] no. [291] 20 Aug. 62; Charnay, pp. 276–77.

24. E.g., B2:KM38–43:EA, K4a: no. 11 17 Sep. 32, K4a: no. 19 15 Feb. 33; Layish, *Judaean Desert*; Mohsen, *Conflict*, pp. 31–34.

civil courts system, which in Kufra, as stated, was not fixed and institutionalized. This was encouraged by the police, which regarded customary proceedings as a simple and effective mechanism to dispense justice.[25] In some cases, such as renunciation divorces, a representative of the government, a commissioned officer of police, was present at these proceedings.[26]

In Libya a judgment of a *sharīʿa* court of first instance is appealable to the Supreme Court (*al-maḥkama al-ʿulyā*), which was established in 1929 and was designed to replace the two supreme *sharīʿa* appeal tribunals—in Tripoli and Benghazi—established in the early 1920s.[27] But the author has seen no decisions of the Supreme Court; as might be expected, the *sijill*s of Ajdābiyya and Kufra contain no documents relating to appeals. In some cases judgments of one of the two courts were brought for confirmation or execution before the other. Thus in one case a man stated, by affidavit filed with the court of Ajdābiyya, that he had divorced his wife in the court of Kufra one-and-a-half years previously, and the *qāḍī* of Ajdābiyya "permitted (*ajāza*) this affidavit." In another case the court of Kufra received from the court of Ajdābiyya a judgment concerning the validity of a *khulʿ* divorce, and the *qāḍī* of Kufra ordered the husband to pay maintenance to the divorced wife during her pregnancy. It seems that in the last-mentioned case a further approach to the court was required when it emerged that the woman was pregnant, a fact that had not been known at the time of her divorce in Ajdābiyya.[28] At any rate, no element of appeal is present in these cases.

In one case a committee headed by a commissioned officer of police seemingly acted as a court of appeal in respect of a judgment of the court of Kufra. When the *qāḍī* had declared a woman rebellious, her father complained to a commissioned officer of the Kufra district police, who set up a two-member committee headed by himself. The husband accused the wife's parents of inciting her against him; she denied it, and he asked her to affirm her denial on oath. When she had done so, the committee explained to the husband that the wife was declared "abstinent" (*zāhida*) and would not come back to him; this meant that she was responsible for

25. Davis, *Politics*, pp. 224-25, 228.
26. E.g., KD59-73, K51: p. 11 no. 22 3 Sep. 59.
27. d'Emilia, pp. 15-16.
28. AP:E2, p. 168 no. 162 16 Sep. 47; and KD59-73, K43: p. 218 no. 1 23 Dec. 64, respectively. See below, V2a, VI4b(1).

the dissolution and would bear financial liability accordingly. The husband thereupon divorced her irrevocably, and the *qāḍī* confirmed the validity of the divorce and ordered it to be registered when the matter was brought before him.[29] In other words, the committee acted administratively, as an intermediary, without any judicial power; the divorce was performed by the husband and confirmed by the court.

(2) **Material law.** Parallel to the dual judicial system (the civil and the *sharʿī*), which existed in Libya until its abolition by Qadhdhāfī, there was a dual system of secular and religious law, which until the reinstatement of Islamic law in matters under the jurisdiction of the civil courts applied in the two judicial systems respectively: secular law in the civil system and religious law in the *sharʿī*. The imprint of the Ottoman era is represented by the codes imported from the West and by the effects of the capitulations system on the laws. Italian colonial rule also left its imprint in Libya to a certain extent. At the same time it was guided by the principle of noninterference in matters of personal status and *waqf* of Muslim subjects, in view of the religious character of these matters. However, inhabitants of the colonies who wished to apply Italian law to their matters of personal status could do so by taking out full metropolitan citizenship. Italy's attempt in the early 1920s to give Tripolitania and Cyrenaica constitutional autonomy, under direct rule, with the participation of representative local agencies (who appointed the *sharʿī qāḍīs*), ensured respect for religious law and local custom. In the reign of King Idrīs in the 1950s, in an effort to modernize the law, entire codes were imported from Egypt—which in turn were based on French law.[30]

The Islamization of Libyan law began in 1971, when by an act of October 28 the Legislative Review and Amendment Committee was established to purge the law of provisions conflicting with the *sharīʿa* and to set goals for the reinstatement of fundamental *sharʿī* principles by means of legislation. The intention was to apply the *sharīʿa* not only to matters of personal status but also to civil, criminal, and commercial law. This legislation was to be based on the *takhayyur* method—that is, the adoption of such elements of the legal heritage of different schools as suited the purposes of

29. KD59–73, p. 57 no. 109 10 Sep. 60. For *zāhida* see below, p. 21, and the sources indicated in n. 5.

30. Cicchitti, pp. 484ff.; Mayer, *Criminal law*, p. 5; Mayer, *Resurgence*, p. 197; Mayer, *Interest*, p. 541; Nelsen, p. 193. Cf. Coulson, *History*, pp. 149ff.

the legislator, which were determined with reference to the public interest and prevailing custom. The reinstatement of the *sharīʿa* was concerned not with the *sharīʿa* within the meaning of the classical writings but with the fundamental principles of the *sharīʿa* as conceived by the committee. These principles were general and flexible and could be adapted to the changing circumstances of time and place, so long as matters relating to belief and ritual remained intact. Most of the members of the committee had had no traditional *sharʿī* training (only two of them were *ʿulamāʾ*), which made its work easier. The committee did not use the teachings of Sanūsī jurists, who advocated a cautious reopening of the gates of the *ijtihād* by direct access to the textual sources—namely, the Qurʾān and the *sunna* and their interpretation with reference to the needs of present-day society. It should be noted that Qadhdhāfī's reformist approach to polygamy is technically similar to *ijtihād*, in the sense that he interprets the relevant qurʾānic verse (4:3) literally as to allowing polygamy only to persons in charge of orphans. In actual fact it appears that the Libyan legislator is still greatly indebted to classical *sharʿī* literature. In 1972 the Higher Council for National Guidance was set up, whose tasks included the adaptation of the moral and spiritual teachings of Islam to the present requirements of Libyan society.[31]

The greatest achievement of the Legislative Review and Amendment Committee was in criminal law. Between 1972 and 1974, four statutes were enacted that reinstated the five qurʾānic *ḥadd* punishments, although selectively and in deviation from traditional law.[32] In 1972 the taking of interest, contracts involving risks, and aleatory contracts in civil and commercial transactions were forbidden by law. The prohibition of interest is based on a direct interpretation of qurʾānic provisions, which is why Mayer holds that it is tantamount to *ijtihād*; but the resemblance is of course only technical, since it was imposed by statutory legislation and not by the authorized exponents of the *sharīʿa*. At any rate, the prohibition is selective, and because of business relations with the West is limited to a comparatively unimportant field. Concerning risks, too, there is an attempt to interpret the *sharīʿa* in a manner justifying institutionalized insurance

31. Mayer, *Criminal law*, p. 8; Mayer, *Resurgence*, pp. 197, 202, 211–12; Mayer, *Interest*, p. 542; Ziadeh, pp. 81, 123; Nelsen, pp. 193–94. For more details on the *ijtihād* see below, p. 204.
32. Mayer, *Criminal law*, pp. 10ff.; Mayer, *Sexual mores*, pp. 293ff., 301; Mayer, *Resurgence*, p. 198; Nelsen, pp. 274–75.

contracts.[33] In 1971–72 the Islamic alms tax (*zakāt*) was in a sense reinstated through institutionalization by statute.[34] Various laws, buttressed by penal sanctions, are designed to ensure state control over public morality. They forbid the consumption and transport of and trading in alcohol, breaches of the fast in the month of Ramaḍān, indecent performances in public places, homosexual intercourse even between consenting adults, artificial insemination, the entry into Libya of foreign women unaccompanied by agnates, and marriage between Libyan women and foreigners.[35]

In sum, apart from matters of personal status—in relation to which a comparatively wide codification was reached on the basis of the *sharīʿa*—the extent of the reinstatement of *sharʿī* principles by modern codifications superseding European-inspired legislation has been rather modest. The reinstatement of those principles was selective and sometimes involved deviation from or even clear distortion of the *sharīʿa*; and it seems that the Libyan legislator, besides his desire to create the image of a revival of Islamic law, has also been guided by practical economic and normative considerations. As a matter of fact, the Islamization process was already halted in 1974. Moreover, in the opinion of observers, the actual application of the Islamistic legislation was even more restricted. Thus, for instance, there is no evidence of the application of qurʾānic corporal punishments such as amputation.[36] Furthermore, significant de-Islamization measures may be pointed out. The 1973 abolition of the autonomy of the *sharīʿa* courts and application of Islamic law within the secular courts will in the long run have far-reaching repercussions. In the same year the family *waqf* was also abolished, resulting in violent incidents. Earlier, in 1970, the regime had decided to transfer income of the *waqf* to a "*jihād* fund" for Palestinians, instead of applying it to the purposes stated in the endowment deeds. The *waqf* property of the Sanūsī order was confiscated.[37]

33. Mayer, *Interest*, pp. 542ff., 549, 559; Mayer, *Criminal law*, p. 20; Mayer, *Resurgence*, p. 198. Cf. Layish, *Contribution*, pp. 271ff.
34. Mayer, *Criminal law*, p. 20; Mayer, *Resurgence*, p. 198. Cf. Layish, *Saudi Arabia*, p. 281.
35. Mayer, *Criminal law*, p. 7; Mayer, *Sexual mores*, pp. 288ff., 302–3; Nelsen, p. 275; Ansell & al-Arif, pp. 217–16; Davis, *Politics*, pp. 38, 189, 213 n. 12.
36. Mayer, *Criminal law*, p. 21; Mayer, *Resurgence*, p. 200; Mayer, *Interest*, p. 541. Cf. Davis, *Politics*, p. 45; Harris, p. 16.
37. Evans-Pritchard, pp. 74, 77–78; Nelsen, p. 87; Davis, *Politics*, p. 57; Davis, *Islam*; Harris, pp. 33, 49.

The regime also took care to "purify" the mosques of nests of opposition. Mayer concludes that all in all, in spite of the fundamentalist image of the Libyan regime, the legal system is no more Islamic today than it was in the past and the process of Westernization and modernization is continuing in various fields. Qadhdhāfī only needs the fundamentalist image to legitimize his rule in the eyes of the masses; the reinstatement of the *sharīʿa* is thus not an end in itself but a means to secure power.[38] In this connection we should also interpret the efforts of the regime to enlist *ʿulamāʾ* outside the Sanūsī order, including the appointment of a grand *muftī*, as intended to strengthen the regime.[39] Qadhdhāfī's pragmatic approach is also reflected in his narrow definition of the *sharīʿa* as an ethical, not a legal, scheme, severed from the affairs of this world. This "modernist" approach (some have appraised it as "Muslim Protestantism") was, in Mayer's opinion, intended to prepare the ground for the adoption of the "Green Book" instead of the *sharīʿa* as a positive legal system calculated to solve Libya's social, economic, and political problems. It seems that the rejection of the *sunna* of the Prophet and the equal status granted to religion and custom (*ʿurf*) in Qadhdhāfī's *sharīʿat al-mujtamaʿ* (society) must also be viewed in this context.[40]

In the period of Italian rule there was no interference by substantive legislation in the law applied by the *sharīʿa* courts in matters of personal status; but as noted above, *sharʿī* judgments conflicting with European norms coming within the concept of public policy were not carried out. A person who had acquired Italian citizenship was subject to the Italian law of personal status. The Libyans did not take out Italian citizenship because they were not prepared to forgo the application of the *sharīʿa* to matters of personal status. In the course of time, a special citizenship was introduced enabling local residents to retain their subjection to the *sharīʿa* in matrimonial matters. Legal fields other than personal status were subject to Italian law and justice.

Until Qadhdhāfī's coup, no codification of the laws of personal status, succession, and *waqf* took place. The *qāḍīs*, insofar as they required

38. Mayer, *Criminal law* pp. 3, 20–21; Mayer, *Resurgence*, p. 198; Mayer, *Interest*, p. 541; Davis, *Politics*, pp. 56–57; Ansell & al-Arif, p. 115; Harris, p. 33.

39. Davis, *Politics*, p. 50; Davis, *Islam*.

40. Mayer, *Resurgence*, pp. 199, 208, 217–18; Mayer, *Livre vert*, pp. 9–15, 18ff., 49–50, 56, 58, 67; Ansell & al-Arif, pp. 12–13; Nelsen, pp. 208ff.

guidance in religious law, turned to private treatises on Islamic law according to the Mālikī school. Another possibility open to them (but one that in all probablity they did not make use of) was to seek legal opinions (*fatwās*) from authoritative *muftīs* and *fuqahā*ʾ.[41] The revolutionary regime anchored Islam and the *sharīʿa* in the constitution of the state. Section 2 of the Constitutional Proclamation of the Revolutionary Command Council of 14 December 1969 provides that Islam is the religion of the state. Section 6 of the Constitution of the Federation of Arab Republics of 1971, which indeed was never applied, provides that the *sharīʿa* is the main source of legislation in the Federation. Section 2 of the constitution of 1977 provides that the Qurʾān is the *sharīʿat al-mujtamaʿ*; and Mayer regards this expression as clearly indicating that the *sunna* of the Prophet and the whole corpus of the *sharīʿa* as embodied in the classical *fiqh* writings are not included in the *sharīʿa* in the sense of Qadhdhāfī's narrow definition. A presage of reforms in the law of personal status may be seen in section 3 of the 1969 Constitutional Proclamation, which says: "The family is the basis of Libyan society, anchored in the values of religion, ethics, and nationalism." The proclamation expressly provides that the *sharīʿa* shall be applicable to succession.[42]

The proclamation was indeed followed by Law No. 76 Protecting Some Rights of Women in Marriage, Divorce for Prejudice, and Consensual Divorce (hereinafter "Law No. 76"), enacted on 23 December 1972, and Law No. 18 of 18 March 1973 (hereinafter "Law No. 18"), which supplements and amends Law No. 76. This codification replaces the *sharīʿa* law of personal status based on the Mālikī school, which until then had applied to that legal field. Section 20 of Law No. 76 says "Every provision of law inconsistent with this law is repealed." The main innovations made by this legislation are as follows: maturity of the parties (minimum age) as a condition of marriage; abrogation of the guardian's right to enforce (*jabr*) a marriage; *khulʿ* with compensation by the wife to the husband, imposed by the court, where he vexatiously refuses to divorce her; making the compensation a condition of the validity of the *khulʿ* although payment may be postponed; validation of the divorced wife's renunciation of suckling wages and of the maintenance of minor children in her custody

41. Evans-Pritchard, pp. 203, 212, 216; see below, pp. 201–2.

42. Mayer, *Criminal law*, pp. 6–7; Mayer, *Resurgence*, p. 200; Ansell & al-Arif, pp. 108–9; Nelsen, p. 193.

(*ḥaḍāna*) by the side of invalidation of her renunciation of custody; injury as a ground for judicial divorce available to the husband as well; and procedural deviations from traditional law as to judicial divorce and its legal and financial consequences, with a view to stressing the responsibility of each of the parties and the financial consequences (in simpler language: release of the husband from the obligation to pay the wife's financial rights if she is the guilty party). Compared with reformist personal status legislation in other Arab countries, especially in North Africa—which was the Libyan legislator's source of inspiration, both in substantive respect and as regards the technique of the reforms—the achievements of Libyan legislation in respect of woman's status are rather modest. Mayer correctly notes that the main freedoms of the husband under the *sharīʿa*—the right of polygamy and the unilateral right of divorce—remain intact; in fact in some respects his status has even improved.[43] This is not surprising in view of the tendency to reinstate Islamic law, albeit selectively.

The reinstatement of Islamic law in various fields outside personal status has blurred the distinction between the two judicial domains, the religious and the secular. Henceforth the *sharīʿa*, as far as it had been cast into the mold of statute law, applies also in the civil courts. Since the abolition of the *sharīʿa* courts, the civil courts dispense *sharʿī* justice also in matters of personal status and succession.

c. Social Background

The population of Libya consists of Arabs and of Berbers who have undergone a process of Arabization and Islamization due to the immigration of Muslim Arabs into the region from the seventh century onward. About 90 per cent of the indigenous population speak Arabic and the proportion that is Muslim is still higher.[44] Ajdābiyya, in northern Cyrenaica, has always been an important center, owing to its location at a strategic junction of roads leading to Tripoli in the west, to Benghazi, Alexandria, and Cairo in the east, and to Kufra and Khartum in the south. The town was the seat of the al-Sanūsī government during the short period of the policy of indirect rule under the Italians. The principal tribes are the Maghāriba, "free" members of the Saʿadī federation, and the Zuwaya, immigrants from the Central

43. Mayer, *Marriage*, pp. 31, 39 n. 1, pp. 46–48; Mayer, *Resurgence*, p. 198. For a detailed analysis of the provisions of law concerning divorce see the relevant chapters below.

44. Nelsen, pp. xii, 13ff., 72–76.

Saharan oases who settled in the suburbs of the town in the 1950s but retained their lineage structure. The Zuwaya are spread over a very large area; they own land, and the process of their sedentarization is in a fairly advanced stage. Owing to the town's proximity to the central government, its population is more heterogeneous than that of distant Kufra, and the effects of the 1969 revolution are more marked here. Ajdābiyya had over 30,000 inhabitants in the late 1970s.[45]

Kufra, in Southern Cyrenaica, consists of oases, and it too is located on trade routes. It is comparatively immune from nomad threats because there are no pastures in the vicinity. The Zuwaya tribe is the largest and the dominant population group, but there are other black-skinned and white-skinned tribes, immigrant laborers from Chad and the Sudan, *ikhwān* ("brothers")—that is, descendants of officials and servants of *zāwiya*s of the Sanūsī order who remained in Kufra after the abolition of the order—and slaves liberated under various circumstances and integrated into the social fabric.[46] Many references to liberated slaves (*ʿatīq*, *maʿtūq*, *muʿtaq*)—including those of the *sayyid*s of the Sanūsī order (*al-sāda al-sanūsiyya*), who had become absorbed into the tribes, especially the Zuwaya—are to be found in the *sijill*s of the court of Kufra. Davis notes that the people of Kufra treat the slaves as brothers in economic and political matters but not for the purposes of marriage—because of their origin, not their color; a white man who marries a black girl takes her as his second or third wife.[47] Kufra's attraction in the past was its location in the far south, far from the centers of Ottoman, Italian, and British control. For ecological and political reasons Kufra has retained the organization of a tribal society. The Sanūsī order did not create a state apparatus with all the usual attributes, such as a judicial system. Kufra had a population of about 10,000 in the late 1970s.[48]

In the past the inhabitants of Cyrenaica were strongly influenced by the Sanūsiyya, a fundamentalist Islamic revival movement. The Sanūsī order was considered orthodox (it belonged to the Mālikī school) and contributed greatly to the Islamization of the Cyrenaicans, who were nurtured on non-

45. Davis, *Politics*, pp. 7–8, 80ff., 84–85, 93, 169, 189.
46. Davis, *Politics*, pp. 117ff., 198; Davis, *Koufra*, pp. 549, 551; Anderson, L., pp. 333–34; Tucker, pp. 179ff.
47. E.g., KAMD, no. 49 26 May 39; KD59–73, K48: p. 83 no. 162 13 April 61, K45: p. 88 no. 171 10 May 61; Davis, *Koufra*, p. 553.
48. Davis, *Politics*, pp. 107–8; Davis, *Koufra*, pp. 547, 563.

Muslim Arab custom.[49] The order transferred its center to Kufra in the expectation that Kufra would serve as a basis for its expansion in black Africa and as a dam against French expansion from Algeria. The movement played an important social and political role by means of the network of *zāwiya*s, through which it conducted resistance to the Italian occupation. The secret of its success lay in the fact that it adapted its establishment to the tribal structure of Cyrenaica (the *zāwiya*s were set up within the tribal framework) and that the cohesion of the order was identified with tribal cohesion. The worship of saints—another feature of popular religion common in Cyrenaica—was translated into veneration of the Grand Sanūsī and his successors, with the *baraka* (blessing) being enlisted for this purpose. A supratribal political organization was created through the military and political confrontation with the major powers. In this sense, we may say that the Libyan national state grew out of the Sanūsī order: Idrīs was proclaimed king of a federal constitutional monarchy in 1952.[50] During the wars and the Italian occupation the organization and *zāwiya*s of the Sanūsiyya were destroyed, the Sanūsī family went into exile, the *shaykh*s of the *zāwiya*s scattered in all directions, and the lands of the *zāwiya*s were seized for Italian settlement. Qadhdhāfī's revolutionary regime outlawed the order; tribes and groups closely associated with the Sanūsīs were persecuted; tribal lands and *waqf* properties were confiscated. Nevertheless, the order is still referred to for purposes of social and status classification.[51] Relevant references in the *sijill*s are intended to facilitate identification of the litigants and the *qāḍī*s.

The tribal organization in Cyrenaica is disintegrating. The causes are (1) urbanization, the sedentarization of the Beduin, and the modernization of the administration and the economy—processes that began toward the end of Ottoman rule; (2) the protracted struggle with the Italians and World War II; and (3) the socioeconomic differentiation following the discovery of petroleum in Libya in 1956 and its ensuing intensive exploitation. At the same time, tribal brotherhood continues to play an

49. Ziadeh, pp. 73ff., 126; Evans-Pritchard, pp. 1, 7.

50. Evans-Pritchard, pp. 8, 10, 19, 65, 67, 71, 82, 84; Ziadeh, pp. 109-10, 121-22; Davis, *Koufra*, pp. 561, 563; Davis, *Politics*, pp. 26-27, 189-90; Davis, *Islam*; Mayer, *Criminal law*, p. 4; Mohsen, *Conflict*, pp. 73-74.

51. Evans-Pritchard, pp. 74, 77-78, 191ff.; 200-201; Ziadeh, p. 231; Davis, *Politics*, pp. 189-90; Harris, pp. 15, 33.

important part; it is channeled into new frameworks of social and economic activity and finds expression in mutual aid and the like. The normative system lags, as usual, behind economic changes. The revolutionary regime on the other hand encourages the survival of the normative system, with a view to adapting it to government requirements (legitimation of the regime).[52]

52. Davis, *Politics*, p. 95; Davis, *Koufra*, p. 564; Anderson, L., p. 345.

CHAPTER I

Causes of Divorce

1. DIVORCE ON THE HUSBAND'S INITIATIVE

The specific causes of *ṭalāq* divorces are usually not indicated in judicial decisions. This seems to be due to the fact that in divorces of this kind, which do not involve legal proceedings, the causes are not relevant from a *sharʿī* point of view, since the husband may exercise his right of *ṭalāq* as he pleases and does not have to give reasons for his action. In divorce by mutual consent, which is to all appearances the most frequent form of divorce, the legal and financial consequences are agreed beforehand between the parties. The causes were probably mentioned during the proceedings; but the court, for reasons of privacy and stylistic brevity, does not trouble to state them in its decision, confining itself to general formulas that do not reveal the specific causes of the divorce. Examples of such formulas are: "There has been much discord (*shiqāq*) between them, and each of them blames the other for the deterioration (*isāʾa*) of conjugal relations (*ʿishra*), and relations have not been regularized (*tantaẓim*) as required between spouses according to *sharīʿa* and custom (*ʿādatan*)"; "A dispute (*nizāʿ*) has broken out between the spouses and they have resorted to this court more than once, and in default of reconciliation (*iṣlāḥ*) between them and in the absence of normal conjugal relations (*ḥusn al-muʿāshara*)..."; "The spouses have decided by mutual consent that their marriage cannot succeed (*tatayassar*) in a *sharʿī* way, and as they agree that dissolution (*firāq*) is more fitting (*aṣlaḥ*) and more appropriate (*awfaq*)..."; or "They no longer have any hope of improving their conjugal relations."[1]

1. KD59-73, K51: p. 15 no. 29 27 Sep. 59; AP:E2, p. 182 no. 178 8 Jan. 48; AP:E4, p. 71 no. 70 4 July 46; and AP:E2, p. 11 no. 22 6 Aug. 51, respectively. See also KAMD, p. 29 no. 11 16 Feb. 34; KD59-73, K44: p. 2 no. 4 21 June 59; AP:E4, p. 105 no. 103 13 June 47.

The general inference to be drawn from these and similar formulas is that one or both of the parties had come to the conclusion that their marriage was wrecked beyond repair, that there was no prospect of harmony ever being restored between them, and that divorce was therefore inevitable. Nevertheless, the specific cause of the breakup may sometimes be gathered, with varying degrees of certainty, from data in the *sijill*s. The reasons for the divorce are almost always traditional, as may be expected in a society not yet fully exposed to processes of modernization and Westernization.[2] It happens sometimes that the husband divorces the wife even before consummation of the marriage, but there is only one attested instance of the cause of the divorce being inability of the wife to have intercourse owing to her tender age. The husband's father contended that his son had married a twelve-year-old girl who had fraudulently been registered with the court as seventeen and that it had subsequently been found that she could not consummate the marriage (*mā qadarat ʿalā al-zawāj*). The wife's father confirmed this story and asked that his daughter be given time until she was sexually mature; but the husband and his father preferred to have the matter decided in court and the wife was divorced.[3] In the other cases in which the wife was divorced before consummation (*binā*ʾ, *dukhūl*), the reason may have been different; at any rate, in one of the cases the initiative was taken by the wife, who waived the balance of the dower. In another case it was noted that the wife had been divorced four days after the marriage and that her relative had waived the balance of the dower "without a waiver (*tanāzul*) on my [*scil*, the wife's] part," which may indicate that the reason for the dissolution did not lie with the spouses (it was not stated whether the marriage had been consummated or not). In yet another case, it was said that the man had "given up his betrothed (*makhṭūba*)" before divorcing her and without the marriage having been consummated, which may indicate that the marriage had been of short duration and that the wife had not yet moved into the husband's dwelling.[4]

A rejective attitude of the wife toward the husband is another cause of divorce. Thus in one instance the wife declared "her aversion (*nufūr*) to her

2. Cf. Layish, *Women*, pp. 125ff.
3. KD59-73, K50: p. 3 no. 12 11 Feb. 65.
4. A:E102, p. 16 no. 31 16 Aug. 51; AP:E1, p. 143 no. 254 19 Nov. 52; and AP:E3, p. 348 no. 595 5 July 54. See also AP:E1, p. 147 no. 261 2 Dec. 52. Cf. Charnay, p. 37.

husband" without his having given her reason for it, and in another instance the wife was declared "abstinent" (*zāhid[a]*). Derivatives of the verb *zahada* are used as technical terms in connection with divorce. A husband who initiates a divorce is called *zāhid*, and a wife who does so is called *zāhida*. The status of initiator is of course relevant in assigning liability for the financial consequences of dissolution.[5] Disobedience of the wife to the husband is yet another cause of divorce. According to the *sharʿī* prescription, the wife must stay at the husband's house and not leave it without his permission. Her visits to her relatives must take place at "the *sharʿī* dates." In one case a dispute arose between the spouses when the wife "insisted on traveling [out of town] at the [*sharʿī*] date" while the husband, a soldier, asserted that the date did not suit him. In another case the husband sent the wife, with her brother, to visit her relatives in another town, from where she did not return to him even after he went there and tried to persuade her to do so. The threat of divorce (or of taking a second wife) is a means to ensure the obedience of the wife. Among the Awlād ʿAlī in the Western Desert violation of a *sharʿī* right of the husband by the wife or her relatives is similarly considered a legitimate ground for divorce.[6]

Adultery (*zinā*) of the wife, a grave offense according to both *sharīʿa* and custom, is a further cause of divorce (along with loss of her financial rights). Thus in one instance the husband alleged that the wife "was adulterous and depraved" (*ʿāhir ghayr maḍbūṭa*), and the husband's fears were proved justified. In another case the wife was accused of having committed adultery during a three-year absence of the husband. It was alleged that she had become pregnant by way of adultery (*ḥamalat bi-luqṭat zinā*) and that the child had been killed by her husband's brother. Her guilt was not proved in court, but she was divorced after her father waived her rights (which may be tantamount to an admission of her guilt). Adultery by the wife is a shameful offense; it sullies the honor (*ʿirḍ*) of her family. The duty of cleansing the tainted honor falls on her agnates and not on the

5. KD59-73, K48: p. 65 no. 127 22 Oct. 60, and p. 102 no. 214 7 Nov. 61, respectively; Colucci, *Cirenaica*, col. 43; Colucci, *Tribù*, p. 26.

6. KD59-73, K48: p. 29 no. 56 5 March 60, and K47: p. 44 no. 82 16 May 60, respectively; Mohsen, *Women*, p. 230. Cf. Fluehr-Lobban, p. 143; Charnay, pp. 38-39; Layish, *Women*, p. 128.

husband and his family.[7] In one case it had been stipulated in the marriage contract that the bride must be a virgin, but on the first night of the marriage disputes arose as to the fulfillment of that condition, and the wife was divorced that very night without the marriage having been consummated. After some litigation it was determined that the divorce had been unilateral. D'Emilia remarks that it would have been possible to cancel the marriage contract on the basis of *khiyār al-ʿayb*, the option to rescind a contract by reason of a latent defect existing in the goods or services at the time of the contract; and in the view of the Mālikī jurist Khalīl, if the loss of virginity was due to prenuptial intercourse, the husband can demand dissolution even if virginity has not been stipulated in the marriage contract. In another case a man divorced his wife because she had stolen some coins from him, this too being a disgraceful act. Charnay notes other defects in the wife as a cause of divorce in Algeria under French rule: the husband's suspicion that some ailment of the wife had been concealed from him; failure to bear sons; and housekeeping without proper skill and devotion according to the husband's expectations.[8]

The cause of divorce may lie with the parents of the spouses, who set one against the other. The tensions inherent in the extended family give occasion to numerous and varied disputes among members. Thus in one case the husband confirmed that his father had "spoilt relations between him and the wife" and had indeed forbidden him to marry her. In another case a dispute arose between the wife's father and his son-in-law, and from the latter spread to the wife. In Israel, too, we sometimes see that the dispute has nothing to do with the spouses, except that they have to pay the price.[9]

2. DIVORCE ON THE WIFE'S INITIATIVE

The Mālikī school gives the wife a wide range of grounds (to be discussed at length in chapter IV) for the dissolution of her marriage through legal

7. B2:KM38-43:T41-43, K5: p. 33 no. 84 1 Jan. 42, and K8: p. 40 no. 104 13 Feb. 42, respectively. Cf. Mohsen, *Conflict*, pp. 110–11; Fluehr-Lobban, p. 142; Layish, *Women*, p. 128; Kressel, p. 146.
8. d'Emilia, pp. 36–37, 39, 48–49; Coulson, *Commercial law*, p. 65; Charnay, p. 37. Cf. Fluehr-Lobban, pp. 154–55, 163–64.
9. KD59-73, K51: p. 16 no. 32 10 Oct. 59, and p. 123 no. 262 24 June 62, respectively. Cf. Charnay p. 37; Layish, *Women*, p. 130.

proceedings. Here we shall deal only with the causes of a *ṭalāq* divorce by the husband on the wife's initiative and by mutual consent. A great difference in age between the spouses—or, more exactly, the husband being much older than the wife—may be a cause of divorce, although there is no express evidence to that effect. A great difference in age suggests physical and mental incompatibility and, in extreme cases, perhaps also impotence of the husband. Thus in one case, in which many quarrels had arisen between the spouses, the husband was seventy-five years old and the wife thirty-five. In other cases the age difference was between twenty and thirty years. In one of the aforementioned cases, the divorce took place only eight months after the marriage, which may perhaps strengthen the assumption as to the reason for the divorce.[10]

Impotence of the husband is a ground for dissolution by way of legal proceedings, but it may also be hinted at in *ṭalāq* divorces. Thus in one case the wife stated that the husband had married her two months previously and that she had "called upon him to consummate the marriage but he had not consummated it" (*daʿathu li-dukhūl wa-lam yadkhul bihā*). The husband confirmed her story and eventually divorced her with reference to a disagreement concerning the dower; at any rate, it was not expressly contended that the husband was impotent and that nonconsummation of the marriage was the reason for the divorce. Among the Beduin of Cyrenaica it is dishonorable for a woman to be married to an impotent man. After the ailment has been proved by means of witnesses, her father may compel her husband to divorce her. Similarly, in the Kabyle Mountains under French rule, the husband was compelled to consummate the marriage or, if he could not, to divorce the wife. Among the Awlād ʿAlī of the Western Desert, impotence of the husband is a reason for divorce without the wife having to return the dower. A specific procedure exists for proving impotence by means of witnesses within the framework of what is called "the house of dreadful deeds" (*bayt al-shanāʿa*).[11]

Disputes over nonpayment of the whole or part of the dower are frequent causes of divorce. The husband must pay the dower before consummation of the marriage; and so long as he has not paid, the wife may refuse to

10. KD59-73, p. 45 no. 84 9 June 60, K48: p. 82 no. 160 8 April 61; A:E104, p. 182 no. 314 28 Feb. 53. Cf. Layish, *Women*, p. 127.
11. A:E104, p. 168 no. 294 4 Feb. 53; Peters, *Aspects*, p. 127 n. 7; Bousquet, *Coutumes kabiles*, p. 64; Mohsen, *Conflict*, p. 112; Mohsen, *Women*, pp. 227-28; Layish, *Women*, p. 132.

consummate. Nonpayment of the dower is thus a *sharʿī* ground for disobedience, provided that the wife has not consented to a postponement of payment and that consummation has not already taken place.[12] It seems that nonconsummation (and divorce) must sometimes be understood against this background. Thus in a case that ended in divorce on the wife's initiative, the husband confirmed that he had married the wife six months previously, had paid only part of the dower agreed between them, and had not consummated the marriage. But nonpayment of the dower is a cause of disputes and, as a result, of divorce, even after consummation of the marriage. Thus in one case the husband admitted owing the wife a certain amount of her dower. The wife refused to resume marital relations (*muʿāshara*) unless she was paid that amount; alternatively, she asked that he divorce her by *ṭalāq*, and so long as he did not do either, she asked that he be ordered to pay maintenance.[13]

A further cause of divorce on the wife's initiative is injury caused to her by the nonpayment of proper maintenance[14] or by physical or mental cruelty. Thus in one case the wife demanded "a decent dwelling in the vicinity of honest people" (*maḥall ʿadl bi-jiwār qawm ṣāliḥīn*) within the *sharʿī* meaning of that term; she asserted that she sustained injury (*taḍarrarat*) by living in a place whose inhabitants had no ties of blood relationship (*qarāba*) with her. Some people, including her husband's father, testified that her husband "insulted her by shameful language and sometimes even beat her." Once he had caused her grievous injury and as a result been arrested by the police. The wife complained several times to the *sharīʿa* court of the injury (*ḍarar*) and humiliation inflicted on her. In another case the wife sued for divorce because of a dispute with her husband over the nonsupply of food (*maʾkal*) and drink (*mashrab*), and in a further case the wife faced the husband with the choice between treating her well or divorcing her.[15] In yet another case the wife's father alleged that her clothing (*kiswa*)—that is, part of her maintenance—was in the possession of the husband. The husband denied this, and the court decided that the father must swear to the truth of his allegation before it ordered

12. Linant, *Traité*, pp. 238–39; Anderson, *Africa*, p. 369.
13. AP:E2, p. 17 no. 24 21 Aug. 51. Cf. Layish, *Women*, p. 131.
14. Linant, *Traité*, pp. 259ff.
15. AP:E4, p. 133 no. [126] n.d. [end of document is missing]; AP:E2, p. 5 no. 10 28 July 51; and A:103, p. 126 no. 222 11 Sep. 52, respectively. Cf. Mohsen, *Conflict*, p. 113; Layish, *Women*, p. 132.

the husband to pay the clothing allowance. Since the father did not swear, the matter was returned to the court for another hearing. Each side produced witnesses to confirm its version. The dispute grew more heated, and eventually the husband divorced the wife.[16]

The wife sometimes sues for a divorce because of harassment by relatives of the husband. Thus in one case the wife said: "In view of the lack of good companionship (*ʿishra ḥasana*) on the part of my husband and my lack of tranquillity (*rāḥa*) in the presence of his sister and his father's wife, I demand of him the dissolution (*firāq*) of my marriage and a divorce (*ṭalāq*) with all my conjugal rights; I have no strength to bear the shame (*ʿayb*) inflicted day and night by his sister and his father's wife." This case reflects the distress of a wife in the patrilocal dwelling, in which she is at the mercy of the husband's female relatives.[17] In this connection, mention should perhaps be made of instances of the divorce of spouses who were paternal first cousins. In all these cases the initiative for the divorce was taken by the wife. In some of them she gave up various financial rights in order to obtain her freedom.[18] In one case the wife asked that some persons be allowed to testify that "my cousin married me and divorced me ten months ago" in order to enable her to marry someone else. The decisions do not expressly indicate a connection between the blood relationship and the divorce; but such a connection has been observed in other countries, where there is a tendency to choose one's spouse outside the family, *inter alia* in order to avoid the tensions inherent in the family setup.[19]

Prolonged absence of the husband from Libya (mostly in the Sudan), nonsupply of maintenance to the wife and her children during such absence, and the fear for her chastity and good name during that time are all frequent causes of divorce on the wife's initiative. Thus in one case the wife (aged twenty-seven) said that the husband had gone to the Sudan over ten years before, that she was in a state of "absolute destitution" (*iḥtiyāj kullī*) and that, moreover, she was "afraid of hardship that might be caused to her" (*takhāf ʿalā nafsihā al-ʿanat*).[20] In other cases the wife asserted that

16. A:E102, p. 10 no. 20 6 Aug. 51. Cf. Layish, *Women*, p. 131.
17. A:E103, p. 124 no. 218 27 Aug. 52. Cf. Layish, *Women*, pp. 94ff. and the sources indicated there.
18. E.g., A:103, p. 146 no. 259 9 Nov. 52; KD59–73, K51: p. 12 no. 23 8 Sep. 59.
19. AP:E3, p. 295 no. 495 7 Feb. 54. Cf. Layish, *Women*, p. 130.
20. KD59–73, K51: p. 22 no. 43 28 Nov. 59. See also KD59–73, p. 3 no. 5 1 July 59; B2:KM38–43:T41–43, K6: p. 84 no. 223 1 Jan. 43.

she sustained injury through neediness, absence (*ghiyāb*) of the husband, and lack of means of subsistence (*ḍīq al-maʿīsha*) or through shortage of food (*nafaqa*) and clothing (*kiswa*). It seems that the word *ʿanat* (hardship) here means distress caused by the physical absence of the husband—that is, fear that she might not be able to resist the temptation of extramarital sex to which she was exposed because of her youth. She needed the divorce so that she might be able to remarry and thus preserve her honor.[21] In one case the wife alleged that the husband had divorced her some ten months before. She produced witnesses to confirm her story and asked the *qāḍī* to record their testimony and "to permit me to remarry in order to protect my honor and preserve my dignity (*ṣawnan li-karāmatī wa-ḥifẓan li-sharafī*) because I am a young woman (*shābba*), a juvenile (*ṣaghīra*), and I am afraid of hardship (*ʿanat*) that may be caused to me." In another case, in which the husband had been absent for three years, the wife was accused of adultery (according to one version, the adulterously conceived child was killed), and her own mother hinted at disgraceful conduct (*rishwa*) although nothing had been proved. The husband's brother divorced her on his behalf, and his father "made himself responsible for her (*taḥammala bihā*) pending the arrival of her father." Confirmation of that interpretation of the term *ʿanat* may be found also in a wife's suit for dissolution by legal proceedings on the ground of the husband's absence.[22]

Defamation of the wife, charges against her of immoral behavior (such as adultery), and denial of the paternity of her children are other causes of divorce on her initiative. In one case a dispute arose between the spouses over a slur on the wife's chastity (*bahāta* [*buhtān*?]). She said that she was pregnant, and the husband neither acknowledged nor denied his paternity.[23] It seems that the taking of a second wife is another ground for divorce on the wife's initiative. Davis reports that a wife sometimes strongly objects to the introduction of another wife into her home; her relatives usually suggest that she be divorced and move elsewhere with her children, while having her upkeep assured. In one case the man had forty-six children by different wives, and when he divorced a wife he provided a dwelling for her and her children.[24]

21. E.g., B2:KM38–43:T41–43, K5: p. 16 no. 37 24 Aug. 41, K8: p. 66 no. 165 5 July 42. For *ʿanat* in the sense of fornication see Hava.

22. AP:E3, p. 296 no. 495 7 Feb. 54; and B2:KM38–43:T41–43, K8: p. 40 no. 104 13 Feb. 42, respectively. Cf. Layish, *Women*, p. 132. See below, pp. 91–92.

23. AP:E4, p. [?] no. 6 [?] 1 July 46. Cf. Layish, *Women*, p. 132.

24. Davis, *Politics*, p. 121 n. 20, p. 199.

CHAPTER II

Unilateral Divorce

1. UNILATERAL DIVORCE AND ITS APPLICATION

a. Terminology

The Mālikī school distinguishes clearly between the husband's unilateral right to repudiate the wife, without resort to legal proceedings, and dissolution by the court on *sharʿī* grounds.[1] When divorce by the husband is performed without legal proceedings all he has to do is use expressions commonly meaning divorce; the wife's presence at the repudiation is not required, nor is her consent to the divorce relevant to its validity. The normative expressions are *ṭalāq* and *khulʿ* and their verbal derivatives. Explicit (*ṣarīḥ*) repudiation does not require proof of the husband's intent (*niyya*) to divorce, whereas implicit (*kināya*) repudiation requires such proof. In one case it was stated that the husband had divorced the wife by a single repudiation, "pronouncing it clearly and formulating it unambiguously" (*fa-takallama bihi faṣīḥan fa-talaffaẓa bihi ṣarīḥan*). Charney notes that in Algeria under French rule it was not always possible, in practice, to prove intent by the various divorce formulas, especially as the husband sometimes regretted a rash divorce (while the wife might try to take advantage of it).[2]

Other less frequent expressions denote *khulʿ* divorce by virtue of custom. For instance it was stated: "The husband has undertaken to release her by divorce (*khalāṣ*) in return for all her rights" or "She has thus become released by divorce (*khāliṣa*) in return for her dower."[3] In another case it was said, after dissolution (*firāq*) had been agreed upon between the spouses: "He

1. See below, IV.
2. AP:E1, p. 149 no. 263 7 Dec. 52; Linant, *Traité*, pp. 355ff.; Milliot, pp. 361–62; Anderson, *Africa*, p. 377; Charnay, p. 38.
3. KD59–73, K50: p. 86 no. 168 7 May 61; and AP:E2, p. 178 no. 174 26 Nov. 47, respectively. Cf. Fluehr-Lobban, p. 158.

has dissolved the marriage tie (*ḥallalahā*) in return for her dower." This term is also usual among the Beduin of the Judean Desert, and it seems to have been accepted also in religious-legal literature in relation to customary institutions, such as that of the *al-muḥallil mina'l-ṭalāq*—that is, a man who marries a woman by intermediate marriage, after she has been trebly divorced, in order that he may in turn divorce her so as to render her lawfully permitted to return to her former husband.[4]

A rarer form of customary divorce is the archaic *ẓihār*, in which the husband swears that the wife is forbidden to him, comparing her to a kinswoman of a prohibited degree (the reference is usually to the back —*ẓahr*— of the mother). In the pre-Islamic period this oath was considered a genuine divorce. Muḥammad condemned and forbade this form of divorce (Qur'ān 33:4; 58:2ff.) but could not bring himself to invalidate it altogether. A procedure was devised for retracting the oath by expiation (*kaffāra*), which included the freeing of a slave or, in the absence of a slave, a two-month fast or the feeding of sixty poor people. Of all the schools, only the Mālikī holds that he who has taken a *ẓihār* oath and does not discontinue intercourse with his wife until the requirements of the expiation are fulfilled creates a ground for dissolution by legal proceedings. Under these circumstances the procedure of an *īlā'* (abstention from intercourse) oath is applied: the *qāḍī* calls upon the husband to divorce the wife and, if he refuses to do so, does so in his stead, and the divorce is regarded as revocable. The author has come across only one instance of a *ẓihār* oath. The husband divorced the wife by a triple repudiation, saying: "You are trebly divorced and forbidden to me like my mother (*ḥarām ʿalayya kayfa ummī*)." This phenomenon was also observed in Algeria.[5]

b. Divorce out of Court and in Court, and Registration

As stated, a *ṭalāq* divorce does not require legal proceedings to be valid. There is in fact much evidence of husbands divorcing their wives out of court. Witnesses confirm the husband's story in court, and the wife sometimes confirms that she has been divorced.[6] If many years have gone

4. KD59-73, K48: p. 38 no. 72 22 April 60; Layish, *Judaean Desert*; Lane, p. 622; Wehr, p. 198; Layish, *Women*, pp. 174-75.
5. KDP, K45: p. [?] no. 135 23 Nov. 60; Linant, *Traité*, pp. 374, 379-81; Milliot, pp. 370ff.; Stern. pp. 127-29; Charnay, p. 39. Cf. Anderson, *Africa*, p. 380; Layish, *Women*, p. 235 n. 372.
6. E.g., KD59-73, K51: p. 13 no. 25 19 Sep. 59, K43: p. 47 no. 89 23 June 60.

by since the alleged divorce and if the wife denies it, the husband may find difficulty in proving the divorce. Yet he may need the plea of divorce to evade the fulfillment of his financial obligations toward the wife. Thus in one case the husband countered the allegation that he had neglected (*muhmil*) his wife by not paying maintenance with the plea that he had divorced her ten years previously. The wife denied this, claiming that she was still his lawful wife (*bāqiya ʿalā ʿiṣmatihi*). The husband was unable to prove his allegation by means of witnesses.[7]

Where the divorce is performed out of court, the court is resorted to, sometimes years later, "in order to register it [the divorce]" (*li-nusajjilahu*).[8] This is done for reasons of legal certainty. Both spouses are interested in a declaratory judgment as to their marital status and as to the regulation of their mutual property rights. A clarification of marital status is essential, especially for the wife; because without an official document certifying her as divorced she cannot remarry. In one case the wife alleged in court that she had been divorced about a year before; she produced witnesses who confirmed her story and applied to the court "to record their testimony and permit her to remarry." In another case, the wife said that the husband had divorced her before going away; she produced a witness who confirmed her story. It seems that she was concerned that she might be reduced to the status of a woman tied to an absent husband whose whereabouts were unknown.[9]

The husband is interested in a declaratory judgment as to the divorce showing that he has fulfilled his financial obligations toward the wife, lest she raise a claim in this regard in the future. In one case the husband said that the marriage had failed, and therefore "I paid all that was due to her, including waiting-period maintenance, and repudiated her by *ṭalāq* before the month of Ramaḍān last year." His brother-in-law, in his testimony, confirmed the story as to the divorce "and the receipt, before and after the *ṭalāq*, of everything that was due." In another case the husband declared that he had divorced his wife and that "he claimed nothing from her and she claimed no conjugal rights (*ḥuqūq zawjiyya*) from him." Witnesses confirmed the fact of the divorce and the mutual waiver of conjugal rights.[10]

7. AP:E2, p. 19 no. 38 23 Aug. 51.
8. E.g., A:E104, p. 200 no. 338 16 April 53; KD59-73, K48: p. 29 no. 56 5 March 60.
9. AP:E3, p. 296 no. 495 7 Feb. 54; and B2:KM38-43:T43, K6: p. 6 no. 18 22 April 43, respectively. See below, IV1a, 2a.
10. A:E104, p. 162 no. 282 21 Jan. 53; and KD59-73, K43: p. 47 no. 89 23 June 60, respectively.

It seems that considerations of legal certainty prompt the spouses to get divorced in court after agreeing out of court on the financial arrangements between them. Thus in one case the husband told the court that following a dispute between himself and his wife a month earlier, he had handed her over to her brother in Benghazi and had given up some jewelry (*ḥaly*) owned by him that was in her possession, in return for her waiver of waiting-period maintenance, "and I have come to the court in order to register (*li-usajjil*) her divorce." He afterward divorced her in court.[11]

It seems that sometimes the husband divorces the wife twice: once out of court and once in court. Thus in one case the husband appeared in court "in order to register the repudiation of my wife," adding, "I have delivered to her all her dower and the waiting-period maintenance, and nothing more is due to her from me." He then launched a repudiation (*arsala ṭalāq*) against his wife, who was absent from court. The twofold divorce is apparently a security measure, although the whole proceeding is reckoned as a single divorce, since the court orders the wife to observe the waiting period from the date of the divorce performed in court.[12] In a tribal society, certainty as to the divorce and as to the regulation of the financial claims of the parties is obtained through the guarantor (*kafīl*) of the divorce.[13]

Resort to the court in matters of divorce is, as in matters of marriage, due to civil exigencies. The registration of divorce is not essential to its *sharʿī* validity. Registration or a declaratory judgment is a condition for a formal change of marital status. It is thus civil exigencies that cause a tribal population in process of settling down and still adhering to customary law to turn to the *sharīʿa* court. Several countries have anchored the registration and confirmation of divorces in law for reasons of orderly administration, the inevitable result being that secular legislation, which has no basis in the *sharīʿa*, makes for increased resort to the *sharīʿa* courts. In Israel criminal legislation forbids divorce against the wife's will, and in the absence of the wife's consent, the husband applies to the *sharīʿa* court for permission to divorce her.[14]

11. AP:E1, p. 147 no. 260 2 Dec. 52.
12. A:E102, p. 351 no. 601 26 July 54. See below, pp. 106ff., 153ff.
13. Shuqayr, p. 417; al-ʿĀrif, pp. 91ff.; Layish, *Judaean Desert*.
14. Anderson, *Reform*, p. 126; Coulson, *History*, p. 211; Layish, *Women*, pp. 133ff. 151–52. For more details on the civil exigencies see below, pp. 182–83.

2. SUSPENDED REPUDIATION

The Mālikī school, unlike other schools, does not recognize a divorce whose validity is delayed until a specific future date; according to it, such a stipulation is of no effect and the divorce takes effect immediately. Like other schools, the Mālikīs recognize a divorce whose validity is conditional on the uncertain occurrence of a specific event in the future, depending on the volition of the wife or the husband, provided that the condition is capable of fulfillment; if it is not, both the condition and the divorce are void. If the condition is supposed not to have been met and is designed to serve a purpose improper from a *sharʿī* point of view, the condition is void and the divorce takes effect immediately.[15]

Suspended repudiation is one of the most impressive manifestations of the husband's unilateral freedom of divorce. Two kinds of suspended repudiation must be distinguished, according to the object in view. One is a threat by the husband to divorce the wife in order to ensure her obedience to him, the other a means to demonstrate, by an "oath of repudiation," the husband's determination to carry out a decision in some matter not connected with the wife at all. In other words, the element of intent (*niyya*) to divorce is absent here.[16] It seems that only repudiation of the first-mentioned kind is recognized in Cyrenaica. Suspended repudiation may serve also for the protection of the wife when she stipulates in the marriage contract that if the husband deviates from certain norms agreed between them (e.g., takes a second wife or treats her cruelly or deserts her), she shall be regarded as divorced.[17] But the Cyrenaican *sijill*s contain no evidence of the application of suspended repudiation already at the conclusion of the marriage contract.

The use of the mechanism of suspended repudiation is not frequent. When it is applied on the husband's initiative, it is designed to achieve two objectives. One is to ensure the wife's obedience by making her divorce conditional on an act constituting disobedience. Thus in one case the husband said in the course of the proceedings: "I made her divorce conditional on her leaving [the house] without being instructed by me to do so, and she actually did so leave [the house]" (*jaʿaltu ṭalāqahā fī khurūjihā*

15. Linant, *Traité*, pp. 384-90; Milliot, pp. 366ff.; Anderson, *Africa*, p. 377.
16. Layish, *Women*, pp. 137ff., 238 n. 446; Anderson, *Africa*, pp. 21, 29, 377.
17. Anderson, *Africa*, pp. 29, 72, 377; Layish, *Women*, pp. 156–57.

bi-dūn amrī wa-kharajat fiʿlan). From a formal point of view, it is not certain that this was an instance of suspended repudiation, since the exact formula of divorce used by the husband was not indicated there, neither in the first person nor even in the third. In fact after a discussion of the wife's conjugal rights, he divorced her by simple repudiation in the presence of the court. In another case the husband swore to divorce the wife by triple repudiation if the maidservant (*khādima*) did not remain in the house. The servant left four days later, and the wife hurried to the court asking to be regarded as divorced since the condition had been fulfilled, whereas the husband claimed that the divorce had not taken place since the servant had remained in the house for some time.[18]

The other objective is slightly more frequent: the divorce is made conditional on the wife's waiver of various financial rights and on compensation to the husband—an arrangement that may be defined as suspended *khulʿ*. Thus in one case the wife waived all her financial rights, including dower and waiting-period maintenance, and undertook to pay the husband three pounds "at the earliest date" in return for her divorce. The husband agreed to this condition and said: "The divorce is conditional (*muʿallaq*) on the bringing of the said three pounds; on the day on which she pays three pounds into this court, she is to be regarded as divorced (*fa-hiya ṭāliq*)." The wife agreed to this, and the *qāḍī* confirmed the occurrence of the divorce (*wuqūʿ al-ṭalāq*) while expressly making its validity dependent on the fulfillment of the condition.[19]

Suspended *khulʿ* is frequent, in a substantive though not always in a formal respect, in cases where the husband is far away and willing to divorce the wife on certain conditions. Thus in one case it was stated in the husband's letter (*jawāb*), which was read out in court: "If (*idhā*) my wife returns all the money she received from me, she is divorced (*fa-hiya muṭallaqa*)." In another case the husband, who had been in the Sudan for about ten years, wrote to his brother, who acted as his representative: "If (*idhā*) my wife . . . wishes [to redeem] herself and if she gives up all her financial rights and has no plea or claim against me, then divorce her (*ṭalliqhā*) as my representative by a single repudiation." The wife agreed to

18. A:E104, p. 175 no. 305 17 Feb. 53; and d'Emilia, pp. 37, 49, respectively. Cf. Layish, *Women*, pp. 137ff., 156–57; Fluehr-Lobban, p. 142.

19. A:E102, p. 357 no. 611 7 Aug. 54. Cf. Layish, *Women*, pp. 139, 148–49, 161. On the *khulʿ* see below, III4.

these conditions "in return for her divorce; she redeemed herself from him (*khālaʿathu*) in return for all her dower, which she delivered to him." The husband's representative agreed to this and divorced her by a single repudiation, saying: "You are divorced (*ṭāliqa*) in virtue of my brother's power of attorney."[20] In another case the husband, who was in the Sudan, said in a letter to his representative: "If (*in*) my [two] wives redeem themselves (*khalaʿūhunna* [*khalaʿatā*]) in return for all their rights, then buy or hire camels for them with my money and send them to me in the Sudan; the one that lingers (*tataʾakhkhar*) and refuses to travel, [if] she gives up all her rights and all my household effects (*athāth*) in her possession, divorce her (*ṭalliqhā*) on my behalf." The letter was read to each of the wives separately and its content explained. Both refused to travel to the Sudan; they delivered the whole of their dowers to the representative and undertook to deliver the other household goods to him; the representative then divorced each of the wives separately, saying: "You are divorced by a single repudiation on behalf of your husband." In the above cases the divorce is conditional on compensation to the husband. In this respect it may be classified as suspended repudiation, although formally it is not a suspended repudiation with all that this term implies. In the Somaliland Protectorate, suspended *khulʿ* was formulated negatively: "If you do not demand maintenance, living accommodation, a dower, etc., you are divorced," and jurists disagreed as to the validity of the divorce because the consideration was not properly defined. In Israel, the mechanism of suspended repudiation is, with the encouragement of the *qāḍī*s, applied as a device to circumvent the prohibition, by penal law, of divorcing one's wife against her will. It is argued that in such cases the husband does not divorce the wife but she "chooses divorce for herself (*ikhtārat al-ṭalāq li-nafsihā*)" by not obeying the husband.[21]

It seems, however, that in most cases the mechanism of suspended repudiation is used by the wife to improve her status in the husband's house. It is applied, following a crisis in their relations in connection with living accommodation, family quarrels, the form of the marriage, and so on, as a part of an amicable settlement (*ṣulḥ*) approved by the court. Thus in

20. B2:KM38-43:T41-43, K7: p. 77 no. 203 1 Nov. 42; and KD59-73, K51: p. 22 no. 43 28 Nov. 59, respectively. See also B2:KM38-43:T43, K7: p. 18 no. 55 14 Aug. 43.

21. KD59-73, K47: p. 52 no. 100 1 Aug. 60 and p. 53 no. 101 2 Aug. 60; Anderson, *Africa*, p. 54; Layish, *Women*, pp. 141-42, 189-90.

one case it was agreed between the spouses that the husband would divorce the wife in return for her dower and maintenance, and at the same time he stipulated that if he subsequently took her back (*idhā rajaʿūhā* [*rajaʿahā*]) his second wife would be divorced (*takūn... muṭallaqa*) in return for her dower. In other words the divorced wife agreed to return to him only on condition that the second wife was divorced, her divorce too being conditional on the waiver of her dower. In another case the wife had the status of an "angry wife" (*mughāḍiba*); she was staying with her brothers, and when she agreed to return to the husband's house and "repair their married life" (*tuḥsin ʿishratahā*), the husband undertook to buy her some silk clothes with the clothes money from the deferred dower and a silver bracelet after the ploughing season; he also undertook to install her in separate living quarters equipped with everything necessary. "From a desire to protect my wife's rights," the undertaking was registered in the presence of witnesses. The husband added: "Therefore, if (*idhā*) I do not pay what I have undertaken to pay at the aforementioned date, my wife shall be regarded as divorced (*fa-takūn muṭallaqa*) with all her rights." In this instance the suspended repudiation is thus part of a reconciliation agreement arrived at out of court; it seems that the parties resorted to the court in order to register the agreement and have it supported by a *sharʿī* sanction. In another case it was stated: "Following a lengthy dispute, which has caused a deterioration of marital relations, the parties have reached the following amicable settlement: (1) The wife agrees to return to the husband's house on condition that he returns to her a bracelet from her dower and gives up certain articles in her possession; (2) if (*idhā*) he assaults and beats her in the future and this is duly established [i.e., by the court], she shall be considered divorced (*takūn muṭallaqa*) with all her rights." The husband agreed to the conditions, relinquished the articles, and undertook to return the bracelet at the earliest opportunity. He also undertook that "if (*idhā*) he should in the future lay hands on her and beat her, she would be regarded as divorced (*takūn ṭāliqa*) and he would give her all that was due to her." Formally speaking, it is not certain that what we have here is a suspended repudiation, since the repudiation is not expressed in the first person.[22]

22. KD59–73, K45: p. 128 no. 264 27 June 62; AP:E2, p. 176 no. 172 30 Oct. 47; and A:E102, p. 26 no. 51 5 Sep. 51, respectively.

In the following cases it seems certain that we have to do with an *undertaking* by the husband to divorce the wife if any of the conditions of the reconciliation agreement between them is infringed; technically, there is no suspended repudiation here. In one case the spouses became reconciled (*taṣālaḥā*), and the husband undertook "to treat her companiably, not to ill-use her by neglecting her (*yataraddad ʿalayhā*).... If it was proved (*idhā thabata*) that he had again neglected her, the wife would be divorced while retaining all her rights; but if it was proved that she was to blame, she would have no right to the sheep and he would be permitted to divorce her at will." Similarly, in another case, the wife alleged that the husband "always ill-treats and beats her without any *sharʿī* necessity." The husband undertook that "if (*idhā*) he beats or ill-treats her in the future, he will divorce her (*sa-yuṭalliquhā*) after conceding all the conjugal rights." In consequence, the spouses made peace on those conditions. The prefix *sa-* stresses the fact that the undertaking relates to the future.[23]

In Zanzibar under colonial rule, too, suspended repudiation was used for the benefit of the wife during the period of the marriage (and was not stipulated in the marriage contract). In the Aden Protectorate, it was usual to ensure the wife's maintenance, prior to a prolonged absence of the husband, by a suspended repudiation that would become effective if the husband did not supply maintenance as required. This practice was anchored in an order of the sultan of 1942.[24]

3. DELEGATED REPUDIATION

All the schools recognize the husband's right to transfer the power to divorce the wife to a third party or even to the wife herself. There is a fundamental difference between giving someone a mandate (*tawkīl*) to divorce the wife and the husband's cession of the right of divorce in favor of the wife (*tafwīḍ al-ṭalāq*). The legal consequences differ accordingly. In the Mālikī school a mandate to divorce the wife is conditional on the nonfulfillment of a specific undertaking by the husband to the wife (e.g., that he will not take an additional wife). If he transfers to the first wife the power to divorce herself or her rival, he cannot go back on this act. The

23. AP:E2, p. 31 no. 59 20 Sep. 51; and A:E102, p. 331 no. 363 19 June 54, respectively.
24. Anderson, *Africa*, pp. 17, 20, 25–26.

husband's cession of the right of divorce in favor of the wife is a unilateral act not requiring her consent and is irrevocable. In the Mālikī school a distinction, though a rather vague one, is made between two kinds of *tafwīḍ* as to their legal consequences: one grants to the wife the exclusive option (*takhyīr*) between continuance of the marriage and dissolution. If she opts for the second alternative, the divorce is irrevocable (and, according to some, triple); but the husband may stipulate that it shall be revocable. A *tafwīḍ* of the second kind is a genuine cession by the husband of the right of divorce in favor of the wife or a third party. In this case the dissolution is a revocable repudiation.[25]

a. *Tafwīḍ al-Ṭalāq*

The mechanism of ***tafwīḍ al-ṭalāq*** is designed for the protection of a wife who wishes to obtain her freedom; she may apply it as a stipulation in the marriage contract or by virtue of an agreement in the course of the marriage. Although she ostensibly acts in the name of the husband and by virtue of his right of *ṭalāq*, this mechanism may in fact be regarded as a refined means to dissolve the marriage on her initiative otherwise than by legal proceedings. There are various formulas for the application of this mechanism, and they are different as to their legal consequences. It seems that *tafwīḍ al-ṭalāq* is not frequent in Cyrenaica, where it is never stipulated in the marriage contract but always in the course of the marriage as part of a reconciliation agreement between the spouses following a dispute between them, and its application is made dependent on a specified condition. In one case the husband admitted beating the wife unlawfully, causing a wrong (*ẓulm*); he demanded that she return to him and promised to buy her various pieces of jewelry. He also undertook that "If (*in*) he again beats her, her divorce shall be in her hand (*yakūn ṭalāquhā bi-yadihā*); if she so wishes, she shall divorce herself (*in shāʾa[t] tuṭalliq nafsahā*)." The wife accepted this undertaking and returned to the husband's house, and the *qāḍī* "permitted (*ajāza*) the reconciliation (*ṣulḥ*)." The expressions usual in legal literature are *yakūn amruhā bi-yadihā* (she will be responsible for herself) and *li-mashīʾatihā* (as she wishes), and elements of these two expressions are to be found in the present case. A combination of delegated repudiation and judicial divorce in cases of nonprovision of maintenance by an absent husband will be dealt with

25. Linant, *Traité*, pp. 330–33; Milliot, pp. 359–60; Anderson, *Africa*, p. 377.

below. Delegated repudiation was unknown in most of the African countries studied by Anderson. In Ibāḍī Zanzibar it was rare. In Israel it is rather frequent, particularly as a stipulation in the marriage contract; but it also occurrs in the course of the marriage. The delegation is either absolute or subject to conditions—such as the husband's departure for abroad, the transfer of his residence to another locality, or the taking of a second wife.[26]

b. Divorce by Proxy

More frequent are cases in which the husband empowers a person other than the wife to act as his *wakīl* (proxy) or *nā'ib* (deputy) in order to divorce her. The two terms are used alternatively, sometimes in the same document, and are apparently synonymous. The term *wakīl* is more frequent; it is applied in connection with matters of a legal nature.[27] A *wakīl* is appointed by a formal proceeding in court (*tawkīl sharʿī*). The function of the *wakīl* or *nā'ib*, who is usually an agnate (the father or an uncle or brother) is not only to divorce the wife but also to settle all financial claims connected with the divorce—that is, to give the wife her financial rights or to accept from her the waiver of those rights or compensation for her release. In one case the husband's father produced a *tawkīl sharʿī* from his son authorizing him to divorce the wife and to demand financial rights. In another case the husband directed his brother, who acted as his *wakīl*, to divorce the wife on condition that she waived her rights: "If my wife demands to redeem herself, then, if she gives up all her financial rights and there is no plea or claim against me, you shall divorce her on my behalf (*bi'l-niyāba ʿannī*) by a single repudiation." The wife agreed to the conditions "in return for her divorce; she redeemed herself (*khalaʿathu*) from her husband in return for all her dower and delivered it to him." The *wakīl* received it, saying: "You are divorced on behalf of my brother."[28]

A power of attorney is usually given when the husband is abroad, especially in the Sudan, sometimes for an extended period, and is unable to

26. AP:E2, p. 11 no. 21 6 Aug. 51; d'Emilia, pp. 44–45; Milliot, pp. 359–60, 385; Anderson, *Africa*, p. 74, also pp. 21, 29, 54, 109, 142, 155, 168, 213, 233; Layish, *Women*, pp. 153ff. See below, pp. 86, 141–42.

27. Schacht, *Introduction*, pp. 119–20, 190.

28. A:E104, p. 188 no. 322 [?] March 53; and KD59–73, K51: p. 22 no. 43 28 Nov. 59, respectively. For further examples see II2 (suspended *khulʿ*).

divorce the wife in court. He appoints an agnate to handle his affairs, including the divorce. Thus in one case the wife stated that the husband had gone to the Sudan ten years previously and that she was in dire straits and feared for her chastity. She said that the husband's brother was his *wakīl* "for this and other matters"; it seems that she was referring to maintenance and, if necessary, divorce. The brother confirmed her statements. In another case the wife said that the husband "had been absent for years and had left her nothing and sent her nothing... and that he had a brother... whom he had appointed *wakīl* for us." The brother confirmed her story and divorced her "on behalf of his brother... he being his *wakīl*."[29] The husband is sometimes present and shares functions with the *wakīl*: he divorces the wife, and the *wakīl* (or agnate) settles the financial claims. Thus in one case, following the wife's divorce by the husband, "his father and his *wakīl* for the purposes of the *ṭalāq*" undertook to pay the balance of the dower later. Similarly, in another case, the husband's brother undertook to pay the balance of the dower one month after the divorce.[30]

Occasionally we find a combination of divorce by proxy and by letter. In one case the wife's father appeared in court with a letter from his son-in-law, who apologized for being unable to come to Kufra, "and for this reason I have asked our father to divorce our wife (*yufāriq zawjatanā*)... and may this be known to you from this day onward... and anything she claims from me by right our father will give her." The father confirmed in court receipt of the letter and the divorce of the wife. In another case the wife's brother appeared in court with a letter (*jawāb*) from the Sudan which said that his brother-in-law had asked a certain person to divorce his sister and that that person had done so, waiving on his principal's behalf the return of anything he had given her, except a bracelet, which her brother would deliver to him.[31] In other cases it was stipulated in the *jawāb* that the spouses would waive their mutual rights or that the wife would compensate the husband for the divorce. Thus in one case the *wakīl* of the husband, who had been absent for three years, received a *jawāb* from him

29. KD59-73, K51, p. 22 no. 43 28 Nov. 59; and B2:KM38-43:T41-43, K6: p. 84 no. 224 5 Jan. 43, respectively. See also B2:KM38-43:T41-43, K8: p. 40 no. 104 13 Feb. 42; KD59-73, p. 206 no. 497 12 Sep. 64; K48: p. 51 no. 95 19 Dec. 65.
30. KD59-73, K45: p. 112 no. 235 21 March 62 and K47: p. 28 no. 55 24 Feb. 60, respectively.
31. KD59-73, K48: p. 7 no. 13 23 July 59; and B2:KM38-43:T41-43, K7: p. 94 no. 250 3 March 43, respectively. See below, II4.

that said: "Divorce my wife, provided that nothing is demanded from me and that we demand nothing from her." By virtue only of the *jawāb* and the agreement between them, the *wakīl* divorced the wife, after he had waived the husband's rights. In another case the *jawāb*, which had been sent from another locality, said: "If my wife waives all that is due to her from me, divorce her on my behalf." The *qāḍī* explained to the wife the meaning of the *jawāb*, she gave up all her dower, and he divorced her on the husband's behalf.[32]

Frequently the wife, too, is represented in a divorce by a *wakīl* or *nā᾿ib*, usually an agnate (her father or brother). In one case a wife's maternal grandfather represented her.[33] The function of the *wakīl* or *nā᾿ib* is to take her place throughout the proceedings, from consent to the divorce to negotiations on the terms to the settling of financial claims. In one case the wife's father produced a *tawkīl sharʿī* from his daughter, issued by the court, authorizing him to claim her rights from her husband and vesting him with "absolute freedom of disposal" (*taṣarruf muṭlaq*) on her behalf. In another case it was stated that the husband had divorced the wife and that "the marriage between them was dissolved through her *wakīl*, her brother." In yet another case it was said that the wife's brother had "divorced her... by virtue of a power of attorney from her (*bi᾿l-wakāla minhā*)"; it seems that the wife had been given an option by the court to divorce herself from her absent husband and that "she chose (*ikhtārat*) *ṭalāq*," or rather, her brother chose it for her.[34]

The wife's *wakīl* receives from the husband what is due to her as a divorced woman, or he waives her rights or compensates the husband for the divorce, as may have been agreed between them prior to the divorce.[35] The status of the agnate may be inferred from the following case, as described by the husband in court: Following a dispute "between us... I took and delivered her (*naqaltuhā wa-waṣṣaltuhā*) to her brother in Benghazi; I gave her to him (*sallamtuhā lahu*)... [I divorced her] and paid to

32. B2:KM38–43:T41–43, K8: p. 66 no. 165 5 July 42 and K7: p. 18 no. 55 14 Aug. 43, respectively.
33. KPD, K45: p. [15] no. 132 10 Nov. 60.
34. A:E104, p. 188 no. 322 [?] March 53; KD59–73, K45: p. 112 no. 236 22 March 62; and KD59–73, p. 93 no. 206 1 Nov. 61, respectively. On the dissolution of the marriage by the wife see below, pp. 141–42.
35. E.g., KD59–73, K50: p. 90 no. 176 18 May 61, p. 152 no. 332 17 Jan. 63, K42: p. 158 no. 334 24 March 63.

her the waiting-period maintenance."[36] The terms used by the husband were borrowed from the terminology of customary marriage, under which the bride is not a party to the contract, though there is some support for them in the *sharīʿa*: a woman whose marriage has not been consummated cannot be a party to divorce proceedings and must be represented by her father or guardian; only the loss of her virginity in a lawful manner—that is, in matrimony—vests her with legal competence and frees her from her agnates' right of *jabr*—namely, the right to give her compulsorily in marriage. Moreover, if she is physically mature but under age as regards the disposal of property, she may be a party to divorce by legal proceedings (e.g., on the ground of injury); but she needs the consent of her legal representative or her guardian for any act involving financial interests. In fact it seems that the agnate, even where his status is not based on an appointment as a *wakīl* or *nāʾib* by the court, decides upon and regulates the actual divorce with the husband out of court.[37] Finally, the spouses may be jointly represented by agnates, as *wakīl*s,[38] or their fathers may appear beside them in divorce proceedings in court.[39]

4. DIVORCE BY LETTER

The question of the registration of a divorce after it has been verbally pronounced by the husband or a person authorized by him is irrelevant in traditional law, since registration is not required for its validity or proof. But it is a moot point whether a divorce in writing, not verbally pronounced, is valid. Most jurists of the various schools hold, although with minor variations, that it is valid even where the husband is not mute and the wife is not absent. The jurists of the Mālikī school go furthest in permitting a divorce in writing without any of the restrictions imposed by other schools. The letter, whether addressed or not (a distinction made by the Ḥanafī school), by itself dissolves the marriage, provided that the husband desires this result. And according to this school if the husband

36. AP:E1, p. 147 no. 260 2 Dec. 52.

37. E.g., KD59–73, K48: p. 29 no. 56 5 March 60; Milliot, p. 384; Coulson, *Commercial law*, p. 36.

38. E.g., KD59–73, p. 100 no. 210 [?] Nov. 61, K51: p. 180 no. 427 29 Oct. 63.

39. E.g., KD59–73, K48: p. 38 no. 72 26 April 60, K47: p. 51 no. 97 9 July 60.

changes his mind about the divorce between the time of the writing of the letter and the time of its delivery, the divorce is still valid.[40]

Divorce by writing seems to be widely applied where the spouses are far distant from each other: either the husband is not at his permanent place of residence or the wife is in another locality. The letter is described as a *risāla* (message) or *jawāb* (answer); the latter is probably a borrowing from popular appellations of the *fatwā* in tribal society, since the letter is apparently drawn up or certified by a *faqīh*. Thus in one case it was said that the *jawāb* had been certified by "the writer of the letter (*kātib al-ḥurūf*), the *faqīh*...[and others]."[41] Sometimes the husband divorces the wife in the presence of "the congregation" (*jamāʿa*) and sends a document to that effect, signed by him, to the marriage solemnizer (*maʾdhūn*), who confirms the *ṭalāq*. In one case, following a demand by the wife, who was in another town, that the husband pay her the balance of the dower, the husband wrote a *jawāb* to the *qāḍī* of that town. The *qāḍī* summoned her to court "and read to her the husband's letter of divorce," and she "responded by consenting." It seems that she consented to the divorce on condition that she received what was due to her, for it is said in what follows that the husband was summoned to court in his town, divorced the wife, and paid her the balance of the dower.[42]

The husband sometimes announces the divorce to the wife's agnates, and they or she hasten to court to confirm it. In one case the husband sent a *risāla* to his father-in-law saying: "Your daughter..., my wife, is divorced by a single repudiation." In another case the wife produced in court a *risāla* that the husband, who was in Benghazi, had sent to her through her brother and that said: "My wife...is divorced (*mufāraqa*)." The letter was undated, and the husband afterward stated that the divorce had taken place four months previously.[43] As noted earlier, the husband may divorce the wife by letter on condition that she waives her rights or compensates him ("suspended *khulʿ*").[44] The author has not come across a case of

40. Linant, *Traité*, pp. 360–62.
41. B2:KM38–43:T41–43, K7: p. 94 no. 250 3 March 43; Layish, *Judaean Desert*. See below, VII3e. Cf. Berque, p. 428.
42. KD59–73, K48: p. 85 no. 166 25 April 61; and B2:KM38–43:T41–43, K5: p. 53 no. 133 30 April 42, respectively.
43. KD59–73, K51: p. 17 no. 34 17 Oct. 59, and K45: p. 81 no. 158 28 March 61, respectively.
44. B2:KM38–43:T41–43, K7: p. 77 no. 203 1 Nov. 42. On the suspended *khulʿ* see above, pp. 32ff.

divorce in writing where the spouses were not distant from each other. Charnay reports a practice prevailing among Algerian Muslims under French rule of providing the spouses, at the time of the marriage, with a card. A husband who divorced his wife returned the card to the *qāḍī*, who declared the divorce and sent the wife another card certifying the divorce; hence the expressions "cancel the card" and "return the card," frequent in Algerian *sijill*s.[45]

45. Charnay, p. 37 n. 2.

CHAPTER III

Divorce by Consent

1. DEFINITIONS AND TERMINOLOGY

In divorces by consent, which are anchored in the Qurʾān and the *ḥadīth*, two elements must be distinguished as to their financial consequences: mutual renunciation (*mubāraʾa* or *ibrāʾ*) of the matrimonial rights—that is, the dower and the waiting-period maintenance (*nafaqat al-ʿidda*), and the payment of compensation (*ʿiwaḍ* or *badal*) to the husband by the wife (*khulʿ*, "divestiture," or derivatives of this term, and other expressions of similar meaning; some use the term *ṭalāq* or a metaphorical expression [*kināya*] while also indicating compensation). The accepted rule is that the wife returns to the husband the dower she received at the time of the marriage. Some jurists hold that this distinction between *mubāraʾa* and *khulʿ* is legally immaterial and that a renunciation divorce is a variant of a compensation divorce. Others hold that a renunciation divorce is a separate kind of divorce. At any rate, the terms *mubāraʾa* and *khulʿ* are not synonymous (except according to the Ḥanafī school); the former refers only to situations not involving compensation. The schools disagree as to whether compensation is a condition of *khulʿ*. The Mālikīs hold that a *khulʿ* is valid even without compensation and that the husband's consent to effect the divorce is sufficient. The Shāfiʿīs hold that the *khulʿ* is not possible without compensation, while the matter is controversial among the Ḥanafīs. Modern jurists, such as the Egyptian Qadrī Pasha, hold that the *khulʿ* can be valid even without compensation, and this position is reflected in the modern legislation of several Middle Eastern countries. In any case, the wife's matrimonial rights are not affected beyond what is included in the compensation. Some call both forms of divorce *ṭalāq ʿalā māl*, "divorce in return for property." The husband must be competent to effect the divorce, and the wife must be a lawful spouse competent to be a party to proceedings for divorce for consideration. Both spouses may initiate this form of divorce and agree to it either themselves or through their representatives. If the husband is not an adult, he cannot effect a divorce by mutual consent. Only his father, who has a right to marry him off compulsorily (*jabr*), or his guardian can do so. According to the Mālikī school, the wife can free herself from the coercive power of her marriage guardian, and achieve legal competence, only through the lawful loss of her virginity (i.e., through consummation of her marriage); but even then she needs a matrimonial representative or a guardian for divorce by consent. However, if she consents directly, the divorce is valid.[1]

Law No. 76, whose reformist features were mainly inspired by the Ḥanafī school simplified the definitions of the types of divorce by consent, included *mubāraʾa* in *khulʿ*, and provided that compensation should be a condition of the validity of *khulʿ*. The significance of this reform is that it permits the husband to prevent a *khulʿ* divorce if the wife is unable to compensate him on the spot. Law No. 18 eases the position somewhat by enabling the court to postpone the date of payment if the wife is destitute and the husband refuses to grant a delay in order to harass her. Law No. 76 permits the opening of *khulʿ* proceedings even if one of the parties is still a minor, provided that the father or grandfather appointed as guardian of the minor's financial interests consents thereto; in the absence of such an appointment, the consent of the *qāḍī* is required. The full age of legal puberty is twenty-one years, and it is expected that women below that age will, in practice, be able to perform *khulʿ* in accordance with the provisions of that law. The *sharīʿa* protects a minor female by providing that the dissolution of her marriage shall not involve the alienation of property to compensate the husband. The new law enables either party to withdraw the offer of a *khulʿ* divorce as long as the other party has not accepted it; this constitutes an amendment in favor of the husband. Law No. 76 further provides that the mutual obligations of the spouses shall be unaffected by *khulʿ* except for the compensation agreed upon between them.[2]

A *khulʿ* divorce is effected by voluntary agreement between the parties, and what is more important, the husband divorces the wife of his own free will. There is no support in the Mālikī school, even in a "weak" opinion, for

1. Linant, *Traité*, pp. 421–25, 431, 437–38, 442; Linant, *khulʿ*, pp. 185ff., 191–92; Milliot, pp. 372–73, 384; Anderson, *Africa* pp. 141, 366, 367; Stern, p. 129 and the reference there to Robertson Smith.
2. Mayer, *Marriage*, p. 39 n. 1, p. 41 n. 3, pp. 41–46.

the view that the wife can force a divorce upon the husband if she is able to compensate him by returning the dower and other payments.[3] A drastic amendment introduced by Law No. 76 is that if the husband refuses to consent to the *khulʿ* in order to harass the wife, and as a result it is to be feared that the spouses will not observe Allāh's precepts (i.e., that the wife will disobey the husband and he will mistreat her), the *qāḍī* may decree *khulʿ* in return for appropriate compensation to the husband. The object of the reform is to enable the wife to dissolve the marriage after all possibilities of dissolution by legal proceedings on the ground of injury (*ḍarar*)—recognized by the Mālikī school—have been exhausted; such proceedings are, to all appearances, not a simple matter. The reform seems to be based on the view prevailing in the Mālikī school that a judicial decree of *khulʿ* might be granted for specific consideration—usually the whole or part of the dower—on the recommendation of arbitrators appointed by the court in the case of marital discord, provided that the wife is the guilty party.[4]

The use of the term *ibrāʾ* or *mubāraʾa* for a mutual-renunciation divorce is attested though not particularly frequent. It occurs in such formulas as: "Each of the spouses renounces (*abraʾa*) in favor of the other." It may occur with a slightly different meaning: being free from obligations—for example, "Each of the spouses was free (*bariʾa*) from any obligation to the other."[5] The term *khulʿ* and its verbal derivatives refer to *ṭalāq* by consent, whether with renunciation of rights or with payment of compensation to the husband. The most usual formula is: "The wife redeemed herself from him in return for the whole of her dower" (*khālaʿathu bi-kāffat ṣadāqihā* or *khālaʿat nafsahā bi-jamīʿ ṣadāqihā*).[6] Divorce by consent is frequently called *ṭalāq khulʿī*, *ṭalqa khulʿiyya*, or *mukhālaʿa*.[7] The verb *fadā* in the eighth form, in the sense of "to redeem," may be used to describe the freeing of the wife through divorce by consent. Thus in one case it was said: "The wife redeemed herself (*khālaʿat*)... from her husband in return for the whole of

3. Anderson, *Nigeria*, p. 25; Schacht, *Report*, p. 1.

4. Mayer, *Marriage*, pp. 42, 44; Anderson, *Africa*, pp. 140, 209; Coulson, *History*, p. 187. Cf. Fluehr-Lobban, pp. 157ff.

5. E.g., AP:E2, p. 13 no. 26 13 Aug. 51; AP:E3, p. 308 no. 520 21 March 54.

6. E.g., KD59-73, K43: p. 46 no. 88 21 June 60, p. 56 no. 108 27 Aug. 60, K45: p. 97 no. 201 29 July 61, p. 98 no. 204 17 Oct. 61.

7. E.g., AP:E2, p. 11 no. 22 6 Aug. 51; KD59-73, K50: p. 141 no. 311 25 Oct. 62; AP:E4, p. 85 no. 84 17 Sep. 64.

her dower... and freed herself (*iftadat nafsahā*) from him in exchange for all that has been mentioned." The husband took delivery (*taslīm*) of the deferred dower and seized the redemption price from her (*qabaḍa minhā al-iftidā*[ʾ]).[8] Other terms for divorce by consent are *aṭlaqa sarāḥ* and *khāliṣ*. Thus in one case it was said: "I have redeemed myself from my husband... in exchange for all my *sharʿī* rights, so that he may divorce me and free me (*li-yuṭalliqanī wa-yuṭliq sarāḥī*)."[9] In another case it was said: "The husband stated that she was freed (*khāliṣ*) in exchange for all her dower and rights."[10] Law No. 76 also classified renunciation divorces under the heading of *khulʿ*. Several African countries likewise use the two terms synonymously.[11]

2. CONSENT OF THE PARTIES

Although no quantitative study has been conducted, there can be no doubt that most of the divorces recorded in the *sijill*s are by mutual consent of the parties.[12] This finding gives no indication as to which side initiated the divorce. It may have been either side. The husband is interested in divorce by consent because of the advantages involved as regards the financial consequences. But it seems that this mechanism is mainly resorted to by the wife (or her agnates), since the husband can divorce her even without her consent. The possibility of dissolution by legal proceedings (judicial *ṭalāq*) is limited because it requires a *sharʿī* ground. Of course, the agreement of the husband is a condition of divorce by consent.

The Cyrenaican *sijill*s contain no evidence of compulsory *khulʿ*, either before or after the adoption of Law No. 76, and it seems to be unknown. On the other hand it was known, with some variations, in several parts of Africa, including North Africa under colonial rule. But it was not anchored there in the *sharīʿa* or in statutory legislation but in custom. Its *raison d'être* was that a wife who leaves the husband's house and refuses to return cannot be forced to obey him by a decree for restitution of conjugal rights; the institution of *bayt al-ṭāʿa* was unknown. The mere fact of refusing to return was, under certain circumstances, deemed to be adultery, especially if she

8. KAMD, p. 25 no. 8 3 March 33 [?]. Cf. Fluehr-Lobban, pp. 157ff.
9. A:E103, p. 130 no. 231 23 Sep. 52.
10. E.g., KD59–73, K44: p. 135 no. 299 7 Oct. 62, K47: p. 138 no. 305 18 Oct. 62.
11. Mayer, *Marriage*, p. 41; Anderson, *Africa*, e.g., p. 54.
12. Cf. Layish, *Women*, p. 162.

threatened expressly to turn prostitute[13] in order to extort a divorce. Under these circumstances, plain common sense prompted the husband to agree to release the wife by *khulʿ* in return for appropriate or even excessive compensation.[14] The courts recognized the wife's right to obtain her release from an unwanted marriage by returning the dower, wholly or in part, moneys expended by the husband before or during the marriage, gifts, etc. The *qāḍī*s sometimes (e.g., in northern Nigeria) tried to represent the divorce as a *sharʿī khulʿ* when in fact it was purely customary. In West Africa, enforced *khulʿ* was supported by the Mālikī doctrine (which permits such a mechanism of dissolution where it is recommended by the family arbitral council—anchored in the Qurʾān—in cases of disputes between spouses) and was reinforced by the reluctance of the British administration to enforce judgments for obedience by execution proceedings. In practice, the *khulʿ* was enforced upon the husband without recourse to arbitrators; this too is proof that it was rooted in custom.[15] The Awlād ʿAlī of the Western Desert recognize a wife's customary right to obtain her freedom by compensating the husband. Where she cannot expect her father to help her dissolve her marriage, especially when she is married to her paternal cousin, she takes her belongings and sometimes her children and seeks the protection of an influential person (in picturesque language, "throws herself before him")—that is to say, she seeks his mediation in dissolving her marriage on the basis of compensation to the husband.[16]

The usual formula in divorce by consent is: "Agreement has been reached (*taqarrara al-ittifāq*) between the spouses for dissolution without discord (*firāq min ghayr shiqāq*)."[17] Sometimes the spouses agree that "the most appropriate thing for them to do is to dissolve their marriage by way of an amicable settlement (*ʿalā wajh al-ṣulḥ*)"—that is to say, an arrangement not involving legal proceedings.[18] Sometimes it is expressly stated that dissolution was achieved without the intervention of the *qāḍī*.[19] Even in divorces by consent, the husband may give the wife her financial rights, as agreed between them prior to the divorce—that is, the dower,

13. Schacht, *Report*, p. 1; Anderson, *Africa*, pp. 54, 146.
14. Anderson, *Africa*, pp. 140, 209, 292–93.
15. Coulson, *History*, pp. 137–38; Anderson, *Africa*, pp. 140, 232; Anderson, *Nigeria*, p. 26.
16. Mohsen, *Conflict*, p. 116; Mohsen, *Women*, pp. 230ff. Cf. Stewart, *Texts*, pp. 11ff.
17. E.g., KD59–73, K44: p. 1 no. 1 7 June 59.
18. E.g., AP:E4, p. 121 no. 118 9 April 47.
19. KD59–73, p. 159 no. 335 25 March 63.

wholly or in part; maintenance for the waiting period or, if she is pregnant, until she has given birth; allowances for clothing and bedding; etc.[20]

3. "RENUNCIATION DIVORCE"

a. Renunciation by the Wife

As a rule, in divorces by consent the financial consequences are mainly borne by the wife (or her relatives).

(1) **Dower.** The wife renounces the whole of the dower if she has not yet received it, or the balance of the dower if she has received part of it. Thus in one case it was said that the wife and her father "have renounced her specified (*muʿayyan*) dower"; this seems to refer to the dower agreed upon (*musammā*) between them at the time of the marriage. In another case it was said: "She renounces (*tatanāzal*) the balance (*bāqī*) of her dower, which in any case she had already waived (*samaḥat*) in order that he might divorce her." In another case it was said that at the time of the marriage the husband had paid the wife only part of the dower and that it had been agreed between them that "she renounces the part that is still a financial liability (*dhimma*) of the husband."[21]

Occasionally the wife renounces the deferred dower. In some cases it was said that upon their divorce it was agreed between them that the husband would renounce the prompt (*muʿajjal*) dower and the wife the deferred (*muʾajjal*) dower. But it is not certain that these terms are used here in the conventional sense. Thus in one case it was said that the husband had paid to the wife "[part] of the dower and still owed [part] of the dower" and that "they have agreed that he shall renounce the prompt dower and she the deferred dower." In other words, the "prompt dower" is here the part of the prompt dower actually paid and the "deferred dower" is here the part of the prompt dower still outstanding.[22] The *sijill*s indeed mention many instances of "customary" deferred dower—that is, not dower in the normative sense, which is paid upon divorce or death, "whichever is the earlier" (*li-aqrab al-ajalayn*), but that part of the prompt dower which it is

20. KD59–73, K44: p. 1 no. 1 7 June 59, p. 159 no. 335 25 March 63; KM63DP:EP, p. 50 no. 95 6 July 60; and KD59–73, K44: p. 134 no. 279 26 July 62, respectively.

21. KD59–73, K45: p. 118 no. 247 26 April 62; A:E103, p. 122 no. 215 24 Aug. 52; and A:E104, p. 168 no. 293 4 Feb. 53, respectively. Cf. Linant, *Traité*, p. 406.

22. KD59–73, K45: p. 97 no. 198 17 July 61, K45: p. 97 no. 202 [?] June 61.

agreed shall be paid at a later date during the existence of the marriage. A marriage contract usually specifies the types and quantities of this dower and indicates when each of its types is to be paid (e.g., "one silver bracelet in four months" and another bracelet "after the sowing season"; or "four rotls of silver, one rotl at the end of every year, and a silk costume at the end of a year."[23] Sometimes no specific date is mentioned but the phrase "[shall be paid] when it is convenient (*ʿalā al-maysara*)" is used; the reference is of course to the time when the marriage is still in existence,[24] and it may be expressly stated that the matter in question is deferred dower "according to Beduin custom." Thus in one case the marriage contract provided that the deferred dower would be 12,000 francs, to be paid as follows: 6,000 francs "in two years" and 6,000 francs "at the end of ten years according to the custom of the desert dwellers in the case of shame or absence (*ka-ʿādat ahl al-bādiya ʿalā ʿayb aw ghayb*)" or "according to the custom of the country dwellers" (*ka-ʿādat ahl al-balad*).[25] In some cases it is said that the wife "has delivered" (*sallamat*) the balance of the dower to the husband or that "she has redeemed herself from him in return for the balance of the dower."[26] In these cases, it is not clear whether the wife waived something she had not yet received or returned something she had already received; the dividing line between renunciation (*mubāraʾa*) and compensation (*khulʿ*) is thus blurred, although what is meant here is probably renunciation.

23. E.g., AMR42–44, A2: p. 14 no. 14 16 June 42, p. 54 no. 54 1 April 53.

24. AMR42–44, A3: p. 68 no. 68 4 Aug. 43.

25. E.g., AMR42–44, A5: p. 129 no. 129 10 Feb. 44, A5: p. 103 no. 103 21 Nov. 43, A5: p. 114 no. 114 21 Dec. 43, A3: p. 122 no. 122 20 Jan. 44. Cf. Anderson, *Africa*, p. 369. Peters came across the expression *ʿalā ʿayb aw ghayb* in Cyrenaican Beduin society in the context of the payment of dower. Where animals are offered as dower, they are not all delivered on the spot but part are delivered only "in the lambing season" or "at the time of the next harvest," when it will probably have been established that the union is fertile. The terms of the agreement between the parties are: "We will put so many in front of you (*quddāmak*) and leave so many in case of shame or absence (*ʿalā ʿayb aw ghayb*)." In Peters' opinion, the word *ʿayb* refers to the shame the wife may bring upon the husband by persistently flaunting her sexuality or by having sexual congress with another man, so that she is regarded as an adulteress. The word *ghayb* means absence through either death or desertion (Peters, *Bridewealth*, pp. 145–46). *Ghayb* may mean absence of the husband, who has gone to a distant place and thus causes injury to the wife by not providing maintenance and by endangering her chastity; it is frequent in Cyrenaica, as we have seen. In either case—shame or absence—a ground for dissolution is created and the husband must pay the deferred dower immediately.

26. E.g., KD59–73, p. 101 nos. 212 and 213 14 Dec. 61.

Khulᶜ is not the only term for renunciation; the verb *sallama* seems to have the same meaning. Thus in one case it is said that the wife "delivered to him all her rights" (*sallamat lahu kāffat ḥuqūqihā*), and it makes no sense to say that she returned the waiting-period maintenance, or the dower, that she had not yet received. The word *sallamat* seems to be synonymous with *asqaṭat* in *asqaṭat kāffat ḥuqūqihā al-bāqiya ᶜalā zawjihā* (she renounced all the other rights her husband still owed her).[27]

(2) **Clothing.** Renunciation of the dower is often accompanied by renunciation of the clothing allowance (*kiswa*). Thus it was said: "She renounced the balance of her dower . . . and her clothing" or "She claimed neither dower nor clothing"; or the wife's father renounced "a large outfit of clothing (*badla*)" on her behalf.[28] These cases seem to suggest that the wife renounced something she had not yet received. Still, it is possible that the reference was not to renunciation but to the return of the value of the clothing. Thus in one case it was said that the wife "redeemed herself in return for the price (*thaman*) of the clothing."[29]

(3) **Waiting-period maintenance.** The wife renounces the waiting-period maintenance (*nafaqat al-ᶜidda*). She renounces maintenance specifically or as part of "all her matrimonial rights."[30] She may undertake to "support herself" (*al-infāq ᶜalā nafsihā*) during that three-month waiting period,[31] or her father may undertake to support her during that time.[32] Only in one case did the wife renounce maintenance that had been awarded her by the court while the marriage was in existence and that had not been paid by the time of the divorce. Such maintenance was here described as *nafaqat ihmāl* (maintenance for neglect).[33]

27. KD59–73, K44: p. 135 no. 300 7 Oct. 62; and B2:KM38–43:T41–43, K6: p. 84 no. 223 1 Jan. 43, respectively.
28. E.g., KD59–73, K50: p. 129 no. 285 15 Aug. 62, K48: p. 177 no. 383 18 Aug. 63, K48: p. 187 no. 405 24 Oct. 63; AP:E2, p. 178 no. 174 26 Nov. 47.
29. KD59–73, K47: p. 25 no. 49 2 Feb. 60.
30. E.g., AP:E4, p. 101 no. 99 18 Nov. 46, p. 107 no. 105 18 Jan. 47, p. 184 no. 180 12 Jan. 48; KD59–73, p. 104 no. 218 21 Dec. 61, p. 102 no. 251 21 May 62, K45: p. 129 no. 265 4 July 62.
31. E.g., A:E103, p. 150 no. 265 13 Dec. 52; AP:E1, p. 153 no. 269 6 Jan. 53; A:E104, p. 168 no. 293 4 Feb. 53.
32. E.g., A:E104, p. 200 no. 338 16 April 53, p. 204 no. 343 4 May 53. On maintenance during the waiting period see below, V2a.
33. A:102, p. 28 no. 54 9 Sep. 51. Cf. Linant *Traité*, pp. 406, 436; Layish, *Women*, p. 159.

(4) **Suckling wages and custody maintenance.** To obtain her freedom, the wife is sometimes ready to waive the wages for suckling her children (*ujrat raḍāʿ*) and the maintenance of minor children in her custody (*ḥaḍāna*), which she is by law entitled to receive from the children's father. She may even renounce her right of custody and be prepared to hand the children over to their father. Thus in one case the wife, in addition to the balance of her dower, waived the wages for suckling her infant son (*raḍīʿ*). In another case she waived the wages for suckling one of her daughters, undertaking to maintain her gratuitously, and renounced the custody of her other daughters in favor of their father. In yet another case it was agreed between the spouses upon their divorce that the child should remain in the custody of the mother until his weaning (*infiṭām*) without any payment whatsoever and then pass to his father. In a further case the spouses agreed that the wife might take her small daughter to another town on condition that she demanded nothing from the father as long as the daughter was still at the age of *sharʿī* custody. In another case the wife, while still pregnant, waived pregnancy maintenance and the wages for suckling and left the husband the option (*ikhtiyār*) of assuming custody if he so wished. Similarly, a pregnant wife gave up a daughter and a son, and "their father took them from her."[34] In another case the husband agreed to divorce the wife only after she undertook to support her daughter at the suckling age "with her own money (*min khāṣṣ mālihā*) until her father claimed her."[35] At times the wife's father or proxy (*wakīl*) undertakes to maintain the child as long as he is in his mother's custody and to hand him over to his father or paternal grandfather when they claim him—but in any case without delay at the end of the custody period.[36]

According to the Mālikī school, the wife's renunciation of wages for the suckling and maintenance of minor children in her custody is invalid. Law No. 76, in reliance on the Ḥanafī school, seeks to ensure, by conferring legal validity on the wife's renunciation of her rights, that the husband derives

34. KD59-73, K48: p. 73 no. 143 14 Dec. 60; AP:E2, p. 13 no. 26 13 Aug. 51; KD59-73, K50: p. 13 no. 34 12 May 65; A:E103, p. 158 no. 276 12 Jan. 53; KD59-73, K45: p. 78 no. 152 12 Feb. 61; and KD59-73, K48: p. 47 no. 88 6 Dec. 65, respectively. See also KD59-73, p. 102 no. 251 21 May 62; A:E104, p. 224 no. 358 [?] June 53; AP:E3, p. 302 no. 507 25 Feb. 54. Cf. Charnay, p. 53.

35. AP:E4, p. 101 no. 99 18 Nov. 46. See also KD59-73, p. 152 no. 332 17 Jan. 63.

36. AP:E2, p. 162 no. 156 3 Sep. 47. See also AP:E3, p. 308 no. 520 21 March 54; KD59-73, p. 99 no. 208 13 Nov. 61. Cf. Linant, *Traité*, pp. 406, 440.

the full benefit of his consent to release her. Moreover, the husband may claim the monetary value of those services if it appears that the wife, owing to lack of means, did not fulfill her undertaking to maintain the children and the husband had to do it instead. He may even collect this debt from her estate (art. 16). On the other hand the law seeks to ensure, also in reliance on the Ḥanafī school, the wife's right to the custody of minor children. The Mālikī school recognizes the validity of her renunciation of *ḥaḍāna*, although some make it subject to the condition that no harm is caused to the child by his removal from the mother. The law provides that the wife's renunciation of *ḥaḍāna* in the divorce agreement is void regardless of the child's interest (art. 17).[37]

b. Renunciation by the Husband

(1) **Dower and clothing.** Although the wife bears the greater burden of the financial consequences of divorce by consent, the husband too sometimes waives matrimonial rights in the divorce agreement. He renounces the part of the dower that he has already paid to the wife or the clothing he has already given her. Thus in one case it was said: "The husband and his father renounce in favor of the wife's father everything he has received from them [as dower]—twenty-two sheep and one camel—and they also renounce the clothing allotted to the wife [in the marriage contract]."[38] We have already seen that it may be agreed between the parties that the husband renounces the prompt dower and the wife the customary "deferred dower," (i.e., the part of the dower that the husband did not pay during the period of the marriage.[39] Sometimes the husband gets back part of the dower he has paid and waives the remainder.[40]

(2) ***Khasāra, maṣārīf al-marʾa, walīmat al-faraḥ.*** The husband sometimes waives losses (*khasāra*) and expenses (*maṣārīf*) incurred in consequence of the marriage. This includes dower and clothing; the entertainment of guests, such as sheep slaughtered (*dhabāʾiḥ*) as part of the wedding festivities (*walīmat al-faraḥ*); everything spent on or given to the woman before or during the marriage, such as jewelry and consumable (*hālika*)

37. Mayer, *Marriage*, pp. 45–46; Linant, *Traité*, pp. 440–41.

38. AP:E2, p. 162 no. 156 3 Sep. 47.

39. E.g., KD59–73, K45: p. 97 no. 198 17 July 61, K45: p. 97 no. 202 [?] June 61. See above, pp. 48–49.

40. E.g., KD59–73, K42: p. 157 no. 332 2 March 63.

goods; and various household effects, such as bedding.[41] These expenses are sometimes called "the woman's expenses" (*maṣārīf al-marʾa*).[42]

c. Mutual Renunciation

Occasionally, general formulas expressing mutual renunciation of matrimonial rights are used without specifying those rights. Thus, for instance, it is said: "Each of them renounces (*abraʾa*) in favor of the other" or "Each of the spouses was free (*bariʾa*) of the rights of the other." Following the mutual renunciation, it is said: "Neither of us will demand anything of the other, contrary to what is mentioned in the *sijill*" or "Neither of us will demand anything, much or little" or "No claim (*daʿwā*), demand (*ṭalab*), or matrimonial right remains between them."[43] Some try to ensure themselves against future claims by saying: "Whichever [of the spouses] claims [matrimonial rights against the other] shall be a *ẓālim* who has no right (*ḥaqq*)." It seems that the term *ẓālim* should not be interpreted here in a religious-ethical sense—sinner—but in a customary-legal sense—offender—that is to say, one against whom a cause of action is created.[44] It is sometimes possible to trace the stages of negotiations that end in the mutual renunciation of rights. Thus in one case the wife's father demanded waiting-period (pregnancy) maintenance and the husband's father demanded compensation for "losses" caused to him; eventually the parties settled for mutual renunciation, and the husband effected the divorce. In Israel, mutual renunciation upon divorce has been noted also in matters unconnected with the marriage, such as monetary debts, obligations based on bills of exchange, and civil and criminal actions conducted in civil courts, sometimes in relation to the prohibition of divorce against the wife's will.[45]

41. E.g., AP:E4, p. 139 no. 129 2 June 47; KD59-73, p. 101 no. 212 14 Dec. 61, K47: p. 182 no. 430 21 Jan. 64, no. 431 27 Jan. 64; AP:E2, p. 182 no. 178 8 Jan. 48, p. 184 no. 180 12 Jan. 48; AP:E4, p. [?] no. [?] 1 July 46.

42. E.g., KD59-73, p. 150 no. 331 12 Jan. 63. See also K44: p. 135 no. 300 7 Oct. 62, K43: p. 139 no. 306 18 Oct. 62, K43: p. 170 no. 368 13 June 63.

43. E.g., AP:E2, p. 13 no. 26 13 Aug. 51; AP:E3, p. 308 no. 520 21 March 54; AP:E4, p. 139 no. 129 2 June 47; KD59-73, K51: p. 11 no. 22 3 Sep. 59, K51: p. 19 no. 37 2 Nov. 59, K45: p. 89 no. 173 13 May 61.

44. KD59-73, K48: p. 85 no. 166 25 April 61. Cf. Layish, *Judaean Desert*.

45. KD59-73, K50: p. 4 no. 13 15 Feb. 65; Layish, *Women*, p. 160.

4. "COMPENSATION DIVORCE"

a. Compensation on the Wife's Initiative

As one would expect, the initiative for dissolution with compensation to the husband is chiefly taken by the wife, since the husband does not require her consent to a divorce.[46] The stages of a *khul*ʿ divorce on the wife's initiative can frequently be traced. At the first stage, she proposes that the husband release her, specifying the conditions of the compensation. Thus in one case the wife offered to pay to the husband "the whole of the dower I have received from him and all the expenses [caused to him by the marriage]...and she redeemed herself from him in return for all her matrimonial rights, in order that he might divorce her (*fi naẓīr an yuṭalliqahā*)." In this case, the husband accepted (*qabila*) the entire offer and divorced the wife.[47] Occasionally the husband rejects the wife's initiative because he is not really interested in a divorce; under these circumstances, he may have her declared rebellious (*nāshiza*).[48] But if she insists, he will sooner or later agree to release her against compensation. In fact, his initial refusal may be a tactical move to obtain more compensation. In one case the parties at first agreed upon "divorce without a dispute"; but it seems that in the further course of the negotiations the husband withdrew his consent: "The wife wanted a divorce and the husband wanted their married life to continue; the wife did not agree to return." At this stage the wife's father joined in the negotiations, and both offered to compensate the husband for the divorce with various items of jewelry and a sum of money (the dower) that the father had received from the husband at the time. The husband agreed and divorced the wife.[49]

Occasionally the wife, on her way to the desired freedom, has to overcome attempts of the *qāḍī* to reconcile the spouses. Thus in one case the judgment says: "The wife demanding dissolution, the *qāḍī* tried to reconcile them...reconciliation (*ṣulḥ*) being designated as a blessing (*khayr*) by Allāh, but the wife only wanted dissolution, and the husband granted her request." In Israel there have been cases of a wife offering to renounce

46. See above, p. 27.
47. KD59–73, K48: p. 65 no. 127 22 Oct. 60. See also K51: p. 114 no. 239 4 April 62; AP:E4, p. 107 no. 105 18 Jan. 47.
48. E.g., AP:E2, p. 5 no. 10 28 July 51.
49. KD59–73, K47: p. 28 no. 54 22 Feb. 60. Cf. Anderson, *Africa*, p. 209.

various matrimonial rights and compensate the husband on condition that he divorce her.[50]

A compensation divorce, in the narrow technical sense of the term, means that the wife not only renounces various matrimonial rights but also compensates the husband for her release. In practice, it is difficult to draw a dividing line between the two. Compensation is usually bound up with the renunciation of rights. The dower due to the wife, which has been paid to her wholly or in part, is full compensation to the husband for his consent to release her by divorce. The sociophilosophical justification for this is that the dower entitles the husband to have lawful sexual intercourse with the wife and therefore that if she wishes to be released by him, she must return the dower to him. Anything fit to be given to the wife as dower is fit also to be used by the wife as compensation for her divorce: money, fruit, livestock, etc.—but not goods forbidden by religion such as wine or pork. If these are agreed upon between the parties as compensation the husband's right to compensation ceases.[51]

(1) **Dower.** There is express, albeit scanty, evidence of a wife returning (or a husband getting back) the dower that was paid in full on contraction of the marriage[52] or of a wife asking the husband to receive back "out of her money" that part of the dower which is proved to have been paid to her marriage guardian.[53] There is more evidence of a wife "redeeming herself by waiving the whole dower which she is entitled [to receive] from him [the husband] and which is his financial liability and by delivering it to him." It is difficult to assess in the above-mentioned cases whether the wife returns dower actually received or waives the right to receive dower. The evidence points in both directions. Thus, following the above formula, it was said in one case that the wife "paid" (*dafaʿat*) to the husband a certain sum and a silver bracelet[54] but in another case that "the wife renounced (*tanāzalat*) all her dower."[55] Occasionally, it is said that the wife redeems herself in

50. AP:E4, p. 121 no. 118 9 April 47; Layish, *Women*, p. 161.
51. Linant, *Traité*, pp. 422, 437–39.
52. E.g., B2:KM38–43:T41–43, K5: p. 16 no. 37 24 Aug. 41; AP:E1, p. 145 no. 257 24 Nov. 52.
53. AP:E2, p. 23 no. 46 29 Aug. 51.
54. KD59-73, K47: p. 42 no. 77 22 Oct. 65.
55. KDP, K45: p. 12 no. 30 16 May 65. See also KM63DP:EP, K6: no. 251 23 [June] 43; KD59–73, K44: p. 1 no. 2 9 June 59, K44: p. 2 no. 3 13 June 59, p. 3 no. 5 13 July 59, K48: p. 38 no. 73 2 May 60.

return for all her dower, the prompt and the deferred (*muqaddam wa-mu*ʾ*akhkhar*), as stipulated upon the conclusion of the marriage contract.[56] Sometimes she redeems herself only with the deferred dower or part thereof, in which case we may assume that the reference is to a right not yet realized. Even then, it is said at times: "She delivered (*sallamat*) or sent (*arsalat*) it [the dower] to her husband."[57] Occasionally the spouses agree upon a compromise as to the apportionment of the dower: the wife will redeem herself with the prompt dower, and the husband will pay her the deferred dower (i.e., the balance of the prompt dower not paid during the marriage). Thus in one case the husband said: "My wife has redeemed herself from me with the whole of the registered dower . . . and an amount which I shall pay when I have it is left of the dower to her credit with me."[58]

In several cases the wife redeemed herself by *khul*ʿ with half the dower, but there is no evidence connecting this with the question of the consummation of the marriage. Where the marriage has not been consummated, the wife is entitled to half the dower.[59] In one case, in which the wife was divorced by *khul*ʿ before consummation, the wife redeemed herself with the whole of the dower.[60] The parties may agree in writing that the dower shall be returned to the husband in monthly instalments (*taqsīṭ*). In one case it was proved that the husband owed the wife (on account of the dower?) the sum of eight pounds. To clear the debt the husband sold (*bā*ʿ*a*) to the wife some agricultural land worth ten pounds, so that she now owed him two pounds. It was agreed between them that she should pay that sum in two equal instalments at the end of two consecutive cane harvesting seasons, whereupon the husband divorced her by *ṭalāq*.[61]

The wife usually compensates the husband with money, but sometimes it may be with livestock (she-camels, cows, sheep, goats, etc., of different

56. E.g., AP:E2, p. 180 no. 186 24 Dec. 47; KD59–73, K47: p. 39 no. 75 4 May 60, K47: p. 5 no. 9 9 July 59, K48: p. 8 no. 16 10 Aug. 59.

57. KD59–73, K51: p. 35 no. 66 11 April 60; KAMD, p. 29 no. 11 16 Feb. 34. See also KD59–73, K51: p. 13 no. 26 21 Sep. 59, K51: p. 21 no. 42 19 Nov. 59.

58. KD59–73, K45: p. 106 no. 222 15 Jan. 62. See also KD59–73, K43: p. 63 no. 122 11 Oct. 60, K45: p. 66 no. 129 1 Nov. 60, K50: p. 90 no. 175 18 May 61. On the customary dower see above, pp. 48–49.

59. E.g., KD59–73, K43: p. 63 no. 123 13 Oct. 60, K45: p. 68 no. 133 12 Nov. 60, K45: p. 161 no. 341 30 March 63. Cf. Bousquet, *Précis*, pp. 157ff.

60. KD59–73, K43: p. 60 no. 116 5 Oct. 60. Cf. Layish, *Women*, p. 160.

61. KD59–73, K44: p. 2 no. 4 21 June 59. See also KD59–73, p. 24 no. 55 4 Aug. 55.

kinds and ages); it seems that the compensation is paid in the same form as the dower was, although there is no evidence of this in the *sijill*s.[62] Other forms of compensation are raw foodstuffs (barley, cane, etc., in units of weight).[63]

(2) **Clothing.** Compensation by dower is at times coupled with compensation by clothing (*kiswa*), which includes wearing apparel of different types. There is express evidence of wives returning, in kind, clothing received from their husbands. In one case it was said that the wife delivered to the husband "part of all the new clothes" in return for a *khulʿ* divorce, although clothing is regarded as the wife's personal property.[64] But it is sometimes difficult to escape the impression that the reference is to a right not yet realized. Thus in one case it was said that the wife "renounced (*tanāzalat*) the dower and the clothing."[65]

(3) **Household effects.** Similarly, the wife returns various household effects (*athāth*) to the husband as part of the compensation,[66] but she sometimes takes with her "all that belongs to him in the house": mattresses (*farsha*), blankets (*baṭṭāniyya*), and the like.[67]

(4) **Jewelry.** Compensation by dower is often accompanied by the return of silver (*fiḍḍa*) ornaments of various kinds, such as bracelets and necklaces (*dumluj*, *siwār*, *ʿiqd*), received by the wife as prompt dower or part thereof[68] or separately before or during the marriage. She may return them, "under his examining eye, at the divorce session (*muʿāyana biʾl-majlis*) in order that he may divorce her on that account."[69]

62. E.g., AP:E102, p. 10 no. 19 4 Aug. 51; KD59-73, K48: p. 47 no. 88 6 Dec. 65.
63. E.g., KAMD, p. 25 no. 8 3 March 33 [?].
64. KD59-73, K47: p. 5 no. 9 9 July 59. See also KD59-73, K50: p. 93 no. 181 11 June 61, no. 182 13 June 61.
65. KD59-73, K48: p. 52 no. [98] 9 Jan. 66. See also B2:KM38-43:EA, K4a: no. 28 28 Sep. 32; KD59-73, K43: p. 75 no. 147 27 Dec. 60, K48: p. 8 no. 16 10 Aug. 59.
66. E.g., KD59-73, K48: p. 47 no. 88 6 Dec. 65.
67. E.g., KD59-73, K44: p. 127 no. 281 2 Aug. 62, K43: p. 182 no. 394 12 Aug. 63.
68. E.g., A:E104, p. 194 no. 330 4 April 53; KD59-73, K44: p. 62 no. 119 6 Oct. 60.
69. AP:E4, p. 101 no. 99 18 Nov. 46. Cf. Coulson, *Commercial law*, p. 65. See also B2:KM38-43:T41-43, K7: p. 94 no. 250 3 March 43; AP:E2, p. 184 no. 180 12 Jan. 48; KD59-73, K51: p. 16 no. 32 10 Oct. 59, K47: p. 58 no. 111 15 Sep. 60, K45: p. 129 no. 266 7 July 62, K47: p. 138 no. 304 17 Oct. 62; KDP, K45: p. 12 no. 29 16 May 65.

(5) ***Khasāra.*** In addition to returning the dower, the wife sometimes compensates the husband for loss (*khasāra*)—that is, expenses incurred by him in consequence of the marriage, and the husband occasionally states exactly what he claims under this heading: sheep (slaughtered for the wedding feast), jewelry and clothing given to the wife, etc.[70] There is no evidence in the *sijill*s of a wife compensating her husband with immovable property or with her share in her father's estate,[71] probably because she is not actually competent to own or dispose of property.

b. Compensation on the Husband's Initiative

Occasionally, a *khulᶜ* divorce is initiated by the husband. Thus it was said in one instance that he was "determined (*ᶜāzim*) to divorce his wife . . . and he released her (*khālaᶜahā*) in return for her dower," and in another that the spouses "agreed on dissolution (*firāq*) after he had released her in return for the whole of the dower he owed her."[72] One of the advantages of this mode of divorce is that the husband is not only saved expenses for which he would be liable in the case of a unilateral divorce but is likely to be compensated on terms that he himself has set. Thus in one case a dispute arose between the spouses and the husband "divorced her (*ṭallaqahā*) and released her (*khalaᶜahā*) against her prompt dower." In another case the husband "released her in return for all her financial claims against him; she gave them up and he divorced her by *ṭalāq*."[73] The husband occasionally ill-treats the wife until she demands her freedom, but he agrees to divorce her only after his conditions as to compensation are fulfilled. Thus in one case the husband beat the wife with a stick until she was hospitalized, and he was jailed for it. The wife's father, acting as her proxy, asked the court for dissolution of the marriage (*taṭlīq*) in view of the suffering caused to her. The court instructed the husband to divorce the wife, but he "refused to do so until the father returned the dower he had paid to him; only then would he divorce his daughter."[74]

In some places in Africa under colonial rule, it was observed that a husband desirous of a divorce with compensation provoked the wife into

70. E.g., KD59–73, K45: p. 216 no. 517 27 Dec. 64, p. 220 no. 5 26 Dec. 64. Cf. Layish, ***Women***, p. 160.

71. Cf. Layish, ***Women***, p. 161.

72. KD59–73, p. 104 no. 218 21 Dec. 61, and K45: p. 118 no. 248 28 April 62, respectively.

73. KM63DP:EP, p. 50 no. 96 14 July 60; and KD59–73, K48: p. 171 no. 381 15 Aug. 63, respectively.

74. A:E102, p. 345 no. 589 12 July 54.

initiating a divorce. The provocation might consist in his refusal to eat with her, the supply of inferior food and clothing, and similar forms of ill-treatment. The husband might thus extort compensation of twice the amount of the dower. In Tanganyika it was sometimes observed that a husband, despising the aging wife who bore him children, annoyed her so that she might redeem herself by *khulᶜ* with monetary compensation, which would enable him to take another wife instead. In the Kabyle Mountains, on the other hand, it was observed that an angry, contemptuous, and vindictive husband divorced his wife "for nothing" (*berroû bātᶜel*)—that is, without stating any price for her redemption. Such a release was regarded as a grave slight to the wife and her family; the intervention of an influential mediator was sometimes sought to persuade the husband to fix a price, lest a suspicion arise as to her reputation, reducing her chances of remarriage. Linant de Bellefonds, on the other hand, estimates that a wife prefers *khulᶜ* without compensation—since the divorce agreement in itself affords some moral satisfaction—to the humiliation of a unilateral divorce, whereas the husband may prefer *khulᶜ* without compensation for fear of moral censure if he exercises his right.[75]

Occasionally, a *khulᶜ* divorce will—in substance if not in form—have the character of a suspended repudiation. Thus in one case the husband divorced his wife "by *khulᶜī* divorce; she was to be legally permitted (*taḥill*) to him only by a new marriage, after her brother had delivered her dower to him." In another case the wife renounced her "marital rights"—dower and waiting-period maintenance—and undertook to pay a certain sum to the husband "at the earliest date in order that he may divorce her for it." The husband agreed to divorce her on these conditions, saying: "On the day that she pays . . . into court, she will be a divorced woman (*fa-hiya ṭāliqa*)."[76] In a case of a different kind the wife alleged in court that the husband had traveled to another locality four months previously and prior to his departure had "released me (*khalaᶜanī*) in return for my dower and divorced me in the presence of [or through] (*ᶜalā yad*) . . .," and they confirmed her story. The reference may be to the deposit of a suspended *khulᶜ*, in the full sense of the term, with a third party. In another case the spouses were at odds because of the husband's refusal to install the wife in

75. Anderson, *Africa*, pp. 54, 155, 209; Schacht, *Papers*, File: "Islamic law in practice"; Bousquet, *Coutumes kabiles*, p. 78; Charnay, p. 53; Linant, *Khulᶜ*, pp. 194–95.

76. B2:KM38-43:EA, K4a: no. [28] 28 Sep. 32; and A:E102, p. 357 no. 611 7 Aug. 54, respectively.

an adequate dwelling on the plea that he was poor. They eventually agreed on divorce, but he subsequently withdrew his consent and then again agreed to a divorce on condition that his wife give him "all her property."[77] In another case (described earlier in detail) the husband, who was in the Sudan, instructed his proxy in writing to release his two wives in return for all their dower and all household effects if they refused to join him: "If she who lingers and refuses to travel delivers all her rights and all the household effects in her possession that belong to me, divorce her (*ṭalliqhā*) on my behalf." The letter was read to the two wives; both refused to join the husband and delivered or undertook to deliver all the dower and the household effects in their possession. The proxy thereupon divorced them as he had been instructed.[78]

5. DIVORCE THROUGH AGNATES

a. Relatives of the Wife

(1) **Their functions and financial liabilities.** As stated, the Mālikī school recognizes the father's or guardian's competence to conduct divorce negotiations, with binding effect, on behalf of his daughter or ward and to compensate her husband with his money; the father or guardian generally returns the dower he has received. That school also permits a divorce agreement to be negotiated, even against the wife's will, between the husband and a third party who has no mandate on her behalf and is not her guardian.[79] In many cases all the proceedings for divorce by consent are taken by the intermediary of agnates of the spouses, especially of the wife. The wife's relatives are the father (in most cases), the paternal grandfather, a germane brother (*shaqīq*), a paternal uncle, and a paternal cousin.[80] The functions of the wife's relative are to initiate the divorce in her name, to conduct negotiations with the husband or his proxy on the renunciation of various "marital rights" (such as the dower and the waiting-period

77. B2:KM38-43:T43, K7: p. 16 no. 46 16 July 43; and AP:E4, p. 133 no. [126] n.d., respectively.
78. KD59-73, K47, p. 52 no. 100 1 Aug.60, K47: p. 53 no. 101 2 Aug.60. For more details see above, p. 33.
79. Linant, *Traité*, pp. 428–29, 431. For more references see above, n. 1.
80. E.g., B2:KM38-43:EA, K4a: no. [28] 28 Sep. 32; AP:E2, p. 170 no. 164 22 Sep. 47; AP:E1, p. 145 no. 257 24 Nov. 52; KD59-73, K47: p. 6 no. 12 14 July 59, K48: p. 32 no. 62 24 March 60, K45: p. 81 no. 157 21 March 61, K48: p. 82 no. 160 8 April 61. Cf. Charnay, p. 53; Layish, *Women*, p. 161.

maintenance) or the compensation to the husband (the return of the whole or part of the dower and other expenses incurred by the husband) in the manner most favorable to the wife (e.g., by ensuring her maintenance in the event of pregnancy), to assume financial obligations where the compensation is not paid in full at the time of the divorce, and to accept the divorce from the husband.[81] In one case the wife's father renounced her financial rights in view of a suspicion of adultery. She was charged with committing adultery in the absence of the husband and the illegitimate offspring was said to have died or been killed. Although the charge was not proved, it seems to have been sufficient to tarnish her reputation and she was divorced with the consent of her father, who waived her rights. The father's intervention under these circumstances fits the customary norm, according to which a woman's misbehavior is the concern of her agnates, whose honor is sullied, and not that of her husband. The husband is entitled to divorce her and to receive compensation, and the father or another agnate assumes full financial and moral responsibility for her conduct.[82]

Occasionally, the agnate or guardian performs all the above-mentioned acts as the representative (*nāʾib*) or proxy (*wakīl*) of the kinswoman or ward (*rabība*) (until she reaches the age of puberty) and is in that case given official status by the court.[83] It may happen that the wife is an orphan and that her guardian renounces her rights in her name, as well as undertaking to pay out of his own pocket anything that may be due to her from her husband.[84] The agnate also undertakes to satisfy any monetary claim she may make against the husband in the future contrary to the agreement between the husband and himself. For instance, if the wife claims the balance of her dower or "something of the deferred dower" and "it is proved that this is due to her by law," or "if his daughter demands something [from her husband] contrary to what has been agreed between them, ... then he [the agnate] is responsible to her [for that claim]" (*fa-huwa al-masʾūl bihi*) or "is obliged to satisfy it" (*yakūn malzūman bihi*);

81. E.g., KAMD, p. 25 no. 8 3 March 33[?]; AP:E2, p. 83 no. 82 13 Sep. 46, p. 164 no. 158 [?] Sep. 47[?], p. 170 no. 164 22 Sep. 47; A:E103, p. 136 no. 241 9 Oct. 52; KD59–73, K48: p. 32 no. 62 24 March 60.

82. B2:KM38–43:T41–43, K8: p. 40 no. 104 13 Feb. 42; Kressel, pp. 142ff.

83. E.g., AP:E4, p. 79 no. 78 14 Aug. 46, p. 139 no. 129 2 June 47; AP:E2, p. 178 no. 174 26 Nov. 47; B2:KM38–43:T41–43, K8: p. 66 no. 165 5 July 42; A:E103 p. 96 no. 178 3 July 52; A:E104, p. 228 no. 378 [?] July 53. For *rabība* see Lane.

84. A:E104, p. 208 no. 349 20 May 53.

occasionally, he states expressly that "he will pay out of his own money."[85] The agnate sometimes adds that he is responsible "to the noble *sharīʿa* court" or "to the *sharīʿa* court and the [statute] law (*qānūn*)"—which means that the undertaking is enforceable by sanctions of the *sharīʿa* court and the civil court in case a civil action is brought to implement a financial agreement transcending the domain of personal status.[86] It is probably the husband who demands that these undertakings be included in the divorce instrument issued by the court, as a precaution against any possible financial claims by the wife. Such claims are indeed to be anticipated.

These findings indicate that divorce by consent reflects a customary conception of marriage under which the woman is not a party to the contract although formal measures are sometimes taken to bring it into line with *sharʿī* requirements by granting agnates power to act on the wife's behalf. There is no certainty at all that the wife consents to the divorce or to the terms of the renunciation and compensation, and it may be that the agnates initiate the divorce while guided by considerations that have nothing to do with the wife and try to force it, on the conditions set for it, on the wife. There is in fact evidence of relatives acting against the will of the wife. Thus in one case a woman complained that she had been divorced four days after her consummated marriage and that the agnate, who was present in court, "renounced the balance of my dower without renunciation on my part." She asked the court to award her her due, which consisted of various ornaments, "either from this my relative or from my divorcer." The relative alleged that he had "renounced her dower with her consent" but was unable to prove this, and eventually the woman was reunited with her husband in a new marriage. In another case a father took his minor (*ṣaghīra*) daughter from her husband's house and kept her at his house against the husband's will. The woman's brother reached an agreement with the husband, after the latter had taken a second wife, for her return to him or, alternatively, her divorce by *ṭalāq*, while undertaking to obtain his father's permission for that agreement; "and if the girl's father does not consent to that agreement, he should bring a claim against

85. AP:E4, p. 83 no. 82 13 Sep. 46, p. 119 no. 116 24 March 47, p. 139 no. 129 2 June 47; AP:E1, p. 145 no. 257 24 Nov. 52; AP:E2, p. 162 no. 156 3 Sep. 47[?]; A:E104, p. 200 no. 338 16 April 53, p. 201 no. 340[?] 20 April 53, p. 228 no. 378 [?] July 53; AP:E4, p. 85 no. 84 17 Sep. 64.

86. AP:E2, p. 168 no. 162 16 Sep. 47, p. 180 no. 186 24 Dec. 47.

his son." It seems that we have to do here with monetary claims in connection with divorce. These two cases also illustrate why an undertaking of the agnate is required to meet possible undertakings of the wife to the husband.[87]

(2) **Agnates by the side of the wife.** Occasionally, the wife and her agnate together conduct the negotiations with the husband for a divorce by consent and together renounce rights and pay compensation to the husband in respect of the divorce. Thus in one case the wife and her father pleaded economic distress resulting from the husband's absence; the wife and her father redeemed her from him in return for all her dower, which they delivered to him, and renounced all her financial rights. In other cases the wife and her grandfather compensated the husband.[88] In one case the husband said that following the worsening of relations with his wife several days previously, "I agreed with my wife and her father on divorce by way of amicable settlement (*ṣulḥan*)" (i.e., a settlement not involving legal proceedings), under which "my wife's father, by virtue of a power of attorney from his daughter, redeemed her with her deferred dower."[89] Occasionally the wife "redeems herself from him" with the whole or part of her dower, and her agnate repays or returns the dower.[90] In one case it was noted that the wife had redeemed herself with the whole of her dower and that the husband "had debited her father with the sum of...."[91] The wife occasionally compensates the husband in the presence of an agnate, who in turn makes himself responsible to the court for any claim of the wife against the husband.[92] Although there may certainly have been cases in which the wife herself conducted the negotiations for her redemption, the very presence of the agnate and his role in the divorce proceedings suggest that his function is a dominant one, as is to be expected in a traditional society.

87. AP:E1, p. 143 no. 254 19 Nov. 52; and KD59–73, p. 48 no. 90 12 Dec. 65, respectively.
88. B2:KM38–43:T41–43, K5: p. 16 no. 37 24 Aug. 41.
89. AP:E4, p. 119 no. 116 24 March 47.
90. E.g., KD59–73, K51, p. 12 no. 24 4 Sep. 59, K48: p. 30 no. 58 15 March 60, K48: p. 31 no. 60 21 March 60, K51: p. 197 no. 424 21 Dec. 63, K44: p. 204 no. 493 25 Aug. 64.
91. KD59–73, p. 24 no. 55 4 Aug. 65.
92. E.g., AP:E2, p. 180 no. 186 24 Dec. 46.

(3) **Cognates by the side of the wife.** In rare cases the wife appears in court with her mother, but the wife alone performs the act required for her redemption from the husband: renunciation or return of the dower.[93] In one case the mother represented her daughter as *nāʾiba* in the divorce proceedings but was careful to emphasize that they were acting jointly. When the daughter learned of the *khulʿī ṭalāq* pronounced by her husband, the mother said: "I am responsible for and chargeable with whatever she [my daughter] or her proxy demands from him [her husband]." She requested that her son-in-law pay the divorce fee, whereupon her daughter would move into the mother's residence. This phenomenon was observed in Algeria under French rule in cases in which the wife was rather elderly.[94] The presence in court of the mother rather than an agnate demonstrates the wife's competence to conduct negotiations for her redemption. Indeed, in many cases the wife appears alone in divorce proceedings. The situation is perhaps different if—as happens even more rarely—another cognate appears by the side of the wife—namely, the maternal grandfather[95] or, in particular, a maternal uncle (*khāl*), who in tribal society has a special status of intimate kinship free from considerations of agnatic consanguinity. Thus in one case the husband said that he had settled the question of the wife's financial rights with her uncle; the uncle confirmed the husband's version of the matter, received a sum of money as the balance of the wife's financial rights, and undertook that "if she claims any right from her husband contrary to what is stated above, he [the uncle] will pay what is due to her after her right has been proved in accordance with law"—which indicates that the cognatic uncle, too, may play an important part in divorce proceedings.[96]

b. Relatives of the Husband

In some cases of divorce by consent, the wife is divorced by an agnate of the husband: his father or paternal uncle or some relative of unspecified degree. In all such cases the relative acts in the official capacity of authorized representative (*nāʾib*) or proxy (*wakīl*) of the husband. The only reason for this practice is the husband's absence from Libya, generally in

93. KD59–73, K48: p. 8 no. 16 10 Aug. 59, K51: p. 12 no. 23 8 Sep. 59.
94. AP:E4, p. 105 no. 103 13 June 47; Charnay, p. 323.
95. KD59–73, K48: p. 31 no. 61 22 March 60.
96. A:E104, p. 164 no. 286 28 Jan. 53. On the position of the *khāl* see Peters, *Aspects*, p. 135; Obermeyer, pp. 125–26, 130; Oweidi, pp. 107–8.

the Sudan, and his inability to divorce the wife himself at her place of abode. The agnate conducts the negotiations on the financial conditions of the wife's redemption in the husband's name and, when agreement has been reached, divorces her on his behalf. D'Emilia reports a case in which a man had demanded that his wife comply with his request to move to another town near the army base where he was serving. It emerged that the wife had redeemed herself from him by *khul*ʿ after his brother had received a special mandate from the husband for this purpose and had exercised his power, apparently without informing the husband in time, and that she had married another man in reliance on the *qāḍī*'s permission.[97]

c. Relatives of Both Spouses

Occasionally both spouses are represented by their fathers or other agnates with the status of *wakīl* or *nāʾib*. The wife's representative, in her name, renounces various financial rights before the husband's representative or compensates the husband, and the husband's representative divorces her in the husband's name.[98] The representation of both spouses by agnates additionally underlines the dominant status of these relatives in divorce-by-consent proceedings.

6. CUSTOMARY *KHUL*ʿ

a. The Customary Origin of *Khul*ʿ

*Khul*ʿ, according to its *sharʿī* definition, is a wife's "redemption of herself" from the marriage tie, with the husband's consent, by the use of the word *khul*ʿ, or a verbal derivative of it, in return for some consideration. The husband, not the wife, dissolves the marriage tie; he must be legally competent to divorce the wife, and the wife must be legally competent to enter into a contractual divorce agreement for a consideration. She is a party to the proceedings for divorce by *sharʿī khul*ʿ, just as she is a party to the marriage contract. She generally compensates the husband by

97. E.g., B2:KM38-43:T41-43, K5: p. 16 no. 37 24 Aug. 41, K8: p. 66 no. 165 5 July 42, K6: p. 84 no. 223 1 Jan. 43; KD59-73, K44: p. 1 no. 2 9 June 59, p. 3 no. 5 1 July 59; d'Emilia, pp. 31-33, 48.

98. E.g., KD59-73, p. 57 no. 110 11 Sep. 60, K51, p. 114 no. 239 4 April 62, K45: p. 128 no. 263 [?] June 62, K43, p. 140 no. 308 21 Oct. 62; KDP, K45: p. 13 no. 31 19 May 65. Cf. Layish, *Women*, p. 162.

returning the dower (which is her property under the *sharīʿa*), wholly or in part, in exchange for her freedom. This is the picture emerging from the *sijill*s and confirmed by research elsewhere.[99]

However, the *sijill*s show far-reaching deviations from *sharʿī khulʿ*. These consist mainly in compensating the husband by assigning to him the dower the woman is due to receive upon her marriage to another man or even in making the remarriage conditional on the return of the dower to the first husband. This is attested by dozens of instances and it seems that we have not to do here with a marginal phenomenon. Although these practices have already been observed elsewhere,[100] the Cyrenaican *sijill*s make it possible to study more exactly the mechanism of this *khulʿ*—hereinafter referred to as "customary *khulʿ*" since it is mainly inspired by custom. In fact the *sharīʿa* has deviated from it by adapting its mechanism to the norms required by the transformation of the wife from a nonparty to a marriage contract under customary law into a party to a marriage contract under the *sharīʿa*.

Scholars agree that *khulʿ* is rooted in pre-Islamic custom, except that according to the latter the dower was not returned by the wife but by her clan. There is no express reference to *khulʿ* in the Qurʾān, although a trace of it may perhaps be found in the wife's right to redeem herself by returning the dower (2:229). Orthodox exegesis, too, relates that right to the *khulʿ* custom. A hint of *khulʿ* may be found in the *ḥadīth* as well, although the reference here is only to the wife's initiative for dissolution while dissolution itself is reserved to the husband.[101] The customary *khulʿ* was observed in other parts of North Africa under French rule as well.[102]

b. Features and Application of Customary *Khulʿ*

Most customary *khulʿ* divorces involve mutual renunciation of "marital rights"—such as waiting-period maintenance and dower—arising out of the dissolution of the marriage tie.[103] However, the special characteristic of customary *khulʿ* is the undertaking to return the balance of the dower, or to pay compensation in addition to the dower, "upon her marriage to

99. Anderson, *Africa*, p. 367. For more details see above, III1, 4a.

100. Layish & Shmueli, p. 38 and the sources indicated in n. 39.

101. Stern, pp. 129–32 and the sources indicated there; Linant, *Traité*, p. 422.

102. Bousquet, *Coutumes kabiles*, pp. 52–53, 59, 64, 68; Bousquet, *Islamic & customary law*, p. 64; Colucci, *Cirenaica*, cols. 38ff.

103. E.g., A:E104, p. 184 nos. 314–15 28 Feb. 53, p. 210 no. 352 16 May 53.

another man so that he may divorce her for it" (*ʿinda iqtirānihā bi-zawj ākhar* [or *ghayrihi*] *li-yuṭalliqahā ʿalā dhālika*).[104] Sometimes the wife is a full-fledged, exclusive party to the customary *khulʿ* proceedings. She conducts negotiations with the husband on the exact terms of the *khulʿ*, and each side carries out its part. For example, in one case the wife said: "I redeem myself (*khalaʿtu*) from my husband for my whole dower, the prompt and the deferred, specified in my marriage contract, and I undertake to pay him... when I am able to marry someone else.... I have delivered to him all I have received of the prompt dower and the clothing (*kiswa*), and there is nothing left of my financial liability (*dhimma*) but these... so that he may divorce me in return." The husband "consented to this and agreed to wait for the said payment." Eventually he divorced her by a single *khulʿī* repudiation. In another case the wife initiated dissolution after eight months of marriage and undertook to support herself during the waiting period, as well as to pay the husband eight pounds "upon her marriage to another husband in order that he may divorce her in return." The husband agreed to these terms and divorced her.[105]

According to the *sharīʿa*, the freedom of marriage of a divorced woman is unlimited provided that there are no *sharʿī* impediments to the marriage—such as nonobservance of the waiting period or a forbidden degree of kinship (*maḥram*) to the intended husband. Her marriage to another man cannot be made conditional on the payment of a debt to her former husband; nonpayment of a debt is merely a ground for a civil claim. Any restrictions on remarriage are apparently imposed by the woman of her own free will. In this respect we have to do here with a compromise between the *sharīʿa*, according to which the wife is a party to the divorce proceedings, and the custom adopted by the wife of her own choice. However, it is not certain that the *sharʿī* norm appearing from the above examples as to the wife's personal involvement in *khulʿ* proceedings reflects the actual facts. It is possible that the court is trying to couch proceedings conducted according to custom in terms fitting the *sharīʿa* and that the wife is not in fact a party to the proceedings or at any rate not an exclusive party, as we shall see below.

104. E.g., KD59-73, K51: p. 20 no. 39 8 Nov. 59.
105. AP:E4, p. 137 no. 127 23 May 47; and A:E104, p. 182 no. 314 28 Feb 53, respectively. See also A:E104, no. 315 28 Feb. 53; B2:KM38-43:T41-43, K8: p. 62 no. 157 14 June 42; AP:E2, p. 174 no. 169 11 Oct. 47; A:E103, p. 150 no. 265 13 Dec. 52.

In some cases in which the wife is presented in the *sijill*s as a full partner in the negotiations for a customary *khulʿ* divorce, it seems that owing to difficulties in raising the necessary funds for compensating the husband or because the latter demands it as security for the fulfillment of her financial obligation, she enlists the help of her father in the compensation arrangement. Thus in one case the wife redeemed herself by compensating her spouse with the whole of her dower and financial rights. After "he proved against her that she still owed him seven pounds of her prompt dower, she and her father undertook to pay them to him upon her marriage to another man"—all this in return for (*fī naẓīr*) his divorcing her by *ṭalāq*. Similarly, it was stated in another case that the wife "redeemed herself with her deferred dower and she and her father undertook to return the prompt dower to him ... upon her marriage to another man."[106] Cases of this kind, too, represent a compromise between custom and *sharīʿa*: the financial arrangement is purely customary, but it is the wife, not her father, who conducts the negotiations. And although the father's support is enlisted he is not a formal party to the transaction. From a technical legal point of view, the obligation to return the dower falls on the wife alone. In this sense we may see here a transitional stage between customary and *sharʿī khulʿ*, provided that the *qāḍī* does not intervene by smoothing custom so as to adapt it as far as possible to the *sharʿī* norm. In one case the wife appeared in court with her mother (rather than with her father or some other agnate), which demonstrates a wife's competence to conduct negotiations for her freedom.[107]

Still, in most cases of customary *khulʿ*, the wife's agnates, and especially her father, are directly involved in the proceedings, assuming every financial and other liability for the fulfillment of the conditions agreed upon with the divorcing husband. Thus in one case the husband alleged in court, in the absence of the wife, that his father-in-law had undertaken to give him some camels, a sum of money in cash, and some jewelry upon his daughter's marriage to another man. The father-in-law confirmed this version and undertook that if his daughter claimed anything from the divorcing husband in contravention of the agreement between them, he, the father-in-law, would indemnify the husband for any monetary damage incurred through filing the claim in court. In a further case the wife's

106. KD59-73, K51: p. 15 no. 29 27 Sep. 59, and K48: p. 64 no. 125 18 Oct. 60, respectively.
107. KD59-73, p. 206 no. 496 10 Sep. 64.

father waived all his daughter's financial rights and undertook to pay to the divorcing husband "what he received of his daughter's dower... upon her marriage to another man." He added: "If my daughter demands any financial rights from this her husband, we shall satisfy her out of my own money." In a similar case the divorced woman's father undertook to pay a certain amount "upon my daughter's marriage to another man." He added: "Furthermore, if, breaking away from my control, she marries without my permission... for less than that amount, I undertake to pay it in full of my own volition without any resistance or delay."[108] The instances before us reflect the customary norm in its full supremacy, with a slight concession to the *sharīʿa* prompted by the character of the authority before which the matter is brought: the wife is not a party to the *khulʿ* proceedings but the object of a transaction between her father (who receives her dower upon her remarriage) and her former husband. But since, in the *sharīʿa* court, the wife may, under the *sharīʿa*, claim the fulfillment of her financial rights as a divorced woman, an undertaking by her father to satisfy such claims is required.

Occasionally a male agnate (usually the father) acts as the wife's deputy (*nāʾib*) or proxy (*wakīl*) in divorce proceedings. Thus in one case the wife's father, by virtue of a power of attorney from her, waived all her financial rights and undertook to his son-in-law to pay a certain sum "when his daughter is able to marry another man." He also undertook that if his daughter claimed anything contrary to the agreement between them "he will be liable for it [the claim] to the honorable *sharīʿa* court." In a further case the father, as his daughter's *nāʾib*, undertook to pay a certain sum upon her marriage to another man, adding that if she claimed anything from her former husband "by virtue of a right due to her under the *sharīʿa*" he would pay it to her out of his own money.[109] According to the Mālikī school, no legal status is required in order to conduct negotiations with the husband concerning *khulʿ*. Even a third party who has no family or legal ties with the wife may stipulate with the husband that he shall divorce her by *khulʿ*—even against her will—provided that he, the third party—and not the wife—pays compensation to the husband.[110] This is a carryover from

108. AP:E4, p. 117 no. 114 20 March 47; A:E104, p. 197 no. 335 8 April 53; and AP:E3, p. 326 no. 355 29 May 54, respectively. Cf. Layish, *Women*, p. 160.

109. AP:E2, p. 182 no. 178 8 Jan. 48; and A:E102, p. 333 no. 567 23 June 54, respectively.

110. Linant, *Traité*, pp. 423, 428–29.

the customary concept of marriage, according to which the wife is not a party to the divorce negotiations.

Sometimes both spouses are represented by their fathers, which stresses even more the customary character of the proceedings. Thus in one case the two fathers agreed on customary *khulʿ*; the husband's father, as his son's *wakīl*, agreed to the conditions, saying: "I have already divorced (*qad ṭallaqtu*) [the name of the wife] from her husband, my son [name], who is absent from the session of the court."[111] In another case, in which the husband was represented by his father and the wife was herself a party to the negotiations, it was stated that the husband's father had divorced his daughter-in-law, saying: "The woman has redeemed herself [with] the specific dower, which she has delivered to him [the husband's father], and he has entered to her debit [as compensation] the financial loss (*khasāra*) caused to him [the dower, gifts, and a certain sum]...; when she finds a husband, he shall pay that sum before the reading of *al-Fātiḥa* [the solemnization of the marriage]." It is not clear from this document whether the reference is to the loss caused to the husband or the loss caused to his father as the person who financed the dower and the other expenses connected with the marriage.[112] In one case the wife was represented in customary *khulʿ* proceedings by her guardian. It was agreed between the husband and the guardian that the latter should pay the husband a certain sum out of his own money when the ward (*rabība*) married another man. The guardian also undertook to maintain her during the waiting period. It seems that the guardian, in accordance with the customary norm, treats the ward's dower as his own money, whence his readiness to compensate the husband upon her remarriage. It is also quite possible that the guardian holds succession rights of the ward and is therefore prepared to maintain her during the waiting period. This phenomenon was also observed in northern Nigeria under colonial rule. Anderson notes that the wife was seldom able to raise funds of her own for her redemption; much more often her guardian or her family paid the dower to her husband, expecting to

111. A:E104, p. 226 no. 375 [?] July 53. See also KD59–73, K48: p. 82 no. 159 28 March 61, p. 178 no. 385 19 Aug. 63, K50: p. 20 no. 48 14 July 65, p. 131 no. 269 8 July 72. Cf. Colucci, *Cirenaica*, col. 39.

112. KD59–73, K50: p. 131 no. 270 11 July 62. On the *al-Fātiḥa* see Layish & Shmueli, p. 33 and the sources indicated there.

recoup themselves by an identical amount upon her remarriage or to collect it secretly from her new husband.[113]

The particulars of the financial arrangement between the parties to a customary *khulᶜ* are, as one may expect, settled outside the *sharīᶜa* court on a voluntary basis. The arrangement is recorded in the *quṣṣa* or *quṣṣat al-marʾa*, (literally: "lock of hair" or "wife's lock of hair"). This term, which has been found only in the *sijill* of Kufra, is a popular customary expression. It describes a kind of promissory note drawn up to guard against the unexpected. Colucci explains that the father's obligation, "written [on his daughter's] lock of hair," to pay an agreed amount to the husband on her marriage to another man, is contracted in case of a divorce where the woman or her family are in the wrong and it is decided by the assembly (*mīᶜād*) that the husband should be given back the dower and other expenses connected with the marriage. This direct obligation is needed, since the woman's father cannot pay all the expenses on the spot. Moreover, it is usual also to stipulate that the father has such an obligation even if the daughter should die before she remarries, lest the husband lose his financial right. The usual formula is: "Entered (*kutiba*) [or: recorded (*sujjila*)] to her [the wife's] debit (*ᶜalayhā*) the amount of...in her 'lock of hair' [as follows]: 'When she marries another man, he shall pay the said amount.'"[114] All the kinds of compensation that the wife owes to her divorcer—various jewelry, household effects, livestock, etc.—are sometimes specified, with an indication of their total monetary value; "they are recorded in the arrangement until he who seeks her hand is caused to pay the said amount."[115] It is sometimes expressly noted—again, apparently, for reasons of legal certainty—that the compensation shall be paid "before the making of the marriage contract with her [by the new husband]" or—more frequently—"before the public reading of [*Ṣūrat*] *al-Fātiḥa*," which is equivalent to the formation of the marriage tie. In other words, the payment of the compensation is a condition of the woman's

113. A:E103, p. 96 no. 178 3 July 52; Anderson, *Africa*, p. 209.

114. E.g., KD59–73, K48: p. 176 no. 382 15 Aug. 63, K47: p. 196 no. 464 16 June 64, p. 206 no. 496 10 Sep. 64, K44: p. 213 no. 511 n.d., p. 217 no. 518 26 Dec. 64, p. 24 no. 56 4 Aug. 65, p. 207 no. 498 7 Aug. 65; Colucci, *Cirenaica*, col. 43; Colucci, *Tribù*, p. 26. Cf. Bousquet, *Coutumes kabiles*, pp. 76, 78. For *quṣṣa* see Lane, pp. 2527–28.

115. E.g., KD59–73, K50: p. 10 no. 25 14 April 65.

remarriage.[116] In one case it was expressly noted that it was "not permitted (*mā yajūz*) to anyone to read *al-Fātiḥa* before payment of the above-mentioned." Among the Berbers in the Kabyle Mountains of Algeria under French rule, a woman divorced by customary *khulᶜ* also could not marry another man before the former husband had been compensated. The same phenomenon has also been observed in Israel.[117] In another case it was said: "If the *Fātiḥa* is read to her without this amount having been paid, he who reads it shall be regarded as a transgressor (*ḍālim*) [*ẓālim*, that is to say, there shall be a ground for a monetary claim against him under the rules of customary law]; and he shall be compelled to pay that amount."[118]

Moreover, there are those who—in the best tradition of customary contracts drawn up by arbitrators without statutory status or power of enforcement—demand a guarantee for the payment of compensation upon the woman's marriage to another man. Thus in one case it was said: "Thirty pounds have been entered in her *quṣṣa* with the guarantee (*kafāla*) of her *wakīl*; upon her marriage to another man, the *wakīl* shall pay." The *wakīl* delivered the power of attorney to the husband's father (who represented the husband in the *khulᶜ* proceedings); only then did the husband divorce the wife. According to customary law, the *kafīl* (guarantor) is required to pay out of his own pocket only if the party he represents does not fulfill his obligation under the agreement. In another case the wife's maternal uncle (*khāl*) guaranteed for her.[119] Instances of security being given for the return of the dower in customary *khulᶜ* have been observed among the Beduin of the Judean Desert. In one case arbitrators decided that the woman's father must upon her remarriage pay a certain amount of dinars in consideration of her divorce; if she did not remarry within ten months, her father must raise that amount from some other source. As security for the implementation of this award, all the property of the woman's father was pledged pending taking possession

116. E.g., B2:KM38-43:T41-43, K6: p. 93 no. 247 27 Feb. 43; KD59-73, K50: p. 131 no. 269 8 July 72, no. 270 11 July 72, p. 20 no. 48 14 July 65.

117. KD59-73, K48: p. 178 no. 385 19 Aug. 63; Bousquet, *Coutumes kabiles*, pp. 75ff.; Charnay, p. 53; Layish, *Women*, p. 160.

118. KD59-73, p. 24 no. 56 4 Aug. 65. On the customary *ẓālim* see above, p. 53 and the reference in n. 44.

119. KD59-73, K48: p. 176 no. 382 15 Aug. 63; and AP:E3, p. 342 no. 582 6 July 54, respectively. On the customary *kafāla* see Stewart, *Texts*, index, s.v. "guarantee." On the position of the *khāl* see Peters, *Aspects*, p. 135; Obermeyer, pp. 125–26; Oweidi, pp. 107–8.

(*qabḍ*) of the dower. A well-known *shaykh* was appointed surety for the implementation of the award. In another case an arbitrator decided that if the woman's father refused to return the dower to her husband, he must return his daughter to him "and there will be no divorce until Allāh puts them out of their misery." In Israel it has been observed that the woman's father gave a promissory note, signed by him, payable on the date of her remarriage.[120]

Finally, resort to the *sharīʿa* court for putting into practice an institution contrary to the *sharīʿa* is evidence of a desire to utilize a judicial power anchored in law to give teeth to the compensation agreement—that is, to enable it to be enforced in the event of one of the parties not doing his part under it. Thus in one case it was noted that the parties had agreed on dissolution "out of court." The court confirmed that the wife must pay a certain sum of money on her marriage to another man; only then did the husband divorce her in the presence of the court.[121] In other cases it was stipulated in the wife's *quṣṣa*, on the husband's demand, that the compensation should be paid, upon her remarriage, "through the medium (*ʿalā yad*)" of the *sharīʿa* court.[122]

The *sijill*s contain almost no information on the implementation of customary *khulʿ* agreements in everyday life, and it therefore seems that they were generally implemented faithfully, in both letter and spirit, without the parties seeking the intervention of the court. At the same time, it is quite possible that upon nonfulfillment of an obligation under such an agreement the parties prefer to resort to arbitration (or to a civil court); but of this, obviously, there is no evidence in the *sijill*. There are some actual testimonies to the fulfillment of the terms of a customary *khulʿ*. Thus in one case a man divorced his wife by *khulʿ*, indicating in her *quṣṣa* a certain amount of money that her fiancé was to pay before the reading of *al-Fātiḥa*. The woman "remarried, her new husband paid her debt (*khallaṣa mā ʿalayhā*),... and there is no more claim against her." In another case, it was said that the wife "returned thirty pounds, which had been entered in the *quṣṣa* to her debit, to the [former] husband after another man had married her."[123]

120. Layish & Shmueli, p. 38; and Layish, *Women*, p. 160, respectively.

121. KD59-73, K48: p. 82 no. 159 28 March 61.

122. KD59-73, p. 203 no. 490 24 Aug. 64, K50: p. 18 no. 42 7 July 65. For more details see below, VI2e.

123. KD59-73, K50: p. 131 no. 269 8 July 72; and K48: p. 50 no. 93 4 Dec. 65, respectively.

Nevertheless, there are occasional hints at problems in connection with the implementation of a customary *khulʿ*. Thus in one case a woman told her new husband that the former husband "claims from you, O Ibrāhīm, eight female riding camels"—that is, her dower. The new husband admitted only that he owed her the deferred dower, and the wife did not succeed in proving that she had not yet received the prompt dower. From this we may infer that the dower was not paid over to the first husband before the woman's remarriage. In another case a woman claimed from her divorcer a certain sum as dower and clothing allowance, about one quarter of it destined for a certain person; "when he comes [to court] and demands it from this my husband, he shall pay it to him." This certain person was not her father or an agnate; he may have been her first husband, who had divorced her by customary *khulʿ* and had not yet been compensated in spite of her remarriage. Now that she had been divorced from her second husband, she wanted to realize her rights and may on this occasion have wished to pay her debt to her first husband. In another case the woman's former husband appointed a *wakīl* to receive a certain sum of money "from the husband of the principal's divorced wife." The *wakīl* was given absolute power of attorney (*tafwīḍ*) and permitted "to apply to all the other official agencies, *sharʿī* and civil," apparently in order to institute legal proceedings for the realization of the debt due to the first husband under the customary *khulʿ* agreement. In this and the preceding case it was noted that the first husband claimed the debt from the second husband and not from the wife or her guardian, although the second husband was not a party to the customary *khulʿ* agreement. Among the Berbers of the Kabyle Mountains under colonial rule it was usual for the first husband to claim the compensation from the wife's father or second husband. The compensation was usually equal to the dower, but the husband sometimes demanded excessive compensation to revenge himself on the wife and make it more difficult for her to remarry; attempts to fight this practice by legislation were unsuccessful.[124]

c. The Causes of Customary *Khulʿ*

Mohsen encountered customary *khulʿ* among the Awlād ʿAlī in the Western Desert in cases where a woman left her husband to marry her lover. A man

124. B2:KM38-43:EA, K4a: no. 1 4 July 32; B2:KM38-43:T41-43, K8: p. 21 no. 49 24 Sep. 41; and B2:KM38-43:T43, K6: p. 37 no. 111 28 Dec. 43, respectively. Cf. *Thâmamth* in Bousquet, *Coutumes kabiles*, p. 77; Bousquet, *Islamic & customary law*, p. 64. On the customary deferred dower see above, pp. 48–49; Anderson, *Africa*, p. 369.

whose "patronage" she sought in order that he might persuade her husband to divorce her tried at the same time to persuade the future husband to pay to the present one the dower that the future husband was to have paid to her before marrying her. Mohsen found that in a number of cases the present husband was prepared to divorce his wife only after the future husband had promised to pay him the dower at the time of marrying her. In one such case, in which the *ᶜumda* mediated, the latter tried at first to persuade the woman's father to return the dower to her husband; when this failed, he paid the husband a certain sum on account out of his own money and undertook that the remainder would be paid upon her marriage to her lover. Only then did the husband divorce her, and a week later she was married to her lover. Customary *khulᶜ* under similar circumstances was observed by Anderson in several places in Africa. On the Gold Coast under colonial rule, for instance, if the wife eloped with her lover and refused to return to the husband, the latter might demand that her father reimburse him for all the expenses incurred by him, and the father in turn would try to recoup himself from the lover, though not by formal litigation.[125]

In the Cyrenaican *sijill*s no references to customary *khulᶜ* following intimacy between the woman and her future husband were found. It may be that, for reasons of discretion or from reluctance to charge the wife with adultery (*zinā*), the qurʾānic punishment for which is most severe (stoning in the case of a married woman), the *qāḍī*s refrain from specifying the circumstances of the divorce or from indicating the identity of the future husband. On the other hand, there are indications that the rationale of customary *khulᶜ* may be financial distress of the wife or her agnates. Thus in one case the wife persuaded the husband to divorce her, "asking him to grant her a delay (*imhāl*) for the payment [of compensation] because of her poverty (*li-faqrihā*)." In another case it was agreed that compensation should be paid "later." In these cases it was not expressly stated that the wife needed the delay in order to remarry. Colucci, too, explains that the father's obligation, "written on her [the daughter's] 'lock of hair,'" to pay an agreed amount to the divorcing husband originates in the father's inability to pay it at the time of the divorce.[126] The money may be raised

125. Mohsen, *Conflict*, pp. 117–18; Mohsen, *Aspects*, p. 231; Anderson, *Africa*, p. 272.

126. AP:E4, p. 121 no. 118 9 April 47; and KD59–73, K43: p. 47 no. 90 27 June 60, respectively; Colucci, *Cirenaica*, col. 43.

also from other sources (e.g., from agnates of the wife). Thus in one case it was agreed at the time of the *khulʿ* that the wife's grandfather should pay the divorcing husband a certain sum "when his son [the wife's brother] returns from the [military?] service." Law No. 18 enables the court to grant a delay for the payment of compensation in a *khulʿ* divorce where the wife is in financial straits and the husband refuses to divorce her out of spite and will not give her time to raise the money.[127]

Some documents dealing with instances of customary *khulʿ* suggest that *khulʿ* in these cases arises from financial distress of the wife and her agnates: the identity of the future husband is never stated, even in the context of security for the payment of the debt. The remarriage as such is shrouded in the mists of the future, and references to the wife's remarriage are cautious and subdued; blind fate or the will of Allāh are not challenged: "When I am able to marry another man" (*ʿindamā yatayassar lī iqtirān bi-ghayrihi*) or "When a fiancé comes her way" (*idhā atāhā khāṭib*).[128] The practice derives from the institution of customary marriage, under which the bride is not a party to the contract; according to this concept the bride's agnate may compensate the first husband, following the cancellation of the marriage, by means of the consideration he receives upon her marriage to another husband. Authentic vestiges of this customary concept survive even after the adoption of the *sharʿī* concept, according to which the woman is a party to the marriage contract: since her competence to own property is limited in practice, the only way open to her—other than requesting assistance from her agnates—is to compensate her first husband by means of the dower she receives from the second. Similarly, among the Berbers of the Kabyle Mountains under French rule the background of customary *khulʿ* was purely financial: the payment of compensation was deferred until the woman's remarriage, and she was forbidden to marry her lover. In Israel, too, customary *khulʿ* is motivated by financial distress. It is an arrangement designed to ensure compensation to the divorcing husband at some other time, when the situation has improved. The woman's father undertakes that upon her marriage to another man he will satisfy her former husband out of the prompt dower.[129]

127. KDP, K45: p. [?] no. 136 26 Nov. 60; Mayer, *Marriage*, p. 39 n. 1, p. 41 n. 3. See above, III1.

128. E.g., AP:E4, p. 137 no. 127 23 May 47; AP:E2, p. 182 no. 178 8 Jan. 48; KD59-73, K50: p. 131 no. 270 11 July 62, p. 10 no. 25 14 April 65.

129. Bousquet, *Coutumes kabiles*, pp. 77-78; Layish, *Women*, p. 160.

7. RESORT TO DIVORCE BY CONSENT

It might seem reasonable to assume, as Linant de Bellefonds and others do, that a correlation exists between the variety of possibilities available to the wife for the dissolution of her marriage and the frequency of her resort to the *khulᶜ* mechanism. *Khulᶜ* is especially frequent in the Ḥanafī school because the latter rarely gives the wife an opportunity to dissolve her marriage by legal proceedings, so that she has no other effective means to this end than to persuade the husband to divorce her for compensation. Mayer holds that *khulᶜ* has not been given attention by Mālikī jurists because it is irrelevant in view of the numerous opportunities to achieve dissolution by legal proceedings. By the same token, it has been asserted that after the Mālikī view on dissolution by legal proceedings on specific grounds has been adopted by modern reformist legislation in Arab countries dominated by the Ḥanafī school, the *khulᶜ* mechanism has become almost redundant because the wife now has a mechanism at her disposal that frees her from dependence on the husband's good will.[130]

These assumptions, whose inner logic cannot be denied, are not confirmed by the findings in the Cyrenaican *sijill*s. In the period under review divorce by consent is the dominant form. Dissolution on specific grounds—especially absence of the husband and nonprovision of maintenance—though recognized, is not widely practiced. Dissolution by reason of injury (*ḍarar*) is even less frequent, probably because of the many difficulties attending the arbitration proceedings—especially as the arbitrators may assign the responsibility for the dissolution to the wife when there is no objective justification for dissolution, and deprive her of her financial rights.

Moreover, even where there are grounds for dissolution by legal proceedings the wife may prefer to obtain her freedom by *khulᶜ*, probably for practical reasons (shortness and efficiency of the proceedings), without resort to the court. There is ample evidence that in cases of absence of the husband or nonprovision of maintenance, when the wife is in economic and mental distress, the marriage is dissolved by *khulᶜ* even though the wife seems to have valid grounds for its dissolution by legal proceedings. Thus for instance a wife complained in such circumstances of "neediness" (*iḥtiyāj*) due to the husband's absence, "a shortage of means of livelihood" (*ḍīq al-*

130. Linant, *Traité*, pp. 422, 447; Mayer, *Marriage*, pp. 40–41.

maᶜīsha), "the fear of hardship" (*takhāf ᶜalā nafsihā al-ᶜanat*), and the like—expressions usually heard in court in matters of dissolution by judicial divorce. In all these cases the marriage was dissolved by *khulᶜ* in return for the renunciation of various financial rights and the payment of compensation to the husband.[131]

It seems that in these circumstances the wife applies to the court only as a last resort, after exhausting the possibilities of redeeming herself by *khulᶜ*. Thus in one case the husband had been away in the Sudan for three years, and the wife asked him by letter to return. He promised to do so as soon as possible, but she then realized that he was a "liar." In her application to the court for the dissolution of her marriage she said that she "gave up to him everything due to her from him that was in his possession: the dower and what else we claim from him." When her renunciation or the readiness for it did not persuade him to divorce her by *khulᶜ*, she applied to the court. In another case the husband had been in Egypt for a long time, leaving the wife without maintenance, without a *wakīl* for maintenance on his behalf, and without property that might have been sold for the provision of maintenance. In her application to the court for the dissolution of her marriage, she explained: "I have not redeemed myself from him with my dower [although I wished to do so], and our marriage still exists." In a further case, in which the husband was absent in similar circumstances, the wife explained in court in her application for dissolution: "I have not taken my dower from him and not waived my rights, and our marriage still exists." From this we may perhaps conclude that there had been an attempt to obtain her freedom by *khulᶜ* or that such a possibility had been considered. The wife must of course prove that the marriage is valid in order that the court may have a standing in the matter.[132]

The husband, too, has good reasons for preferring the *khulᶜ* mechanism to dissolution by judicial proceedings or ordinary *ṭalāq*. In dissolution on the ground of injury, he faces the same danger from the arbitrators or the court as the wife: if he is found responsible for the dissolution, he will have to bear all the financial consequences. In a *khulᶜ* divorce, he may not have to concede

131. E.g., B2:KM38-43:T41-43, K5: p. 16 no. 37 24 Aug. 41, K8: p. 66 no. 165 5 July 42, K6: p. 84 no. 223 1 Jan. 43; KD59-73, p. 3 no. 5 1 July 59. Cf. Fluehr-Lobban, pp. 149, 151-52. See below, IV2.

132. KD59-73, K48: p. 7 no. 14 28 July 59, K47: p. 41 no. 78 9 May 60; and B2:KM38-43:T41-43, K45: p. 8 no. 19 14 June 41, respectively.

all or part of the wife's financial rights, which he would have to concede in an ordinary *ṭalāq* divorce; moreover, he may obtain compensation for consenting to release the wife. A *khulʿ* divorce creates no impediment to a restoration of the marriage, and as we shall see below, it sometimes entails a revocable divorce, which does not sever the marital tie. The impossibility of enforcing a court order for obedience upon a recalcitrant wife is another reason for the husband to agree to dissolution for compensation.[133]

In nineteenth-century Egypt, as is known, *sharīʿa* courts of different schools were functioning, so that it was possible to obtain a judicial divorce on *sharʿī* grounds in a Mālikī court. But Tucker notes that *khulʿ* was very frequent in Egypt in that century; the wife would obtain a divorce by freeing the husband from the financial liabilities that he would have incurred if he had divorced her by *ṭalāq*: the balance of the dower, the waiting-period maintenance, jewelry, and the upkeep of the children. She would also waive her rights in the family property in his favor. If she did not succeed in thus persuading him to divorce her, she would resort to various devices: she would enlist the help of the *shaykh al-balad* or even threaten to prosecute the husband for stealing her jewelry. In Israel, too, which by means of the Ottoman Family Rights Law of 1917 has adopted the Mālikī norm of divorce by legal proceedings, divorce by consent is still the dominant form of dissolution.[134]

133. Linant, *Traité*, p. 425. See below, pp. 98–99, 103ff. Cf. Anderson, *Africa*, p. 209.

134. Tucker, pp. 54–55; Layish, *Women*, p. 162.

CHAPTER IV

Judicial Divorce

1. GROUNDS FOR JUDICIAL DIVORCE—LEGAL BACKGROUND

The usual distinction between unilateral *ṭalāq* divorces and dissolution by *faskh*, which involves legal proceedings—that is, a distinction, accepted by most of the orthodox schools, according to the criterion of recourse to the judicial authority—does not hold good in relation to the Mālikī school. According to that school there are circumstances under which the *ṭalāq* involves legal proceedings. Dissolution by legal proceedings in reliance on *sharʿī* grounds (i.e., by the court on its own authority, as recognized by the other schools) is not accepted by the Mālikī school (which, however, recognizes ***annulment*** by the court under certain circumstances).

The peculiarity of the Mālikī school is its liberal approach in regard to the status of the wife: she is enabled to achieve dissolution through the court, without the husband's consent, in reliance on a wide range of grounds. These grounds may be divided into two main categories. In the first category are specific grounds leaving the *qāḍī* no freedom of discretion: chronic diseases likely to endanger the spouse's health in consequence of sexual intercourse (this ground is available also to the husband); nonpayment of the dower before the consummation of the marriage; absence of the husband; and refusal of the husband to provide maintenance. The second category is a general ground that may be defined comprehensively as injury (*ḍarar*) to the wife; this ground involves the appointment of arbitrators by the court and the dissolution of the marriage by them. When a ground of the first category has been proved to the satisfaction of the *qāḍī*, he invites the husband to divorce the wife by *ṭalāq*; if the husband fails to do so, the *qāḍī* pronounces the *ṭalāq* on the husband's behalf. This mode of dissolution is called judicial divorce (*taṭlīq* or *ṭalāq al-ḥākim*); it is based on the legal fiction that the *qāḍī* exercises the ***husband's power*** to divorce the wife. It is applied also in cases in which the husband uses a repudiation oath of a sacramental nature: *īlā*ʾ (an oath to abstain from sexual intercourse with the wife), *ẓihār* (comparison of the wife to a woman of a forbidden degree of kinship), or *liʿān* (unproven charges of adultery against the wife). As will be seen below, this mode of dissolution (except in the case of a repudiation oath) entails the same legal consequences as an ordinary *ṭalāq* divorce.[1]

a. Absence of the Husband

The husband's absence (*ghayba*)—that is, his being in a distant place—is in itself a ground for judicial divorce even if he continues to provide maintenance or has left property from which maintenance can be collected. Reliance on this ground is subject to three conditions: (1) The wife must affirm that the husband's prolonged absence is "a danger to her chastity" (as the sources put it), since she may be tempted to go astray. This condition reflects the concept that a married woman has a natural right to intercourse with her husband and that very great harm might befall her in a traditional society if she is prevented from having it. The same rationale underlies the wife's right to dissolution if the husband is *present* and provides maintenance but does not fulfill his marital obligations, albeit for religious reasons even if he has not taken an *īlā*ʾ oath to abstain from the wife. (In practice it is of course difficult to prove neglect of the wife when the husband is present.) (2) There must have been a period of absence (including justified absence) long enough for injury to be caused to the wife (the length of that period—variously from four months to three years—is in dispute among jurists). (3) The husband's whereabouts must be unknown; if they are known, the *qāḍī* must call upon him to return to the wife or to invite her to join him. Dissolution on the ground of the husband's absence is considered irrevocable divorce.[2]

1. For more details see Linant, *Traité*, pp. 308, 310, 451, 453–54, 465; Pesle, pp. 116–17, 122–23; Milliot, pp. 375ff.; Coulson, *History*, p. 185; Coulson, *Succession*, pp. 19–20; Bousquet, *Coutumes kabiles*, p. 80.
2. Linant, *Traité*, pp. 457–58; Anderson, *Africa*, p. 212; Coulson, *Succession*, pp. 19–20; d'Emilia, p. 42 n. 4 and the source indicated there.

b. Nonprovision of Maintenance

The Mālikī school holds clearly and unambiguously that nonprovision of adequate maintenance is a ground for judicial divorce. For this purpose it distinguishes between cases where the husband is present and cases where he is absent. When he is *present*, the wife's demand for a divorce is disregarded if (1) at the time of the marriage she knew that he was poor or (2) he ensures her current requirements either himself or through a relative or a stranger or (3) he has visible means from which maintenance may be collected. If the husband is poor and none of the foregoing applies, the *qāḍī* is to give him one month's grace (according to some, two or three months') to pay maintenance, and if he still does not pay, the *qāḍī* is to pronounce the divorce. If the husband has means but refuses to pay maintenance, the *qāḍī* is to order him to pay or to divorce the wife. If he refuses to do either, the *qāḍī* is to pronounce the divorce without delay; some hold that the *qāḍī* shall first order him to be arrested.

If the husband is *absent* but his whereabouts are known to the wife and he is relatively not far away (less than ten days on foot), the *qāḍī* is to order the husband to return to the wife or at least to pay maintenance to her; if he does not comply, the *qāḍī* is to pronounce a divorce. If the husband's whereabouts are not known to the wife or he is far away (more than ten days on foot) and yet he does not come within the definition of "missing person" or "absent person," and if he does not pay maintenance and has not instructed another person to do so in his stead, the *qāḍī* is to swear the wife to the truth of her allegations. If the husband has left property from which maintenance can be collected, the wife may request the *qāḍī* to seize that property and order it to be sold—at first movables, then immovables. If the husband has left no property, the wife may demand dissolution. The *qāḍī* is to give the husband one month or more to pay the maintenance (there are different views as to the length of the period), and if he does not do so, the *qāḍī* is to dissolve the marriage or—according to Milliot—to permit the wife to divorce herself after swearing her again to the truth of her allegations concerning the husband's departure and the nonprovision of maintenance.

Dissolution on the grounds of nonprovision of maintenance is considered a revocable divorce. The husband may reinstate the wife, without a new marriage, during the waiting period before the divorce becomes irrevocable, provided he proves that he is capable of providing maintenance. If the absent husband returns and discloses that his wife has obtained a divorce by false pretences and that he has in fact provided maintenance, he may reinstate the wife even after the waiting period, provided she has not married someone else or, if she has, that the new marriage has not yet been consummated; if it has, the new marriage remains valid.[3]

c. Nonpayment of Dower

Dissolution by judicial divorce on the grounds of nonpayment of the whole or part of the dower is conditional on the marriage not having been consummated. If the wife consents to intercourse although the husband has not paid the part of the dower that he should have paid at the time of the contraction of the marriage, she loses her right to dissolution on this ground. If the husband's refusal to pay takes place *before* consummation and he has no property capable of being seized as dower, the *qāḍī* is to give him one year to pay the dower and, if he does not do so during that period, to pronounce the divorce. The delay is granted only if the husband's poverty is proved; if his refusal to pay the dower is malicious, the *qāḍī* is to imprison him for a short period (lest he cause injury to the wife) and then is to pronounce the divorce and debit him with half the dower.[4]

d. Chronic Diseases

Chronic diseases and mental diseases likely to endanger the spouse are other grounds for judicial divorce on the wife's initiative (these grounds are available also to the husband), and so is impotence; the wife's right to dissolution is not voided even if she knew of the husband's condition before the marriage.[5]

e. Injury

Injury as a ground for judicial divorce is not defined—which is the reason for its effectiveness, since it may be interpreted most widely and liberally in favor of the wife. This ground may include such elements as injury caused to the wife by the husband, by married life as such, and by a dispute between the spouses (without the wife having to prove that the husband caused it). Some regard injury almost as a residual ground covering any not expressly mentioned ground for judicial divorce; in other words, they regard injury as comprising whatever is not permitted by law,

3. Linant, *Traité*, pp. 459–61; Milliot, pp. 382–83; Anderson, *Africa*, p. 371; Coulson, *Succession*, p. 19. Cf. Fluehr-Lobban, pp. 162–63.
4. Linant, *Traité*, p. 457; Milliot, pp. 382, 385.
5. Linant, *Traité*, pp. 454–55; Milliot, pp. 379–81; Coulson, *Succession*, p. 19. Cf. Fluehr-Lobban, pp. 163–64

such as removing the wife from the marital residence, beating her without *sharʿī* cause, insulting her, subjecting her to acts contrary to nature, imprisoning her in the house, and preventing her from visiting her relatives. In sum, this ground may be taken to include physical and mental cruelty of the husband to the wife, as well as incompatibility between the spouses—which in Coulson's opinion is tantamount to a decree of divorce based on the established breakdown of the marriage. The injury concept is anchored in the *ḥadīth* (*lā ḍarar wa-lā ḍirār*), and the mechanism of dissolution on this ground is based on the qurʾānic verse (4:35) prescribing the appointment of arbitrators in the event of a dispute between the spouses. But whereas most of the schools limit the task of the arbitrators to the reconciliation of the spouses, the Mālikī school empowers them to dissolve the marriage at their discretion, as if they were judges, without requiring advance authorization by the spouses for that purpose.

The legal and financial consequences of the proceedings depend on whether the wife succeeds in proving the allegation of injury. If she does not succeed in producing two male witnesses who attest, albeit only from hearsay, that injury has been caused to her, her demand for immediate dissolution is not acceded to and the *qāḍī* appoints two arbitrators, one from the relatives of each party. They at first try to reconcile the spouses; if they fail, they determine the legal and financial consequences in accordance with the degree of responsibility of each party for the injury. If the husband is responsible, they pronounce minor irrevocable divorce without payment of compensation by the wife. If the wife is responsible, they may either dismiss her request for dissolution while advising the husband to be patient and considerate or, if they think that the interests of the parties so requires, pronounce repudiation while ordering the wife to pay damages to the husband at a rate fixed by them. If the responsibility is divided between the spouses, the arbitrators charge the wife with only a modest amount of compensation when pronouncing repudiation. In the event of disagreement between the arbitrators, they coopt a third arbitrator to tip the balance. The arbitrators are sovereign in considering and deciding the matters at issue, and in effect it is they who award dissolution—although their award requires confirmation by the *qāḍī*—and this form of dissolution is regarded as judicial divorce. Milliot indicates the categories of injury that constitute grounds for dissolution on the wife's initiative, by the *qāḍī* rather than through arbitrators, and which entail legal consequences different from the accepted norm, according to the gravity of the injury. In cases of recurrent slight mistreatment not provoked by the wife, the *qāḍī* dissolves the marriage by revocable divorce; in cases of severe cruelty, he awards triple divorce. Other injury-related grounds for dissolution by the *qāḍī* are the husband's forcing the wife to engage in prostitution or some other immoral occupation and his inflicting grievous injury on her. Dissolution by way of a *liʿān* oath is likewise considered a judicial divorce.

In view of the possibility of defining injury (according to the Mālikī school) very widely, the question of whether the husband's imprisonment, cruelty, infliction of grievous injury, and nonfulfillment of marital duties are grounds for dissolution is, in Linant de Bellefonds' opinion, irrelevant, since the wife may in any such circumstances obtain dissolution through an arbitration procedure in reliance on the plea of injury. Linant de Bellefonds further notes, rightly, that the advantage of the Mālikī doctrine consists in its enabling the injury concept to be adapted to the changing social conditions of modern times. And indeed the position of the Mālikī school on this question, as in regard to several other grounds for divorce by legal proceedings, has inspired reformist legislation in Muslim countries; cruelty has become a ground for divorce by means of arbitration proceedings, albeit with certain deviations from the Mālikī doctrine. Moreover, although polygamy is a *sharʿī* right of the husband, several countries have legislated that if the husband takes another wife, the first wife may dissolve her marriage by legal proceedings, through arbitration, on the ground of injury within the meaning of the Mālikī school.[6]

Law No. 76 did not materially improve the position of the wife as regards dissolution on the ground of injury; it perhaps even worsened it in some respects. On the other hand, it made this plea available also to the husband. The procedure of dissolution, and the legal and financial consequences, deviate—sometimes widely—from traditional law. The legislator explains the reform by the need to relieve the husband, where the responsibility for the dissolution lies on the wife, of the financial consequences imposed on him in unilateral divorce. He may also have been prompted by the wish to limit the exercise of the husband's right of

6. Linant, *Traité*, pp. 461–64; Milliot, pp. 354, 375ff., 385; d'Emilia, p. 40 n. 9 and the sources indicated there; Coulson, *History*, pp. 186–87; Coulson, *Succession*, p. 20; Anderson, *Africa*, pp. 312–13; Anderson, *Reform*, pp. 119ff.; Layish, *Maḥkama*, xiii, p. 40. Cf. Fluehr-Lobban, pp. 153ff.

unilateral divorce by encouraging him under such circumstances to resort to legal proceedings. Where the wife is not responsible for the dissolution the husband may still use the *ṭalāq* mechanism. The wife is adversely affected by the reform where the arbitrators find her responsible. The reconciliation of the spouses is given greater attention under this law than under traditional law: they are required to exhaust the reconciliation proceedings before applying to the court for dissolution. This makes things more difficult for the wife compared with the original proceedings. If the three arbitrators do not reach an agreed decision, the case is returned to the court for determination at its discretion. Where the husband alone is responsible for the injury, the *qāḍī* is to dissolve the marriage while burdening the husband with the financial consequences, as in ordinary *ṭalāq* divorces. Where the wife alone is responsible, the marriage is to be dissolved and she is to pay appropriate compensation to the husband. And where the responsibility is shared, the marriage is to be dissolved without any compensation at all or with compensation fitting the responsibility of the wife. Dissolution on the wife's initiative is to be regarded as irrevocable, and dissolution on the husband's initiative as revocable.[7]

f. Conditional Delegation of Power to Divorce

According to Milliot, if the marriage contract contains a certain condition (e.g., that the husband shall not transfer his residence to another locality), and he infringes that condition, the *qāḍī* is to order him to return to his original place of residence. If notice cannot be given because the husband is too far away, the *qāḍī* is to dissolve the marriage, on the wife's demand, even without warning. What seems to be involved here is a combination of delegated repudiation and judicial divorce.[8]

2. JUDICIAL DIVORCE IN PRACTICE

a. Nonprovision of Maintenance by an Absent Husband

The *sijill*s contain several dozen instances of divorce by legal proceedings. The most usual ground is a combination of (1) nonprovision of maintenance, (2) absence of the husband, who is far away but whose whereabouts are mostly known, and (3) fear for the wife's chastity. It seems that in everyday

7. For more details see Mayer, *Marriage*, pp. 36–40.
8. Milliot, pp. 382–83, art. 406d. See below, pp. 89, 139ff.

reality the distinction between the first two submissions is blurred; at any rate, the justifications for divorce are sometimes taken indiscriminately from both, as well as from the plea of injury—which, as stated, is reserved for dissolution through arbitrators.

The absent husband is mostly in the Sudan and sometimes in Egypt. The period of absence ranges from several months (but always more than four months, the minimum period required for dissolution on the ground of the husband's absence) to several years; in one case it was seventeen years. The wife occasionally states simply : "absence" (*ghayba*) or "absent for a long time."[9] It seems that the main reason for the husband's absence is his (and in some cases also the wife's) Sudanese origin. In many cases the husband, and sometimes also the wife, are emancipated slaves (*ʿatīq*), or descendants of emancipated slaves, of Sudanese origin who have become integrated in the Cyrenaican tribal structure without severing their ties with their country of origin.[10] Another frequent cause of the husband's absence (in the early 1940s) was his being a soldier in the Italian army who had fallen into British captivity (apparently in the Western Desert).[11] Enlistment in the army may have been a way out (though not the only one) in a family rift. Thus in one case the husband disappeared after staying with the wife "for a night and a day" after the marriage; when "a dispute broke out between them and she felt a distaste for him," he left the house and joined the Italian army. In another case the husband disappeared for fear of blood vengeance after killing a member of another tribe; "he took his camel and fled to his tribe."[12]

It seems that the wife usually knows where the husband is. She sometimes corresponds regularly with him, urging him to return. Thus in one case the wife alleged that the husband had been in the Sudan for three years; "I sent him letters from time to time and he would write back: 'I shall

9. B2:KM38-43:T41-43, K5: p. 59 no. 148 1 June 42, K6: p. 93 no. 248 27 Feb. 43; KDP, K45: p. 13 no. 32 21 June 65. See also B2:KM38-43:T41-43, K5: p. 8 no. 19 14 June 61, K5: p. 45 no. 116 16 March 42, K7: p. 85 no. 226 6 Jan. 43 (three years), K6: p. 90 no. 240 18 Feb. 43 (seven months); KD59-73, K47: p. 41 no. 78 9 May 60 (Egypt). Cf. Fluehr-Lobban, p. 162.

10. E.g., B2:KM38-43:T41-43, K9: p. 2 no. 5 10 May 41, K5: p. 10 no. 24 24 June 41 (both spouses as well as the witnesses are emancipated slaves), K5: p. 18 no. 41 28 Aug. 41, K5: p. 59 no. 148 1 June 42, K5: p. 65 no. 164 29 June 42, K7: p. 85 no. 226 6 Jan. 43, K6: p. 6 no. 18 April 43; Davis, *Politics*, p. 79. Cf. Tucker, pp. 187ff.; Fluehr-Lobban, p. 163.

11. E.g., B2:KM38-43:T41-43, K8: p. 11 no. 26 27 June 41, K5: p. 18 no. 41 24 Aug. 41, K8: p. 32 no. 83 10 Jan. 42, K8: p. 38 no. 98 1 April 42.

12. B2:KM38-43:T41-43, K8: p. 11 no. 26 27 June 41; and K7: p. 77 no. 204 1 Nov. 42, respectively.

come as soon as possible'; but in fact he was lying."[13] In some cases he sends maintenance—money, food, and clothing—from time to time.[14] But in other cases all trace of him is lost; he does not answer the wife's letters after many (six or seven) years of absence in the Sudan. In the word of one witness: "He is absent from her, she is cut off, and his whereabouts are unknown . . . and she is injured by the lack of factual evidence [as to his fate]" (*ghāʾib ʿanhā munqaṭiʿa lā yuʿraf lahu makānan wa-annahā muḍṭarra bi-ḥuṣūl al-wāqiʿ*).[15] As stated, a ground for dissolution exists in both cases if the husband does not provide maintenance; but if his whereabouts are known and he is not far away, the *qāḍī* must order him to return and provide maintenance before pronouncing a divorce.

Indeed, the main reason for the wife's demand for dissolution of her marriage to an absent husband is nonprovision of maintenance. She describes her economic plight in court: the husband left many years ago; at first he sent her maintenance, but soon he ceased to do so, and for years now "I have supported myself"; throughout the period of his absence "he has sent me nothing"; he left her ten years ago while she was pregnant without maintenance for her or her child. The wife "was injured by complete destitution" (*taḍarrarat minaʾl-iḥtiyāj al-kullī*).[16] She complains that the husband "has left me nothing that would enable me to derive maintenance from it (*al-infāq minhu*) for me and my son" or "there is no salable property of his in my possession."[17] Where there is such property, the wife asks the court's permission to sell it. Thus in one case the wife stated that the husband had gone to the Sudan two years previously and "sent me nothing"; she had little children whom she maintained by her own efforts; she and her children were "injured by lack of food (*muʾna*) and clothing (*kiswa*)." As the husband and another man owned a *sāniya* (water scoop, well, or irrigated garden) in equal shares, she asked the court's permission to sell the husband's share to his partner. Witnesses confirmed her story and she sold

13. KD59–73, K48: p. 7 no. 14 28 July 59.
14. B2:KM38–43:T41–43, K5: p. 8 no. 19 14 June 41; KD59–73, K51: p. 24 no. 47 21 Dec. 59, K45: p. 79 no. 154 11 March 61.
15. KD59–73, K51: p. 146 no. 321 27 Nov. 62; and A:E102, p. [27] no. [53] 9 Sep. 51, respectively.
16. E.g., B2:KM38–43:T41–43, K5: p. 59 no. 148 1 June 42; KD59–73, K47: p. 27 no. 53 17 Feb. 61, K45: p. 79 no. 154 11 March 61; KDP, K45: p. 13 no. 32 21 June 65. Cf. Rosen, p. 236.
17. B2:KM38–43:T41–43, K5: p. 8 no. 19 14 June 41; KD59–73, K47: p. 27 no. 53 17 Feb. 61.

the asset. We may suppose that the proceeds of the sale were intended for her maintenance and that of her children.[18]

The wife's agnates sometimes support her in the absence of the husband. Thus in one case a woman stated that her husband had been absent for eight years and that she and her three children were supported by the children's maternal uncle (*khāl*)—that is, her brother. Sometimes, the wife demands that her absent husband's father support her; but it seems that the latter is not always eager to do so. Thus in one case the father-in-law stated in court: "My son works independently; he gives his wife nothing; there is no partnership or monetary link between him and me; neither of us interferes in the monetary affairs or matters of maintenance of the other."[19]

But this does not seem to be the wife's principal line of approach. Her main contention is that her husband "has not appointed a proxy (*wakīl*) to support us" (*wa-lā lahu wakīl yunfiq* [or *yaṣrif*] *ʿalaynā*) or "a legal supporter" (*munfiq sharʿī*).[20] In one case the wife stated that the husband had emigrated to the Sudan without leaving her anything "and he owes debts (*duyūn*) to people." The nature of these debts is not explained. They may be debts contracted by the husband before his departure or loans taken by the wife for her maintenance in the expectation that the husband would repay them on his return.[21] In Algeria under the French rule the wife ensured dissolution, in the event of the husband's absence beyond an agreed period, by the delegation, inserted in the marriage contract, of power to divorce herself in that case on the husband's behalf.[22] In the Aden Protectorate, where the emigration of men was a well-known phenomenon, dissolution on the initiative of the absent man's wife for nonprovision of maintenance was rare and unpopular; however, it was usual, prior to the husband's departure, to take precautionary measures to ensure the maintenance of the wife. Thus he was sometimes required to leave property from which maintenance could be collected or to appoint a representative to take care of maintenance. In northern Nigeria—although infrequently—husbands left property with their brothers for the purpose of providing maintenance. In the Gambia

18. B2:KM38-43:T41-43, K7: p. 71 no. 175 29 Aug. 42. For *sāniya*, see Dozy, p. 695. Cf. Anderson, *Africa*, p. 21.
19. KD59-73, K43: p. 59 no. 114 2 Oct. 60.
20. E.g., B2:KM38-43:T41-43, K5: p. 8 no. 19 14 June 41, K8: p. 32 no. 83 10 Jan 42; A:E102, p. 27 no. 53 9 Sep. 51; KD59-73, K47: p. 41 no. 78 9 May 60.
21. KD59-73, K43: p. 77 no. 151 11 Feb. 61.
22. Bousquet, *Précis*, pp. 190-91.

under colonial rule the absent husband was urged to return to his wife, and in the meantime the wife was supported by her family. In Israel, where a serious problem of dispersal of families and absence of the husband was created by the 1948 war and from other causes, dissolution for nonprovision of maintenance by an absent husband, whose whereabouts were known in some of the cases, was not unusual; the wife based her application on his having instructed no one to support her and on his having no property from which maintenance might be collected or monetary claims that might be realized for the purposes of maintenance, although she could always rely on her family for support. She sometimes asked that he return to Israel, or that she be enabled to join him, or that he divorce her.[23]

In the Cyrenican *sijill*s the author has not come across a case in which, when a marriage had been dissolved because of the husband's absence, he subsequently returned and found the woman married to another man. Bousquet found that in the Kabyle Mountains the remarriage of a woman whose marriage had been dissolved by reason of the husband's absence was rare because the intended new husband feared violent action on the part of the ex-husband should he return some day. Although the latter could not undo the second marriage (he could only demand that the woman's relatives return the dower to him), it seems that not all husbands were aware of this. That fear may also deter Cyrenaicans who are thinking of marrying a deserted woman. Tucker, in Egyptian *sijill*s of the nineteenth century, came across the case of an absentee husband who returned home and found his wife married to another. She alleged that he had divorced her prior to his departure; but he denied this, and she could not produce witnesses to confirm her story. Under these circumstances the second marriage was annulled, and after a decent interval the woman was duly returned to her first husband.[24]

The author has found no instance in the Cyranaican *sijill*s of dissolution on the ground of nonprovision of maintenance by a *present* husband, whether unable to pay or able but unwilling to pay. Dissolution on such grounds was observed in various places in Africa, such as Nigeria and the Gambia.[25]

23. Anderson, *Africa*, pp. 25–26, 211, 241; Layish, *Women*, pp. 166–67.

24. Bousquet, *Coutumes kabiles*, p. 74; Tucker, p. 55.

25. Anderson, *Africa*, pp. 210, 232.

b. Fear for the Wife's Chastity

Nonprovision of maintenance by an absent husband as a ground for dissolution is often accompanied by a further ground: fear for the wife's chastity due to the husband's physical separation from her. This is reflected in documents in which the wife points out that the husband has been absent for a long time (several years), that she is still young (between eighteen and thirty-two), that she cannot bear his absence, and that she "fears hardship" (here in the sense of temptation) (*nakhāf ʿalā nafsī al-ʿanat*).[26] In one case the wife, in addition to the aforesaid, said that the marriage had not been consummated and that under these circumstances something might happen "the consequences of which were unforeseeable." In another case the wife said that the husband had gone to the Sudan and left her pregnant; "and I am a young woman, and Satan is cunning (*waʾl-shayṭān shāṭir*); I fear temptation, and in six or seven years I shall have reached the limit of my endurance." It seems, however, that in these cases too the dominant element is nonprovision of maintenance, for the court pronounced the divorce revocable. In another case, in which the husband had gone to another town before the consummation of the marriage, the wife alleged that except for a certain amount he had spent nothing on her maintenance since the day he went away and that, of the property her father had left her in his will—some palm trees and some sheep—nothing remained after the payment of government taxes. The *qāḍī* awarded monthly maintenance and an annual payment for clothing to her from the date of the filing of the claim for maintenance. The wife demanded that the maintenance should be retroactive to the date of the contraction of the marriage and eventually declared that she was not prepared to remain at the husband's house without consummation of the marriage, which in fact was eventually dissolved.[27] Sometimes the wife, while expressing fear for her chastity, notes at the same time that injury has been caused her by the husband's absence: "I have been injured by complete deprivation, and I fear temptation because I am young . . ."; but it cannot be stated with certainty whether the injury was

26. E.g., B2:KM38-43:T41-43, K5: p. 65 no. 164 29 June 42; KD59-73, K48: p. 7 no. 14 28 July 59, K43: p. 59 no. 114 2 Oct. 60, K43: p. 70 no. 137 27 Nov. 60, K45: p. 79 no. 154 11 March 61. Cf. Fluehr-Lobban, p. 159.

27. AP:E2, p. [159] no. [153] [?] Aug. 47; and KD59-73, K51: p. 146 no. 321 27 Nov. 62, respectively; d'Emilia, p. 43.

caused by the husband's physical absence or by the nonprovision of maintenance.[28]

Similarly, it was observed in Nigeria and in the Gambia that an absent husband's wife demanded dissolution, even where he provided maintenance, on the ground that she was injured by his absence as such and the denial of his company and that there was danger that she might slip into adultery. In Israel, too, in the early 1950s, the marriage of a deserted wife was dissolved on the ground that her reputation, in terms of the morals of a traditional society, had to be protected. Remarriage is a structural solution to this problem, especially if the wife is young; but she was not always in a hurry to demand dissolution, since the status of a married woman also involved advantages. Here too the dividing line between injury caused by the husband's absence and injury caused by nonprovision of maintenance is blurred; at any rate, there is no evidence of dissolution on the ground of absence alone.[29]

The author has not, in the Cyrenaican *sijill*s, come across an instance of a wife demanding dissolution of her marriage to a present husband on the ground of injury caused to her by his failure to fulfill his marital duties. Such a step was observed in Egypt, where a husband had been in jail for several years and therefore had not had relations with the wife (*hajruhu iyyāhā fī maḍjaʿihā*). There may be at the same time a reference to "a young woman who fears temptation" (*shābba takhshā ʿalā nafsihā al-fitna*).[30]

c. Injury

In other cases, injury (*ḍarar*) was alleged on the ground of cruelty of the husband, which as stated earlier is a separate ground for dissolution through arbitrators. In one case the husband gave the wife some heavy beatings with a stick. The husband was jailed and the wife was hospitalized and afterwards found refuge at her father's house for many months without the husband providing maintenance to her. The wife's father applied to the court to divorce her (*taṭlīq*). In another case, a woman alleged that she had been "injured" (*taḍarrarat*) by the husband's cruelty to her: he humiliated her and beat her in public, causing her bodily harm, and tried to steal her

28. E.g., KD59–73, K48: p. 33 no. 64 4 April 60, K47: p. 43 no. 81 15 May 60.
29. Anderson, *Africa*, pp. 212, 232, 241–42; Layish, *Women*, pp. 166ff.
30. *MSH*, vol. 4, no. 4 (1932), p. 328, no. 105 of 8 Oct. 32. I am most grateful to my student Ron Shaham for drawing my attention to this source. Cf. ʿAbduh, p. 65; *mahjūra* in Layish, *Women*, pp. 168, 204. See also Anderson, *Africa*, p. 241.

jewelry. She complained to the police, and the husband was arrested. Some people, including her father-in-law, testified to the injury (*ḍarar*) caused to her. The wife further said that she lived in a place where she had no blood relations (*qarāba*) and asked to be transferred to "a decent place in the neighborhood of honest people" (*maḥall ʿadl bi-jiwār qawm ṣāliḥīn*). Finally, she demanded dissolution because of "the evident injury (*ḍarar bāʾin*) caused to her." In both cases the marriage was dissolved on the ground of injury, although the arbitration procedure was not applied. In a third case a wife who had been declared rebellious because she had left the husband's house proved in the course of a hearing before two arbitrators (one on behalf of each of the spouses) that she had repeatedly been beaten by the husband. The declaration of rebelliousness (*nushūz*) was quashed because the wife returned to the husband's house, but the court (not the arbitrators) confirmed the dissolution after the husband had not complied when it called upon him to divorce the wife. The decision was reversed at the appeal stage on the ground that the wife had not demanded a divorce, but at a rehearing the wife demanded dissolution on the ground of cruelty. After she had proved that she had sustained "repeated beatings" (*takarrur al-ḍarb*), she was given the choice between dissolution and continuation of the marriage and opted for the former.[31]

The author has not, in the Cyrenaican *sijill*s, encountered any instance of the application of the arbitration mechanism. Nor is there any evidence of dissolution through arbitrators on the ground of injury, on the initiative of the husband, by virtue of Law No. 76, which placed that mechanism at the disposal of the husband as well. It is therefore not possible to assess the extent of its application. Bousquet and Linant de Bellefonds also found, in relation to Algeria, that dissolution through arbitrators on the ground of cruelty to the wife was very rare because she found it difficult to prove injury in court. In Nigeria the wife might obtain dissolution on the ground of injury caused by the husband's cruelty, provided that her ordeal could not be regarded as lawful punishment under the Qurʾān. In the Gambia she might obtain her freedom if she proved that the husband beat her cruelly or continually, insulted her parents, or accused her of adultery. In the Aden Protectorate, on the other hand, such cruelty justified only her flight from

31. A:E102, p. 345 no. 589 12 July 54; AP:E4, p. 133 no. [126] n.d.; and d'Emilia, pp. 40–41, respectively. Cf. Fluehr-Lobban, p. 156.

the husband's house for a day or two.[32] In Israel dissolution through arbitrators on the ground of injury (under the inspiration of the Mālikī school) is the most effective means of dissolution in the case of cruelty of the husband and unwillingness on his part to grant a divorce. The term "dispute and discord" (*nizāᶜ wa-shiqāq*) has been widened to include more than matrimonial rights; the wife has used that mechanism as a device to obtain her freedom even where she had no *sharᶜī* ground for dissolution. She has even been willing to be found responsible for the dissolution and to bear the financial consequences, so long as she obtained her freedom.[33] In Tanganyika under colonial rule cases were observed where the wife refused to obey the husband in order that he should divorce her and she might marry a wealthier man of Indian, Arab, or African origin, or where a wealthy man coveted her and encouraged her to initiate the dissolution of her marriage. In all such cases the wife's parents might be partners in the scheme in the hope of financial gain. The wife sought dissolution on the ground of some dispute (*shiqāq*) and not by customary *khulᶜ*, although there is no visible reason for this; in fact the court did not grant her relief.[34]

d. Other grounds

Although in many cases the *sijill*s, on judicial divorce, note that the wife has not received her dower or part of it, this does not seem to be the *sharᶜī* ground for the divorce, for it is not stated in any instance that the marriage has not been consummated. Moreover, in all these cases the plea of nonpayment of the dower is accompanied by a plea of absence of the husband or nonprovision of maintenance, each of which is by itself a *sharᶜī* ground for judicial divorce.[35] Since nonpayment of the whole or part of the dower at the time of the contraction of the marriage is rather frequent, these findings lead to the conclusion that the wife is not aware of her right or that it is not regarded as a sufficient reason to demand a divorce. It seems that the remedy for nonpayment of the dower is not a demand for divorce but refusal to obey the husband in the conjugal dwelling pending payment; this remedy too is

32. Linant, *Traité*, p. 463 and the reference to Bousquet, *Précis*, there; Anderson, *Africa*, pp. 20–21, 212, 232, 241.
33. Layish, *Women*, pp. 169–71.
34. Schacht, *Papers*, a letter of Liwali's Court, Dar es-Salaam, Tanganyika, to J.N.D. Anderson of 23 July 1952.
35. E.g., B2:KM38–43:T41–43, K8: p. 11 no. 26 27 June 41, K8: p. 48 no. 120 28 March 42, K5: p. 59 no. 148 1 June 42; KD59–73, K51: p. 310 no. 69 [16 April 60], K43: p. 77 no. 151 11 Feb. 61.

lawfully available to the wife—that is, without her being regarded as rebellious and losing her right to maintenance—so long as the marriage has not been consummated.

The author has not encountered any instance of dissolution by judicial proceedings on the ground of impotence or some other ailment of the husband, although impotence is undoubtedly a factor in divorces by consent of the spouses. Mohsen describes it as a recognized ground for divorce among the Awlād ʿAlī. Among the Beduin tribes of Cyrenaica, Peters came across cases where a husband who believed himself to be impotent hired a blood relative to impregnate his wife; he delegated the blood relative for this purpose, ordering the wife to submit lest he depart this world without issue.[36]

3. RESORT TO JUDICIAL DIVORCE

In sum, judicial divorce on *sharʿī* grounds recognized by the Mālikī school, although well known and not merely marginal, is not particularly frequent in Cyrenaica. It seems that the wife prefers to obtain her freedom through divorce by consent, which is probably an easier proceeding even though it involves a renunciation of financial rights or compensation to the husband. We have seen that even where there is apparently a ground for judicial divorce, the wife prefers to obtain her freedom by *khulʿ*.[37]

In nineteenth-century Egypt, too, dissolution by judicial proceedings was not a remedy from the wife's point of view. But this is not surprising because the Ḥanafī school, which was dominant in the *sharīʿa* courts (although there were also courts of other schools), does not recognize this form of dissolution. Still, ways were found to persuade the *qāḍī* to dissolve the marriage on various grounds, including nonprovision of sufficient maintenance and nonfulfillment of marital duties by the husband. There were also those who under these circumstances availed themselves of the assistance of the *muftī*. It seems that owing to the adoption of the Mālikī norm in matters of divorce in reformist modern Egyptian legislation, dissolution by judicial proceedings is becoming increasingly frequent, although its actual incidence can be determined only by careful research. Corroboration of this assumption may

36. Mohsen, *Conflict*, p. 112; Peters, *Aspects*, p. 127.
37. See above, pp. 77–78. Cf. Fluehr-Lobban, p. 152.

be found in the Israeli *sijill*s following the adoption of the Mālikī norm in matters of divorce as embodied in the Ottoman Family Rights Law of 1917.[38]

It is interesting to note that French legislation in Algeria in the early 1930s, which provided women with secular grounds for divorce by legal proceedings, partly recognized by the *sharīʿa* (absence of the husband, nonprovision of maintenance), made no impact in the Kabyle Mountains. There were specific reasons for this: a woman seldom dared to apply to a French civil authority to demand dissolution of her marriage on a secular ground. When a Kabyle had been convicted of blood vengeance, which the French legislator regarded as a ground for dissolution since it involved moral turpitude, it was usual for his wife and her family to undertake not to demand dissolution. Moreover, even if a marriage was dissolved by a civil court, the ex-husband continued to regard the woman as his legal wife in all respects, and potential suitors, in fear of their lives, hesitated to approach her and ask her hand in marriage. In Israel, too, a secular ground for dissolution is not recognized by the Muslim population; the marriage of a girl under seventeen, which is in itself a criminal offence, although its *sharʿī* validity is not affected, creates a ground for dissolution by the husband, to be carried out in accordance with religious law; in fact, dissolution on the husband's initiative is supposed to induce the (civil) court to impose a lighter sentence. However, marriages of girls under age are common in traditional society and are not forbidden by the *sharīʿa*.[39]

38. Tucker, p. 54; Shaham; Layish, *Women*, p. 163.
39. Bousquet, *Coutumes kabiles*, pp. 82–83; Layish, *Women*, pp. 14ff.

CHAPTER V

Consequences of Divorce

1. LEGAL CONSEQUENCES

a. Legal Background

(1) **Revocable divorce.** The Mālikī school, like other schools, distinguishes three kinds of divorce as regards the legal consequences: revocable divorce, minor irrevocable divorce, and major irrevocable divorce.[1] Each of them is determined by several criteria: the divorce formulas, which may be explicit (*ṣarīḥ*) or metaphorical (*kināya*); the element of intent (*niyya*); the degree of finality of the husband's decision to divorce the wife; the side that initiates the divorce; the number of repudiations; the effectuation of the divorce; and the form of the dissolution—that is, *ṭalāq* (unilateral) or legal proceedings.

Revocable (*rajʿī*) divorce does not dissolve the marriage instantly, provided it has been consummated; it only causes legal separation. The mutual duties and rights of the spouses that arise out of the marriage, including the mutual right of succession, continue throughout the waiting period (*ʿidda*), during which the wife is required to remain in the husband's house. The divorce takes effect (and becomes irrevocable) only after expiration of the waiting period. During the waiting period the husband may reinstate the wife twice without need for her consent or for the presence of witnesses, and without the conclusion of another marriage contract or the payment of another dower. It is not necessary to inform the wife of her reinstatement, although it is universally recommended to do so lest she think that she is free to marry another man after expiration of the

1. Unless otherwise indicated, the legal background is based on the following sources: Linant, *Traité*, pp. 307-10, 365-73, 393-417, 423-25, 442-43, 451, 453; Linant, *khulʿ*, p. 186; Milliot, pp. 352, 354-58, 364-65, 374-75, 378; Stern, pp. 135, 139-45; Anderson, *Africa*, pp. 362-64, 367, 376-77; Pesle, pp. 118-21; Bousquet, *Précis*, pp. 187-88; Coulson, *Succession*, p. 20; Layish, *Women*, pp. 173-74.

waiting period. The Mālikī school holds that the reinstatement must in principle be formally declared. If a metaphorical expression is used that does not necessarily mean reinstatement, the husband must make his intention clear. The resumption of marital relations and similar acts are equivalent to reinstatement by a formal expression, provided that they are initiated by the husband and that he really intends to revoke the divorce. The husband may delegate the revocation to a third party and even to the wife herself. The purpose of revocable divorce is to enable a husband who has divorced his wife rashly to restore his marriage without damage. A divorce of this kind is regarded as the most recommended one (*aḥsan*).

There are no special expressions denoting revocable divorce. According to the Mālikī and other schools, if the husband does not express the divorce in terms implying finality or accompany the expression of divorce with the word "three," the first and second divorces are regarded as revocable provided the marriage has been consummated. Most of the divorce formulas that according to the Ḥanafī school entail one irrevocable divorce—unless the husband otherwise intended—are regarded as revocable by the Mālikī school. A divorce by consent may under certain circumstances be revocable (according to the Mālikī school): where it is so stipulated between the spouses and no compensation is paid or where the husband pays compensation to the wife. Judicial divorce on the ground of nonprovision of maintenance is also considered revocable; the wife may be reinstated within the waiting period if maintenance is provided.

(2) **Minor irrevocable divorce.** Minor irrevocable divorce (*bāʾin baynūna ṣughrā*) becomes operative instantly with all its legal and financial consequences: there are no more mutual duties or rights, the spouses do not succeed each other, and the husband must pay to the wife the balance of the dower not paid during the existence of the marriage. After such a divorce the husband may reinstate the wife twice, during or after the waiting period, but only by a new marriage and dower, conditional upon consent of the wife or her guardian and in the presence of witnesses.

According to the Mālikī school, minor irrevocable divorce takes place under the following circumstances: upon revocable divorce if the husband does not reinstate the wife during the waiting period; where the divorce occurs before consummation of the marriage—even if *khalwa* (privacy) has taken place, technically enabling the spouses to have undisturbed marital relations (in both cases, the wife is exempt from the waiting period); where the husband uses a divorce formula suggesting finality, such as *al-battata*; in the case of *khulʿ* or any other divorce involving compensation; in the case of *īlāʾ*, an oath by the husband to abstain from marital relations for a certain period; in the case of *liʿān*, a charge of adultery against the wife that the husband cannot prove; upon judicial divorce on any of the following grounds: chronic illness of one of the spouses, lack of equality between them (*kafāʾa*), nonpayment of dower, defection from Islam, injury to the wife, prolonged absence of the husband, or disharmony between the spouses.

Law No. 76 provides that whenever the court, following a failure of arbitrators to decide a question of injury, pronounces judicial divorce on behalf of the wife, such divorce shall be regarded as irrevocable, whereas divorce on behalf of the husband shall be revocable. According to traditional Mālikī law, judicial divorce on the wife's initiative (except in cases of nonprovision of maintenance) involves irrevocable divorce, whereas if the court pronounces divorce on the husband's initiative, it is deemed to have stepped into the husband's shoes and the divorce may be presumed revocable.[2]

(3) **Major irrevocable divorce.** Major irrevocable divorce (*bāʾin baynūna kubrā*) entails the same consequences as minor irrevocable divorce but in addition creates a temporary impediment to remarriage between the spouses: the marriage cannot be legally restored until the wife has been married to another man and that marriage has been dissolved, either by divorce or by the husband's death, and after the appropriate waiting period. Although all the schools agree that in principle the intermediate marriage must be contracted in good faith, there are differences between them as to the application of that principle. All the schools except the Ḥanafī hold that an intermediate marriage is void if contracted "with intent to render [the woman] lawfully permitted [again to her first husband]" (*bi-qaṣd al-taḥlīl*)—a device that is considered legitimate though reprehensible by the Ḥanafī school even if expressly stipulated in the marriage contract. The schools' view is based on the assumption that such an intermediate marriage is tantamount to a temporary marriage (*mutʿa*) and thus does not

2. Mayer, *Marriage*, p. 38. Cf. Coulson, *History*, p. 188; Anderson, *Reform*, pp. 120ff.

meet the requirement of an intermediate marriage. Moreover, some Mālikī jurists hold that such a marriage is void even if the intent of *taḥlīl* is not expressed, while most jurists permit it so long as the intent is not expressed or, in other words, so long as the unlawful motive by which the husband was actuated is not *formally* agreed upon by the parties. All the schools agree that the intermediate marriage must be consummated and that the woman must strictly observe the waiting period after the dissolution of the first marriage and the intermediate marriage before being permitted again to her first husband. The purpose of the intermediate marriage is to prevent the husband, by the interposition of a deterrent barrier—in terms of traditional morality—from ill-using the wife by alternately divorcing and reinstating her. If the wife is divorced by triple repudiation for adultery, she is forbidden to the husband forever; their marriage cannot be restored even after a consummated intermediate marriage.

Major irrevocable divorce occurs under the following circumstances: after a third repudiation, whether revocable—even if the wife was reinstated within the waiting period—or by minor irrevocable divorce (Mālikī judicial divorce, being *ṭalāq*—but not *faskh* dissolution of other schools—is included in the count of repudiations); in the case of *khulʿ* if the parties so agree; where any of the metaphorical formulas indicating intent on the part of the husband is used (e.g., *ḥarām*, which means that the wife is forbidden to him); and in the case of triple repudiation, which entails the legal consequences of three separate repudiations. Triple repudiation may be by an explicit expression of repudiation accompanied by pronouncement of the numeral three, by three successive pronouncements of the same divorce formula, by the use of three fingers, or by a metaphorical formula suggesting intent. According to the Mālikī school, an element of intent is not necessary in metaphorical formulas.

(4) **Waiting period.** According to the Mālikī school, the waiting period (*ʿidda*) of a divorced woman lasts for three periods of legal purity or, where she is pregnant, until delivery. She may not remarry during the waiting period. The reason for this seems to be the wish to avoid a doubt as to the paternity of a child she may be carrying. A marriage to another man during the waiting period is invalid, and according to the Mālikī school, its consummation bars the couple from ever marrying each other. Where a wife is divorced before the consummation of her marriage, she is exempt

from the requirement of the waiting period unless privacy (*khalwa*) has taken place.[3]

b. Legal Consequences in Practice

(1) **Revocable divorce.** As far as can be gathered from the *sijill*s, revocable divorce, while frequent, is not predominant, although according to the Mālikī school it is supposed to be the accepted norm in the absence of terms suggesting finality. It is interesting to note that among the Berbers of the Kabyle Mountains revocable divorce was also not usual. Divorce was irrevocable and became operative instantly; the idea that a divorced wife might be reinstated in the waiting period without a new marriage was contrary to custom. At the same time, it is possible that revocable divorce is more widely resorted to in Cyrenaica but that the spouses do not trouble to report it to the court when they are not interested in dissolution or other complications; it may be that the spouses in fact ignore the divorce or that the husband reinstates the wife within the waiting period without reporting the event to the court, on the assumption that the divorce has in any case not become operative. As we shall see below, the *qāḍī*s find it difficult to keep count of the divorces.[4] Revocable divorce is expressly referred to as such; it cannot be identified from the vague divorce formula, which does not indicate the legal consequences. Thus in one case the husband said: "My wife... is divorced by one revocable repudiation" (*ṭalqa wāḥida rajᶜiyya*). In another case the husband's father said: "I have divorced my son's wife... by one revocable repudiation," adding: "This is her first revocable (*rajᶜiyyan*) repudiation by him."[5] Sometimes revocability becomes apparent only from the wife's testimony and not from the formula used by the husband. Thus in one case the husband declared: "I have divorced my wife by what is considered her first repudiation by me." The wife confirmed his version as to the repudiation, adding that the repudiation "is considered revocable (*rajᶜī*)." In another case the wife declared: "He has divorced me by a revocable repudiation registered in this court." Revocability is of advantage to a wife interested in the restoration of the marriage. On the other hand it may create a state of legal

3. Pesle, p. 159.
4. Bousquet, *Coutumes kabiles*, pp. 75, 79. Cf. Layish, *Women*, p. 175; Layish, *Druze*, pp. 181ff., 238ff. See below, pp. 153–54.
5. AP:E2, p. 158 no. 152 11 Aug. 47; and KD59–73, K43: p. 139 no. 307 18 Oct. 62, respectively. See also KD59–73, K50: p. 133 no. 273 25 July 62.

uncertainty, lasting many months, as to the wife's status; in this respect it is perhaps the most serious expression of the husband's freedom of divorce. In the days before sedentarization, Beduin in the Judean Desert would divorce and reinstate their wives any number of times—up to twenty according to one testimony.[6]

In some cases, a wife is revocably divorced after she has given up various financial rights—"the whole dower and the waiting-period maintenance" or "all her rights except the waiting-period maintenance."[7] This is not contrary to the legal norm, according to which a divorce by mutual consent may be revocable if the parties so stipulate, so long as it does not involve the payment of compensation by the wife. In one case a revocable divorce followed mutual renunciation of financial rights. Such an occurrence has also been observed in Israel.[8]

In the waiting period following revocable divorce the wife, according to the legal norm, lives in the husband's house, since the marriage tie still exists and he is technically able to reinstate her. Thus in one case in which a man divorced his pregnant wife by revocable repudiation, he undertook to pay monthly maintenance to her until she gave birth and also "undertook to accommodate (*iskān*) her at his house, where she still was, until she gave birth"—that is, until the end of the waiting period.[9] In a case of a different kind the wife was divorced by customary *khulʿ*. She returned the dower and the clothing to the husband and undertook to pay him a certain amount "when I am able to marry someone else ... so that he may divorce me for it." The husband agreed to wait for that amount on the said condition and consented that the wife might "remain at his place [his residence] without mixing with people (*takhtaliṭ bi-aḥad*) before the expiration of the waiting period"; only then did he divorce her by one *khulʿī* repudiation.[10] It is possible that we have to do here with a revocable divorce, since an irrevocable divorce becomes operative instantly, the wife being forbidden to her divorcer save after remarrying him, although the remarriage may take place *before* the end of the waiting period. It may be

6. A:E103, p. 118 no. 208 13 Aug. 52; and AP:E3 p. 302 no. 507 25 Feb. 54, respectively; Layish, *Women*, p. 176; Layish & Shmueli, pp. 38–39.
7. E.g., KD59–73, K50: p. 133 no. 273 25 July 62, K50: p. 142 no. 314 7 Nov. 62, K44: p. 215 no. 515 22 Dec. 64.
8. KD59–73, K43: p. 139 no. 306 18 Oct. 62; Layish, *Women*, p. 176.
9. A:E102, p. 329 no. 560 3 June 54.
10. AP:E4, p. 137 no. 127 23 May 47.

that in this case, too, the husband wished to retain the option of reinstating the wife during the waiting period.

There is indeed evidence, albeit rare, of the reinstatement of wives during the waiting period. Thus in one case the husband stated that he had divorced the wife by revocable repudiation and the wife confirmed his version, whereupon he reinstated (*rājaʿa*) the wife at a session of the court "and the *qāḍī* had us testify (*ashhadanā*) to it." It is not impossible that the spouses had agreed in advance on the story of the revocable divorce in order to facilitate the restoration of their marriage. At the same time the husband undertook to buy the wife a light handmade outer garment "to give her pleasure," and he also undertook "to see to her welfare in future." The wife "returned (*rajaʿat*) with her husband [to his house] contentedly (*rāḍiya*)." The giving of a present to a wife when she is reinstated after a revocable repudiation (or when a second wife is taken) has been observed in Africa; it is called *raḍwa* (propitiation). It is commended but not enjoined by the *sharīʿa*.[11] In another case, the wife was divorced after four years of marriage. She returned to her house with her daughter while her son remained with his father. She alleged that when she had visited her son a year before, "he reinstated me (*rājaʿanī*)... and we had marital relations for twenty days and then he divorced me by *ṭalāq* and then he drove me out." She asked the court "to return (*tarjīʿ*) me to my children and give me my rights or to divorce me by *ṭalāq* with my rights." The husband confirmed the story of the two repudiations but declared that he did not want to reinstate (*irjāʿ*) her once again. From the wife's story, which was not denied by the husband, we gain the impression that following the first repudiation the wife was reinstated *after* the expiration of the waiting period. If this impression is correct, this reinstatement had no *sharʿī* validity.[12]

(2) **Minor irrevocable divorce.** In everyday reality minor irrevocable divorce is prevalent. Judgments generally do not expressly indicate finality in divorce formulas, but it may be deduced from an accompanying statement (in the third person) of the explicit consequence of the

11. AP:E3, p. 328 no. 558 2 June 54; Anderson, *Africa*, pp. 364, 373. Cf. Fluehr-Lobban, pp. 147, 170; Layish, *Women*, pp. 175–76.
12. A:E104, p. 222 no. 369 [?] July 53. It is not possible to verify this impression since the judgment of the *qāḍī* on the following page is missing.

repudiation, such as: the husband "launched one repudiation against her (*arsala ʿalayhā ṭalqa wāḥida*), saying: 'You are divorced,' and she is not legally permitted to him save by means of a new marriage tie" (*antī* [*anti*] *ṭāliqa fa-lā taḥill lahu illā bi-ʿaqd jadīd*) or the husband "divorces his wife by one repudiation... and she is not to be reinstated save by means of a new dower and a new *Fātiḥa* [i.e., marriage tie]" (*wa-lā lahā rujūʿ illā bi-ṣadāq jadīd wa-fātiḥa jadīda*).[13] In the case of divorce by consent, irrevocability is to be expected not only because it is anchored in law but also because it is difficult to assume that a wife who initiated her release from marriage would agree to revocable repudiation after renouncing various financial rights or compensating her husband with a substantial sum of money. Similarly, judicial divorce, except in the case of nonprovision of maintenance, is irrevocable.[14]

Most of the evidence in the *sijill*s concerns the restoration of marriages by means of a new marriage tie after one or two repudiations—that is, after a minor irrevocable divorce.[15] Although it is occasionally said that the man wishes to reinstate his wife or that he has actually reinstated her, it appears from various data in the document that we have to do with the contraction of a new marriage. Thus in one case it is noted that a man "wished to reinstate (*tarjīʿ*) his wife," a member of the same tribe, who is "free from *sharʿī* impediments and from marriage ties (*al-khāliya minaʾl-mawāniʿ al-sharʿiyya waʾl-ʿalāʾiq al-zawjiyya*), after a first repudiation." The *qāḍī* gave "*sharʿī* permission (*idhn*) for the formation of a marriage tie (*ʿaqd*), and by virtue of that permission the tie was formed between them."[16] In another case the wife was repudiated following a quarrel between the spouses. The husband wanted to "bring back (*yarjiʿ*) the wife to her [his] house, and he brought her back for [the price of] her first dower" (*wa-rajaʿahā ʿalā ṣadāqihā al-awwal*). He gave her some silver ornaments "and brought her back to her house with the consent of both

13. KD59–73, p. 103 no. 217 18 Dec. 61; and KDP, K47: p. [?] no. [?] 25 April 67, respectively. On the *Fātiḥa* as part of the marriage rite see, e.g., KAMD, A: p. [?] no. 48 25 May 39; AMR50, A21: p. 50 no. 53 5 May 50; AP:E1, p. 143 no. 254 19 Nov. 52; KDP, K47: p. [?] no. [?] 25 April 67. Cf. Bousquet, *Coutumes kabiles*, p. 63; Mohsen, *Conflict*, pp. 45, 86, 88; al-ʿĀrif, p. 130; ʿAbd Allāh, p. 54; Layish & Shmueli, p. 33.
14. Linant, *Khulʿ*, p. 186. See below, pp. 151ff.
15. E.g., KAMD, A: p. 9 no. 9 15 June 42, A: p. 23 no. 23 9 Sep. 42; AMR42–44, A5: p. 95 no. 95 16 Oct. 43.
16. AMR42–44, A3: p. 76 no. 76 24 Aug. 43. See also A3: p. 82 no. 82 12 Sep. 43.

parties." The reference to the first dower and to his divorced wife's consent indicate that we have to do here with the contraction of a new marriage, since neither is required on reinstatement in the case of a revocable divorce.[17]

A revocable divorce turns into an irrevocable one when the husband does not exercise his right of reinstatement during the waiting period; he then has no choice but to remarry his divorced wife, paying a new dower. Thus in one case the husband wished to "reinstate (*tarjīʿ*) the wife... after a first revocable (*rajʿiyyatan*) repudiation against payment of a dower." Again, payment of the dower indicates that we have to do with a new marriage.[18]

In all the cases recorded in the *sijill*s in which a divorced woman is returned to her former husband by way of a new marriage, it is done through a proxy (*wakīl*)—her father or brother or another agnate; and although it is sometimes said that the new marriage is contracted with the consent of the parties, it seems that the woman is not at liberty to refuse.[19] The husband, too, is sometimes remarried to his divorced wife through a proxy, which strengthens the assumption that the remarriage of divorced spouses is a family matter rather than a personal one.[20] The measure of liberty taken by the agnate may be gauged from the following case. A woman was repudiated four days after her consummated marriage. Her relative, without her consent, waived the balance of the dower due to her, and he may also have brought about the repudiation. The woman claimed her financial rights from the relative or, alternatively, from the husband. In the end "they all agreed"—and it seems that the relative again had a hand in it—on "reinstatement (*tarjīʿ*) of the wife into intimate association (*muʿāshara*) with the husband under the terms of the dower... the prompt and the deferred—registered between them" upon the first marriage; that is to say, the divorced wife was reinstated by way of a new marriage.[21] In fact there is evidence of financial accounting between the spouses continuing from marriage to marriage. Thus in one case the wife was divorced and the husband entered to her debit (probably in the *quṣṣat al-marʾa*) the sum of six pounds. A year later "he reinstated her (*rājaʿahā*) by

17. KD59-73, K50: p. 19 no. 45 7 July 65.
18. KAMD, A: p. 3 no. 3 16 April 42.
19. AMR42-44, A3: p. 82 no. 82 12 Sep. 43, A3: p. 90 no. 90 10 Oct. 43, A5: p. 95 no. 95 16 Oct. 43; AP:E1, p. 143 no. 254 19 Nov. 52; KD59-73, K50: p. 19 no. 45 7 July 65.
20. AMR42-44, A3: p. 76 no. 76 24 Aug. 43.
21. AP:E1, p. 143 no. 254 19 Nov. 52.

means of the said six pounds with an addition of four pounds, which he paid to her." In other words, the dower of the second marriage was in part set off against the amount that the divorced wife owed the former husband upon the dissolution of the first.[22]

(3) **Major irrevocable divorce.** The divorcing husband often declares in court that this is "his first repudiation descending (*wāqiʿ*) upon her" or "my wife... is repudiated by what is considered my first repudiation of her."[23] In some cases the husband declares that the wife's irrevocable or revocable repudiation was "the second repudiation."[24] The author has come across only one instance of double repudiation: "He launched two repudiations (*ṭalaqatayn*) against her." Under French rule, the Berbers in the Kabyle Mountains completely ignored the existence of double repudiation.[25] From these findings, one might gain the impression that the people are aware of the question of the count of repudiations. However, as we shall see, the counting may be the *qāḍī*'s contribution to the enforcement of the *sharʿī* norm. The first and second repudiations and the double repudiation are not critical from the point of view of the spouses, since they leave them the option of restoring their marriage either by reinstating the wife (in the case of revocable repudiation) or by remarrying each other (in the case of irrevocable repudiation) without resort to an intermediate marriage.

There are also instances of third repudiations: the husband divorces the wife by one repudiation and declares that this is "tantamount to her third repudiation by him" (*muṣādif li-thālith ṭalāq wāqiʿ minhu*).[26] Sometimes the husband (or perhaps the *qāḍī*) adds: "and by means thereof [of this repudiation] she is separated from him for the major period of separation and the marriage between them is dissolved" (*wa-bihi qad bānat minhu al-baynūna al-kubrā wa-infaṣalat baynahumā ʿuqdat al-niqāḥ*);[27] that is to say, an intermediate marriage is necessary before the woman may again be

22. A:E103, p. 108 no. 195 29 July 52.
23. E.g., AP:E2, p. 164 no. 158 [? Sep. 47]; A:E103, p. 96 no. 178 3 July 52, p. 134 no. 238 6 Oct. 52, p. 154 no. 270 7 Jan 53; KD59–73, K50: p. 131 no. 270 11 July 62, K50: p. 133 no. 273 25 July 62.
24. E.g., A:E104, p. 190 no. 324 20 March 54; AP:E3, p. 328 no. 558 2 June 54. Cf. Fluehr-Lobban, p. 147.
25. KD59–73, K45: p. 216 no. 516 7 Dec. 64; Bousquet, *Coutumes kabiles*, p. 77.
26. E.g., A:E104, p. 170 no. 297 8 Feb. 53, p. 176 no. [305] 17 Feb. 53; A:E104, p. 202 no. 341 [? April 53], p. 228 no. 378 [?] July 53.
27. A:E104, p. 164 no. 286 28 Jan. 53.

permitted to her first husband. There are also instances of divorce by triple repudiation or, as it is called in judgments, "three repudiations by a single word," which is followed by an explanation (apparently by the *qāḍī*) of the legal consequences: "He has divorced her by three repudiations by a single word and she has become prohibited to him; she is not legally permitted to him from now on until she has been married to another man" (*ṭallaqahā thalāth ṭalaqāt fī kalima wāḥida fa-ṣārat mabtūta ʿalayhi lā taḥill lahu min baʿdi ḥattā tankaḥ zawjan ghayra*[*hu*]). Triple repudiation makes the remedy of intermediate marriage a mockery.[28] Sometimes it is stated that the husband divorces the wife by means of an expression intended for minor irrevocable repudiation in the sense of triple repudiation. Thus in one case it was said: "He launches against her an irrevocable (*bātta*) repudiation; she is not permitted to him from now on until she has been married to another man."[29]

Triple repudiation is especially frequent in the case of divorce by consent; it is then designed to demonstrate an absolute rupture between the spouses.[30] Where triple repudiation is effected out of court and not by consent, it may be due to anger or provocation—at any rate, to some uncontrollable impulse.[31] In one case the wife was repudiated by triple repudiation "by a single word" for adultery, apparently in order to demonstrate the husband's determination to sever his link with her forever. As stated, on triple repudiation under these circumstances, the marriage can never be restored even after a consummated intermediate marriage. The same finality presumably existed where the wife was divorced on her wedding night because the husband suspected her of not being a virgin or where she had stolen money from him.[32] In another case triple repudiation was combined with an archaic *ẓihār* repudiation with the addition of a *ḥarām* oath. The husband said: "You are forbidden to me like my mother" (*wa-ḥar*[*ā*]*m ʿalayya kayfa ummī*). In the view of most jurists,

28. KD59–73, K47: p. 53 no. 102 6 Aug. 60. See also K51: p. 9 no. 18 17 Aug. 59, K47: p. 54 no. 104 16 Aug. 60, K45: p. 144 no. 318 11 Nov. 62; B2:KM38–43:T41–43, K9: p. 3 no. 8 14 May 41. Cf. Fluehr-Lobban, p. 147.

29. KD59–73, K51: p. 145 no. 319 7 Nov. 61.

30. KD59–73, K47: p. 56 no. 107 24 Aug. 60 (renunciation), K47: p. 53 no. 102 6 Aug. 60, K47: p. 191 no. 449 28 March 64 (compensation). Cf. d'Emilia, pp. 35–36.

31. E.g., KD59–73, K48: p. 84 no. 163 19 April 61, p. 100 no. 211 5 Dec. 61. Cf. Layish, *Women*, p. 174.

32. B2:KM38–43:T41–43, K5: p. 33 no. 84 1 Jan 42; d'Emilia, pp. 36–37, 39, 48–49.

repudiation by way of a *ḥarām* oath is by itself equivalent to triple repudiation; it seems that it is expressly stated to be so for the sake of clarity. Repudiation by way of a *ḥarām* oath was observed in Nigeria under colonial rule—pronounced in a fit of anger—and, in combination with a *ẓihār* or *īlāʾ* oath, in Israel. Divorce by triple repudiation, in fits of anger and irritation, occurred also among the Berbers of the Kabyle Mountains.[33]

The *sijill*s contain several instances of divorce by more than triple repudiation at one session. It is probably intended to demonstrate the husband's determination and may be a mode of expression anchored in custom. Thus in one case the wife redeemed herself with her dower, clothing, waiting-period maintenance, and "neglect" (*ihmāl*) maintenance (i.e., maintenance delayed during marriage), and the husband divorced her, saying: "She, my wife..., is divorced by four repudiations (*arbaʿ ṭalaqāt*)." As she had already been repudiated once, the total count of repudiations was five. In another case the husband "repudiated her [the wife] seven times by a single word, saying: 'You are forbidden [to me] seven times' (*innaki ḥarām sabʿa marrāt*)." In a third case the wife "redeemed herself with the whole of her prompt and deferred dower...and renounced all her financial rights in exchange for her divorce" and the husband "divorced her by a third repudiation, saying: 'You are divorced by a hundred repudiations' (*miʾa ṭalāq*)." Divorce by tens of repudiations "by a single word" has been observed among the Beduin of the Judean Desert.[34]

It seems that the husband is sometimes startled by the consequences of his rashness and tries to mitigate the gravity of triple repudiation, not always successfully. Thus in one case the wife said that the husband had "divorced her by triple repudiation and not, as he alleged, by two repudiations." She had pointed this out to the *sharʿī nāʾib* when he registered her divorce a month before, but he had not taken down what she said. Witnesses confirmed her story, and the *qāḍī* amended the judgment to the effect that she had been repudiated three times. A similar occurrence has been observed in Israel. But it has also been observed that a wife objected to a triple repudiation and asked for its mitigation. Similarly in Algeria under French rule the wife, in despair, sometimes applied to the

33. KDP, K45: p. [?] no. [135] 23 Nov. 60; Anderson, *Africa*, p. 213; Layish, *Women*, p. 174; Bousquet, *Coutumes kabiles*, p. 75 and the source indicated there.

34. A:E102, p. 128 no. 54 9 Sep. 51; KD59–73, K44: p. 136 no. 301 14 Oct. 62, and p. 37 no. 71 24 April 60, respectively; Layish, *Judaean Desert*.

court to annul the triple repudiation because her religious beliefs forbade her to have intercourse with her husband after triple repudiation until she was legally permitted to remarry him following an intermediate marriage.[35] The author has not, in the Cyrenaican *sijill*s, come across triple combined with suspended repudiation, although such a combination has been observed in Israel. It is either meant to emphasize the husband's determination to ensure the wife's obedience or to reinforce a statement not necessarily connected with the wife.[36] Neither did he come across an instance of a wife divorced by triple repudiation being reinstated after an intermediate marriage intended to enable her lawfully to remarry her former husband—a form of reinstatement known from other parts of North Africa. Charnay reports that in Tunisia under French rule various devices were used to circumvent an intermediate marriage: a *mariage blanc* to a sexually immature boy, who was laid under a blanket with the woman for a few minutes without, of course, consummating the marriage; a *fatwā* of a *faqīh* or *muftī* stating that the man conceived the idea of the divorce at a time when he was out of his mind; almsgiving and expiation made up for the ill-considered act; etc. The moralistic Mālikī school attaches importance to the element of intent; under these circumstances there is cause to seek the opinion of Mālikī *fuqahāʾ*. In the Kabyle Mountains, too, reinstatement after an intermediate marriage was very rare. Bousquet attributes this to the fact that according to custom such a marriage was not required, although some Kabyles were aware of the *sharʿī* norm in this matter. The Beduin of the Judean Desert are also not very strict about an intermediate marriage after three repudiations.[37]

In sum, it seems that the rules of revocable divorce and of intermediate marriage after the third repudiation have not attained their objective; the Cyrenaicans are not careful to apply *ṭalāq al-sunna* and avoid *ṭalāq al-bidʿa*.[38]

(4) **Waiting-period.** The author has come across only one clear case of a divorced woman remarrying her former husband without having observed the waiting period. She was divorced four days after contracting a *sharʿī* marriage, which was consummated, and about two weeks later she

35. A:E102, p. 361 no. 617 22 Aug. 54; Layish, *Women*, p. 175; Charnay, pp. 37, 39.

36. Layish, *Women*, p. 174.

37. Bousquet, *Précis*, pp. 189–90; Bousquet, *Coutumes kabiles*, pp. 75–76; Charnay, pp. 39–40. Cf. Layish, *Women*, pp. 174, 176; Layish & Shmueli, p. 39; Fluehr-Lobban, p. 148.

38. Cf. Layish, *Women*, p. 177.

remarried her former husband. In minor irrevocable divorce, as stated, a man may reinstate his divorced wife by remarriage even in the waiting period. But we may assume that the Beduin followed this practice in reliance on custom rather than on the *sharīʿa*. In the days before sedentarization, the Beduin of the Judean Desert would divorce and reinstate their wives without strictly observing the waiting period.[39] There is no evidence in the *sijill*s of the marriage of a divorced woman to a man other than her former husband during the waiting period. The lack of evidence does not prove that Cyrenaican society is indeed strict about the waiting period. There may still be causes for its not being strict about it, such as lack of awareness of the legal position, especially where the marriage is not performed by a *sharʿī* solemnizer (*maʾdhūn*), and unwillingness to get involved in dissolution proceedings, especially where the woman was pregnant at the time of the divorce and the question of paternity might thus arise. At the same time the lack of evidence may possibly indicate that the legal norm as to the waiting period is indeed applied in Cyrenaican society.

As stated, where the wife is divorced before consummation of the marriage, she is exempt from observing the waiting period. There are isolated instances of divorce before consummation. Sometimes it is indicated that the marriage was of short duration or that at any rate the wife had not yet moved in with the husband and that thus no privacy (*khalwa*) had taken place. In one case, for instance, it was said that the man "renounced his fiancée (*makhṭūba*)."[40]

2. FINANCIAL CONSEQUENCES

a. Waiting-Period Maintenance

For the purpose of the maintenance of a divorced woman, most of the schools distinguish between revocable and irrevocable divorce. In revocable divorce the wife is entitled to full maintenance—board, lodging, and clothing—during the waiting period, provided she is not a rebellious woman. This view is shared by all the schools. In irrevocable divorce the

39. AP:E1, p. 143 no. 254 19 Nov. 52. See below, pp. 158ff.; Oweidi, pp. 152–53; Layish & Shmueli, p. 39.
40. AP:E3, p. 348 no. 595 5 July 54. See also A:E102, p. 16 no. 31 16 Aug. 51; KD59–73, K43: p. 60 no. 116 5 Oct. 60. Cf. Stern, p. 134.

schools are divided as to the qurʾānic texts in the matter (2:241; 65:6): if the woman is pregnant, all grant her full maintenance until her delivery; if she is not pregnant, the Mālikī school grants her lodging only (not board and clothing). If the marriage has not been consummated, the woman is not entitled to maintenance, since she is not required to observe a waiting period; but it is recommended to give her a present (*mutʿa*) under certain circumstances.[41]

The Mālikī norm for the waiting-period maintenance seems to be followed in practice, although this is not always fully confirmed by the *sijill*s. Where the wife is divorced by revocable repudiation, she is entitled to waiting-period maintenance even though it is not said that this means full maintenance. Thus in one case a man appeared in court to register his wife's divorce, saying: "I have paid her all her dower and her waiting-period maintenance (*nafaqat ʿiddatihā*) and she has no more claim against me," and the *qāḍī* pronounced the wife divorced by revocable repudiation. In another case in which the wife was divorced by revocable repudiation the husband undertook to pay "waiting-period maintenance until the end of the waiting period."[42]

Where a revocably divorced wife is pregnant, she receives full maintenance until her delivery. In one such case the husband undertook to pay an amount in cash as monthly maintenance until she gave birth and also "to accommodate her, until she gave birth, in a house owned by him in which she then was... and to give her a sheep... and a goat." It seems we may infer from this that the reference is to full maintenance. In a case in which the wife was divorced in similar circumstances, she stated that she was two months pregnant by her husband, and he undertook to pay monthly maintenance to her until she gave birth.[43]

A pregnant woman is entitled to full maintenance until delivery even in the case of irrevocable divorce if the divorce is initiated by the husband. However, the difficulty lies in determining whether the woman is indeed pregnant. According to law, her allegation that she is pregnant is not entertained until she has proved it; but once she has proved it, she receives

41. Linant, *Traité*, pp. 270–71; Pesle, pp. 168–69, 172–73, 174; Anderson, *Africa*, p. 364; Stern, pp. 139, 145.

42. A:E102, p. 351 no. 501 26 Feb. 54; and A:E103, p. 124 no. 219 8 Sep. 52, respectively. See also KD59–73, K43: p. 139 no. 307 18 Oct. 62.

43. A:E102, p. 329 no. 560 3 June 54; and AP:E2, p. 158 no. 152 11 Aug. 47, respectively.

maintenance retroactively for the entire period prior to its proof. Where the pregnancy is obvious and therefore not difficult to prove, the man undertakes to pay "pregnancy maintenance" (*nafaqat al-ḥaml*) until delivery without any special proceeding. Thus in one case the woman was, at the time of the divorce, in the eighth month of pregnancy, and the man undertook to pay waiting-period maintenance.[44] But usually it is not certain that the divorced wife is pregnant. Sometimes she states that she thinks she has been pregnant for some time but still has doubts (*shakk*) about it[45] or that she is pregnant but cannot prove it for the time being by outward physical signs. It seems that the woman does not use medical certificates to prove pregnancy. Under these circumstances, the man undertakes that "if the pregnancy is proved" (*idhā thabata al-ḥaml*) he will pay maintenance until the woman gives birth, and some men say expressly (as required by law): "complete maintenance (*kulfa tāmma*) [which includes] board (*maʾūna*), clothing (*kiswa*) [and lodging]."[46] In one case the woman stated that at the time of the divorce she had a "sleeping embryo" (*ḥaml nāʾim*)—that is, prolonged pregnancy, unlimited in time, in which the embryo does not develop. A month later, owing to some disturbance (*inziʿāj*), "the embryo awoke and began to move," and she demanded that the man be ordered to pay maintenance until she gave birth. The man confirmed her story in full. Some Mālikī jurists hold that the maximum waiting period of a pregnant woman is equal to the maximum period of pregnancy, which according to that school is four to five years (others say one year). The concept of the "sleeping embryo," under which the child is affiliated to its natural father or his relatives, was known also in Kabyle law.[47]

Even where the woman renounces the waiting-period maintenance, which is rather frequent in divorce by consent, the right to maintenance subsists if she is pregnant. Thus in one case it was said: the woman "renounces all her rights ... —no dower, no maintenance—unless she is

44. KD59–73, p. 150 no. 331 12 Jan. 63. See also B2:KM38–43: EA, K10: no. 27 13 July 33; KD59–73, p. 123 no. 262 24 June 62, K50: p. 133 no. 296 12 Sep. 62, K44: p. 212 no. 212 8 Nov. 64.

45. KD59–73, K48: p. 65 no. 127 22 Oct. 60.

46. B2:KM38–43:EA, K4a: no. [28] 28 Sep. 32. See also KD59–73, p. 102 no. 215 16 Dec. 61, K48: p. 155 no. 338 7 Feb. 63, K51: p. 114 no. 239 4 April 62; AP:E2, p. 170 no. 164 22 Sep. 47.

47. A:E102, p. 8 no. 15 1 Aug. 51; Milliot, pp. 353–54; Bousquet, *Coutumes kabiles*, pp. 86–87.

pregnant (*illā in kāna bihā ḥaml*)."[48] In another case, it was said that the woman "renounces (*tarakat*) the waiting-period maintenance unless she conceals (*musirra*) her pregnancy until it is fully proved a month later."[49] In a further case the wife renounced all her rights except the waiting-period maintenance in return for her release.[50] A divorce involving renunciation or compensation by the woman is irrevocable; on the other hand, in revocable divorce the wife is entitled to full maintenance even if she is not pregnant.

Sometimes, the woman is willing, upon divorce, to renounce various financial rights but insists on her right to receive waiting-period maintenance if it is proved that she is pregnant at the time of the divorce. Thus in one case it was said that the woman had redeemed herself from her husband in return for her dower "and demands nothing from him but [half] the waiting-period maintenance." In another case, it was said: "Neither of them demands anything from the other but pregnancy maintenance in respect of the child which is in her womb"; and the man, in turn, undertook "to pay to her what is required of him by law—maintenance and so on—if it emerges that she is pregnant by him."[51] The author has not come across a case where an irrevocably divorced woman who was not pregnant received only lodgings, as required by the Mālikī school; but he has come across a case where a man gave his divorced wife "a red blanket as waiting-period expenses (*kulfa*)."[52] There are several possible explanations for this. (1) Most divorces are by consent, with the wife renouncing also the waiting-period maintenance,[53] so that the question of the nature of that maintenance is not relevant. (2) Where the irrevocably divorced marriage has been consummated—which is generally the case—it is not certain that the woman is not pregnant. The author has come across only one case where the woman, in a *khulʿ* divorce, "acknowledged that she was free (*khāliya*) from pregnancy."[54] It is therefore usual under these circumstances for the man to

48. KD59-73, K44: p. 131 no. 289 20 Aug. 62. See also K45: p. 78 no. 153 5 March 61, K45: p. 80 no. 155 15 March 61, p. 124 no. 260 21 June 62.

49. KD59-73, p. 121 no. 254 28 May 62.

50. KD59-73, K50: p. 133 no. 273 25 July 62.

51. KD59-73, p. 99 no. 209 28 Aug. 61; AP:E4, p. 21 no. 70 4 July 47 and A:E104, p. 200 no. 338 16 April 53.

52. KD59-73, K48: p. 155 no. 338 7 Feb. 63.

53. See above, p. 50.

54. KD59-73, K48: p. 83 no. 161 9 April 61.

undertake that he will pay waiting-period maintenance if it is proved that the woman is indeed pregnant, in which case she is, by law, entitled to full maintenance. (3) There are instances of the divorcing husband undertaking to pay what appears to be full waiting-period maintenance to an irrevocably divorced wife without the question of pregnancy arising. He may of course pay full maintenance of his own free will—and perhaps he does so especially where he initiates the divorce—without being tied to *sharīʿa* law.[55]

However, it is not certain that the reference is always to full maintenance; for the divorcing husband sometimes adds that he will make payment in accordance with the wife's financial rights after they have been proved or determined "in conformity with religious law (*sharʿan*)." It is possible that the formula "right proved in conformity with religious law" or "right anchored in religious law" hints that in the case of irrevocable divorce the term "waiting-period maintenance" must be interpreted restrictively—that is, in the sense of lodging only. Still, there is no express support for such an interpretation in the *qāḍīs*' decisions.[56] Clothing (*kiswa*) is sometimes an independent right. The wife may claim "clothing rights in full." This includes bedclothes (*farsha*) and garments (*kisāʾ*, *thawb*, *qināʿ*, *ridāʾ*). The spouses agree upon the value of the different items, and the husband undertakes to pay accordingly.[57]

The rate and the mode of payment of the maintenance are determined by mutual agreement or, in the absence thereof, by the court. Under these circumstances, the woman demands that maintenance be paid to her "as befits persons of his [economic] position" (*uswat amthālihi*).[58] Sometimes the woman demands that payment be made "immediately, not by instalments (*bi-dūn taqsīṭ*), before I complete the waiting period" but then agrees to accept monthly instalments when it emerges that the man finds it difficult to pay at once.[59] Occasionally the woman insists on realizing her

55. AP:E1, p. 164 no. 264 [?] Dec. 52. See also A:E103, p. 158 no. 276 12 Jan. 53; A:E104, p. 162 no. [282] 21 Jan. 53; KD59–73, K45: p. 106 no. 223 25 Jan. 62, p. 121 no. 254 28 May 62, p. 150 no. 330 15 Dec. 62, K45: p. 118 no. 248 28 April 62, K43: p. 167 no. 361 15 May 63, K43: p. 182 no. 394 12 Aug. 63, K47: p. 197 no. 465 16 June 64.
56. E.g., AP:E1, p. 147 no. 260 2 Dec. 52; AP:E1, p. 149 no. 263 7 Dec. 52. See below, VI4b(1).
57. E.g., KD59–73, p. 123 no. 262 24 June 62, K50: p. 133 no. 296 12 Sep. 62, K45: p. 161 no. 339 25 March 63, K47: p. 194 no. 457 14 June 64.
58. E.g., KD59–73, K43: p. 47 no. 89 23 June 60, K51: p. 114 no. 239 4 April 62.
59. E.g., A:E103, p. 130 no. 230 23 Sep. 52.

right to waiting-period maintenance and invokes the authority of the court to enforce payment.[60]

In sum, it seems that the woman enjoys her right to waiting-period maintenance in the case of revocable divorce and, if she is pregnant or the divorce is initiated by the husband, in the case of irrevocable divorce as well. In divorce by consent, which is the most frequent form of divorce, the wife usually renounces that right; hence the small number of claims for its realization. There is no evidence in the *sijill*s of the payment of maintenance beyond the waiting period—until remarriage or until the woman becomes entitled to a pension from a welfare institution. This practice has been noted in Israel, where it is also usual—in view of the prohibition of divorcing a woman against her will—to compensate a wife for her consent to a divorce. According to the custom prevailing among the Berbers of the Kabyle Mountains under French rule, pregnancy did not entitle a divorced woman to waiting-period maintenance.[61]

b. Suckling Wages and Custody Maintenance

It seems that a divorced woman realizes also her right to suckling wages (*ujrat raḍāʿ*) and to the maintenance of her young children during the period of custody (*nafaqat ḥaḍāna*). The man undertakes to pay the amounts involved voluntarily "as long as she [the divorced woman] is legally entitled to them" (*mā dāmat tastaḥiqquhā sharʿan*) or "until the lapse (*suqūṭ*) of the maintenance."[62] Sometimes he undertakes to pay them while she is still pregnant, or in case she should be pregnant.[63] However, the man's willingness to pay maintenance for his small children does not extend beyond the legally fixed period. In fact, there is evidence that he is willing to take them into his charge at the end of the suckling or custody period. In one case it was agreed between the parties that the man would pay the suckling wage and, after the weaning (*infiṭām*), infant maintenance (*nafaqa lil-ʿayyil*) until the child reached the age of five years, when his

60. E.g., A:E102, p. 351 no. 600 25 July 54; KD59–73, p. 1 no. 7 23 Jan. 65.
61. Bousquet, *Coutumes kabiles*, p. 79 and the sources indicated there; Layish, *Women*, pp. 143–49, 177–78.
62. E.g., KD59–73, K47: p. 25 no. 49 2 Feb. 60, K48 p. 38 no. 72 26 April 60, K50: p. 91 no. 177 20 May 61; A:E103, p. 118 no. 208 13 Aug. 52; A:E104, p. 202 no. 341 [?] April 53.
63. E.g., AP:E2, p. 158 no. 152 11 Aug. 47; B2:KM38–43:EA, K4a: no. [28] 28 Sep. 32; A:E104, p. 228 no. 378 [?] July 53; A:E102, p. 329 no. 560 3 June 54; KD59–73, K51: p. 18 no. 35 26 Sep. 59, p. 150 no. 331 12 Jan. 63.

father would take charge of him.[64] But sometimes the parties agree between them that the child shall remain in the charge of the woman and that the man shall pay maintenance for him until she remarries, when he shall pass into the custody of his father unless there is "someone entitled to take charge of him after his mother"; this probably means a female cognate. Linant de Bellefonds says that the woman is sometimes willing to pay a considerable amount of compensation to the man for the right to extend the *ḥaḍāna* period until the son or daughter reaches maturity.[65] It seems that the man does not always fulfill his undertaking, in which case the woman asks the court to realize her right. Thus in one case the wife was divorced while pregnant and it was stipulated in the divorce certificate that the man should pay suckling wages from the date of the child's birth. When the child was born, the man paid nothing and the woman applied to the court "to assess the suckling wages and order him to pay them," and the court did so. The divorcing husband complained that in view of his straitened circumstances and new family commitments the maintenance was excessive. The wife's father took pity on him and agreed to maintenance at a lower rate, provided that "you do not fall behind (*tumāṭil*) with your payments; if you force me to take legal proceedings, I shall demand full maintenance from you at the rate fixed by the court"; the wife agreed to her father's decision. In another case the wife wished to realize her right to custody and to maintenance for the children during custody even before the divorce.[66]

Sometimes the wife is willing to forgo all the financial rights due to her upon divorce except suckling wages, and the spouses agree accordingly.[67] In one case the wife renounced all her financial rights "except the wages for suckling the child after she has borne him" and the husband, in turn, undertook to divorce her by *khulᶜ* on that condition and to pay the wages for suckling the child after he was born as long as she was entitled to them by law.[68] Sometimes the woman leaves the matter of the maintenance of her small children to the conscience and generosity of their father. Thus in

64. A:E102, p. 10 no. 20 6 Aug. 51; KD59-73, K45: p. 216 no. 517 27 Dec. 64; B2:KM38-43:EA, K10: no. 23 14 Feb. 33.
65. KD59-73, K45: p. 216 no. 516 7 Dec. 64; Linant, *Traité*, p. 440.
66. A:E103, p. 115 no. 205 11 Aug. 52; and A:E102 p. 351 no. 600 25 July 54.
67. E.g., AP:E4, p. 79 no. 78 14 Aug. 46; KD59-73, K51: p. 13 no. 25 19 Sep. 59, K50: p. 133 no. 297 12 Sep. 62, K44: p. 186 no. 404 22 Oct. 63.
68. A:E104, p. 194 no. 330 4 April 53.

one case the woman renounced the dower and the clothing "and claimed no maintenance for herself except by virtue of the generosity (*murūʾa*) of the husband."[69] The rate of the suckling wages and the custody maintenance is fixed by agreement between the parties at the time of the divorce. Sometimes they agree that the rate shall go up or down with the cost of living.[70] Occasionally it is agreed that the rate shall be fixed at the discretion of the court.[71] If the child's father is far away, it is agreed that he shall send the *ḥaḍāna* wages or the maintenance, or that he shall pay them, together with arrear charges, on his return.[72]

c. Dower

In *ṭalāq* divorces on the husband's initiative, he undertakes to pay to the woman the part of the prompt dower still owed by him (what remains after the payment made during the marriage, or after her renunciation). Thus in one case part of the dower agreed on in the marriage contract had been paid and the remainder—an amount in cash, some silver by weight, and clothing of a specified kind—was still a debt of the husband, which he undertook to pay upon divorce. In another case, where part of the dower had been paid upon contraction of the marriage, half of it was waived by the wife upon divorce, but she insisted on realizing her right to the other half.[73] Sometimes the woman insists on realizing her right to the dower along with other financial rights, while the man alleges that the amounts involved have already been paid and that he owes her nothing. Sometimes she demands that the *qāḍī* compel the man to appear in court and order him to pay her the dower.[74]

The man usually pays the woman the remainder of the dower in monthly instalments (*taqsīṭ*).[75] He sometimes undertakes to pay the remainder of the prompt dower at specific dates connected with the farming seasons, such

69. KD59-73, K47: p. 182 no. 430 21 Jan. 64. Cf. Layish, *Women*, pp. 159-60.
70. A:E103, p. 122 no. 215 24 Aug. 52.
71. A:E104, p. 220 no. 366 [?] July 53.
72. KD59-73, K48: p. 51 no. 95 19 Dec. 65, K48: p. 179 no. 388 n.d. See above, p. 57 and the reference in n. 69.
73. A:E104, p. [175] no. [305] 17 Sep. 53; and A:E104, p. 190 no. 324 20 March 53, respectively.
74. A:E103, p. 130 no. 230 23 Sep. 52; A:E104, p. 222 no. 369 [?] July 53.
75. E.g., KD59-73, K51: p. 11 no. 21 2 Sep. 59, K47: p. 42 no. 78 29 Sep. 66, K50: p. 132 no. 271 15 July 62; KDP, K45: p. 15 no. 132 10 Nov. 60. Cf. Bousquet, *Précis*, p. 189.

as the reed harvesting season, when he will have the necessary money.[76] Payment is occasionally postponed until such time as the required funds are available. Thus in one case it was stipulated that payment should take place "when he possesses cash or something that can be sold." In another case the husband expressed willingness to pay the outstanding balance of the dower but added that it was impossible for the time being owing to his poverty (*ʿusr*).[77] In other cases the husband asks that collection of the balance of the dower be postponed until "an early date," "one month hence," or "a time when both sides are better off"; in one case it was until he received money from his brother in the Sudan.[78] It may be stipulated that the dower shall be paid "on demand (*ʿindaʾl-ṭalab*) without delay."[79] But on the other hand the wife may wish "to inspect [the dower] at the session" (*muʿāyana biʾl-majlis*)—that is to say, actually to receive the balance of the dower at the time of the divorce.[80] In one case it was said that the man had paid the woman deferred (*muʾajjal*) dower and that "she took possession (*qabḍ*) of it." However, it is not certain that the reference is to deferred dower in the usual sense (i.e., dower paid in the event of divorce or death). For in another case it was said that it had been proved that the man still owed part of the dower; he had paid half of it on the spot and would pay the other, "deferred (*muʾajjalāt*), half at the time of the sugar-cane harvest next following the date [of the divorce]." Milliot says that where the marriage has been consummated the divorced woman is entitled to receive the whole of the dower immediately, including that part which is not usually paid (upon contraction of the marriage) but only after a delay varying from region to region.[81]

We have seen that in some cases the wife is divorced before the consummation of the marriage. The relevant passages of the Qurʾān (2:236, 237; 33:49) recommend that if under these circumstances there is no agreement as to the dower, the man shall compensate the woman, for the

76. E.g., B2:KM38–43:T41–43, K8: p. 21 no. 50 27 Sep. 41.
77. B2:KM38–43:T41–43, K8: p. 21 no. 49 24 Sep. 41; and KD59–73, K45: p. 106 no. 222 15 Jan. 62, respectively.
78. B2:KM38–43:T41–43, K5: p. 53 no. 133 30 April 42; KM63DP:EP, p. 50 no. 96 14 July 60; KD59–73, p. 102 no. 251 21 May 62, K44: p. 211 no. 507 26 Oct. 64.
79. E.g., KD59–73, K51: p. 14 no. 28 27 Sep. 59, K48: p. 72 no. 142 13 Dec. 60, p. 55 no. 105 18 Aug. 60, K45: p. 81 no. 158 28 March 61, K50: p. 86 no. 168 7 May 61.
80. B2:KM38–43:T41–43, K5: p. 4 no. 9 18 May 41. Cf. Coulson, *Commercial law*, p. 65.
81. KD59–73, K47: p. 51 no. 97 9 July 60 and K48: p. 8 no. 15 6 Aug. 59, respectively; Milliot, p. 368. On *mutʿa* in Algeria see Charnay, p. 38.

material and moral injury caused to her by the divorce, with a *mutʿa* (present) to the best of his ability. The prevailing view in the Mālikī school is that the *mutʿa* is obligatory. Some hold that where the amount of the dower has been agreed on, the woman is entitled to one-half of the dower in addition to the *mutʿa* unless she has renounced this right. Similarly, where judicial divorce takes place before consummation of the marriage and the woman is not the responsible party, she is entitled to one-half of the specified dower.[82] There is only one express testimony to a man's being ordered to pay one-half of the dower.[83] Other cases indicate that the man indeed undertook to pay certain amounts, but owing to the absence of sufficient data it is not possible to determine whether these amounts fitted the legal norm.[84] Bousquet reports that in Algeria under French rule the woman's father usually renounced one-half of his daughter's dower where the divorce took place before consummation. On the other hand, among the Berbers of the Kabyle Mountains the man owed no dower at all where the marriage had not been consummated. In the Somaliland Protectorate if the woman renounced the dower it was usual to give her a *mutʿa* at the discretion and according to the means of the man.[85]

It may be that apart from the dower the woman demands various kinds of jewelry, such as a silver bracelet (*siwār fiḍḍa*), or requires the man to renounce some ornaments (*ḥaly*) he has given her, and he sometimes gives her some jewelry in payment of the waiting-period maintenance he owes her.[86] Sometimes the woman, with the man's consent, takes all the household effects that are in the dwelling (*athāth al-manzil*), and sometimes he agrees to pay, out of his own pocket, all the fees connected with the divorce proceedings and even the fare for the taxi that will take her to another town.[87]

Where the wife is divorced for a serious offense of an immoral, disgraceful nature, such as adultery (but not in the case of a *liʿān* divorce, in which her guilt has not been proved), she loses her right to the dower

82. Pesle, pp. 172–73; Stern, pp. 134–35; Milliot, pp. 367–68; Linant *Traité*, p. 308. Cf. Fluehr-Lobban, p. 170.
83. A:E104, p. 168 no. 294 4 Feb. 53.
84. E.g., A:E104, p. 168 no. 294 4 Feb. 53; AP:E3, p. 348 no. 595 5 July 54.
85. Bousquet, *Précis*, p. 188; Bousquet, *Coutumes kabiles*, p. 64; Anderson, *Africa*, p. 54.
86. E.g., AP:E1, p. 147 no. 260 2 Dec. 52; KD59–73, p. 4 no. 7 5 July 59, K45: p. 153 no. 335 23 Oct. 63.
87. AP:E2, p. 173 no. 174 26 Nov. 47; and A:E102, p. 28 no. 54 9 Sep. 51, respectively.

even if the marriage has been consummated. If she has already received it, wholly or in part, she must return it. In fact in one case the husband alleged that the wife *ʿāhir ghayr maḍbūṭa* (had misbehaved), and his accusation was proved; he divorced her without granting her any financial right. In another case the wife was charged with committing adultery during a three-year absence of the husband from home. It was alleged that as a result of her adultery she had given birth and that the child had been killed by her husband's brother. Although her guilt had not been proved in court, she was divorced and her father renounced her rights.[88] Similarly, it has been found among the Awlād ʿAlī of the Western Desert that where the wife is divorced for adultery or some other valid cause, the husband is entitled to receive back from her father the dower and other expenditures incurred on her behalf. Among the Beduin of Iraq, when a woman is accused of adultery her husband usually gives her relatives time "to claim his rights" from the accuser; if they do not use that time to challenge the latter to prove his accusation or, where he is unable to prove it, if they do not take revenge on him, the husband by virtue of tribal custom has the right to divorce the wife and recover from her relatives the dower and the expenditure incurred by him in connection with the marriage.[89]

In sum, there are indeed significant instances of the woman realizing her right to the dower, or to the remainder of it if she has received part of it during the marriage, especially where the divorce is initiated by the man. Under these circumstances the man is prepared to satisfy all her financial claims provided she proves that they are legally (*sharʿan*) well founded.[90] Moreover, even where the wife renounces certain financial rights in return for her freedom, her other rights are not affected. There are quite a few instances of the woman claiming the remainder of those rights.[91]

At the same time, it seems that the dominant feature is the wife's renunciation of the dower upon divorce by consent, which as stated is the most frequent form of divorce in Cyrenaica. Nor is there evidence in the

88. B2:KM38-43:T41-43, K5: p. 33 no. 84 1 Jan. 42, and K8: p. 40 no. 104, respectively; Milliot, pp. 368, 379.
89. Mohsen, *Conflict*, pp. 110–11; Mohsen, *Women*, p. 230; Farīq al-Muzhir, pp. 95–96.
90. E.g., AP:E1, p. 147 no. 260 8 Dec. 52; AP:E1, p. 149 no. 263 7 Dec. 52; A:E104, p. 170 no. 297 8 Feb. 53; KD59-73, K44: p. 9 no. 23 27 July 64.
91. KD59-73, K50: p. 134 no. 298 17 Sep. 62. See also Linant, *Traité*, pp. 442–43.

*sijill*s of a divorced woman receiving deferred dower in the normative sense of this term. Furthermore, even where the woman is entitled to the dower and other financial benefits, these are at times given not to her but, in deviation from the *sharʿī* norm, to her agnates. This reflects the survival of the customary concept of marriage, according to which the woman is not a party to the contract. Thus in one case the woman alleged that the remainder of her dower was still in the hands of the man, and he alleged that he had paid it in full to her brother. In another case the man undertook to pay the remainder of the dower and the waiting-period maintenance to the woman's brother.[92] In one case the man, upon divorce, allotted maintenance to the woman's brother. This may mean not the waiting-period maintenance but compensation to the brother for having supported the wife and her son for some time before the divorce. In a further case the woman's germane brother confirmed that the man had satisfied all her financial claims in connection with the divorce, and he undertook to pay out of his own pocket whatever might yet be demanded by his sister and be proved legally due to her. From this one may perhaps conclude that the amounts due to the woman were paid not to her but to her brother.[93] Occasionally the woman's father intervenes in the matter of the amount of the maintenance of the minor children; and in one case, already mentioned, he took pity on his former son-in-law because of his financial distress and was prepared to accept maintenance from him at a lower rate than had been fixed by the court, provided he paid it on time.[94] Lastly, the husband sometimes divorces the wife "after handing over the dower to her and to her father."[95] These cases may be regarded as a compromise between custom and *sharīʿa*. The conclusion, arising from Tucker's study, that "a woman divorced by *ṭalāq* retains full rights to the property she had brought to the marriage, including the balance of the *mahr*"[96] may fit the social conditions of nineteenth-century Egypt, but it is not confirmed by the Cyrenaican *sijill*s.

92. B2:KM38–43:EA, K10: no. 21 8 March 33; and AP:E1, p. 149 no. 264 [?] Dec. 52, respectively.

93. KD59–73, p. 103 no. 217 18 Dec. 61; and A:E104, p. 162 no. [282] 21 Jan. 53, respectively.

94. A:E103, p. 115 no. 205 11 Aug. 52.

95. B2:KM38–43:EA, K10: no. 27 13 July 33.

96. Tucker, pp. 54–55.

Law No. 76 provides that where the arbitrators have failed to agree on the case, the court shall grant a divorce on the ground of injury if the party who initiated the divorce is able to prove his or her case. If it is the wife, the divorce will have the same financial consequences as ordinary *ṭalāq*; if it is the husband, he will obtain a divorce without incurring the liabilities attendant upon ordinary *ṭalāq*.[97] This reform is not reflected in the *sijill*s under review.

97. Mayer, *Marriage*, p. 38.

CHAPTER VI

Qāḍīs and Divorce

1. RECONCILIATION OF THE SPOUSES

The *qāḍīs* make great efforts to reconcile the parties, seeking to dissuade them from dissolving their marriage even where there appears to be a *sharʿī* ground for divorce. Only if their efforts fail do they agree to sever the marriage tie. Thus in one case the wife applied for dissolution on the ground of injury (*ḍarar*) caused to her by the husband: he beat and humiliated her. "The court sought . . . to bring about agreement (*saʿā . . . fīʾl-wifāq*) between the parties, making every effort (*badhala kāffat al-masāʿī*) to this end." The wife was accessible to the court's exhortations; but in view of the husband's denial and opposition to the efforts at reconciliation, the court was satisfied that the wife had indeed sustained injury. It left her the choice between continuance of the marriage and divorce. In another case a serious quarrel had broken out between the parties, and the husband had frequently applied to the court in the matter. The *qāḍī* exhorted him to concern himself with the wife's well-being: first to let her stay peacefully at her father's house for four months, supporting her during that period, then to bring her back to his own house, humor her, and "wait to see what God will have happen to him" (*mā yajʿaluhu allāh*)—that is, to let time have its healing effect. However, the husband would not listen, whereupon everybody agreed to a divorce.[1]

It seems that the *qāḍīs*, who regard the marriage contract as sacred, wish to enlist religious sanctions in support of their reconciliation effort. Thus they occasionally call on the spouses "to end their quarrel by an amicable settlement (*ṣulḥ*), a settlement that God has elevated to the rank of a meritorious act (*sammāhu allāh khayran*)."[2] Beyond that, no value

1. AP:E4; p. 135 no. [126] n.d.; and KD59-73, K44: p. 134 no. 279 26 July 62, respectively.
2. E.g., AP:E4, p. 121 no. 118 9 April 47. Cf. Layish, *Women*, p. 181.

judgment is discernible in the *qāḍī*s' decisions with regard to divorce as such.[3] The attempts at reconciliation are probably guided by consideratons of *maṣlaḥa*, the public interest, which may be adjusted to a traditional philosophy, and by a long tradition of arbitration and mediation originating in customary law. However, the author has not, in the *sijill*s, come across any instance of recourse for this purpose to the good offices of mediators or, in matters of injury, of the institutionalized mechanism of arbitrators ("family council")—a mechanism that is especially emphasized by the Mālikī school and has been observed in Israel and on the West Bank.[4] It may be that the *qāḍī*s are guided also by a tendency, observed among them already in the Middle Ages, to avoid applying the *sharīʿa* as far as possible for fear of distorting it; but the author has not found any suggestion of this in their decisions. Schacht notes that some prominent *ʿulamāʾ* in northern Nigeria refused to serve as *qāḍī*s in the judicial system, although the latter, inspired by the Fulani movement, was instrumental in the establishment of a pure, uncompromising Islam. In this connection, the chief *qāḍī* quoted the traditional saying: "He who becomes a *qāḍī*... is slaughtered without a knife" (*man juʿila qāḍiyan baynaʾl-nās fa-qad dhubiḥa bi-ghayr sikkīn*). Anderson notes that in Nigeria the *qāḍī*s made persistent efforts to reconcile the parties and prevent divorces. Similarly, ʿAbduh, who proposed a thorough reform of the *sharʿī* judicial system in Egypt in the late nineteenth century, notes that many *qāḍī*s (especially in remote districts) whose knowledge of the *sharīʿa* did not enable them to achieve justice in their decisions, preferred to bring about amicable settlements (*maḥāḍir ṣulḥ*) "so as to avoid the application of religious law" (*tajannuban lil-ḥukm*), although these were artificial solutions that did not prevent the dispute from arising again soon.[5]

2. *ṬALĀQ* DIVORCE

a. Suspended Repudiation

As noted earlier, suspended repudiation is not widespread in Cyrenaica and, as far as it is practiced, occurs mainly in the context of *khulʿ* . In the

3. Cf., on the other hand, Layish, *Women*, pp. 181–84.
4. Layish, *Women*, pp. 180–81; Layish, *Islamization*, pp. 41–42.
5. Goitein & Ben Shemesh, pp. 39–40; Schacht, *Nigeria*, p. 134; Anderson, *Africa*, p. 209; ʿAbduh, p. 13.

few cases appearing in the *sijill*s, the *qāḍī*s, although it is difficult to imagine that they do not know the mechanism, do not refer to important legal aspects of it, such as the element of intent and the fulfillment of the condition under circumstances of constraint. They confirm suspended repudiation as if it were ordinary repudiation in all respects. Thus in one case the husband admitted that he had made the repudiation conditional on the wife leaving his house without his permission and alleged that she had actually done so. After a discussion of the financial rights, the husband divorced the wife again, in the presence of the court, by a repudiation that became operative instantly ("my wife . . . is divorced from me") and the *qāḍī* decided that the wife was divorced "in the manner described above" (i.e., by the repudiation performed in his presence), without referring at all to the suspended repudiation. He ordered the woman to observe the waiting period from the time of the repudiation performed in his presence.[6]

In another case the woman was repudiated by suspended *khulᶜ*. The divorce was conditional on the payment of a certain amount of money: "On the day on which she pays that amount into court, she will be a divorced woman (*fa-hiya ṭāliq*)." The woman agreed to this, and the *qāḍī* said: "In reliance on what has been agreed between the parties, . . . it is decided that the *ṭalāq* shall become operative . . . as a *ṭalāq khulᶜī* upon payment of the cash on which the *ṭalāq* is conditional." Although there may be a reference here to a suspended repudiation, it seems that the *khulᶜ* is regarded by the *qāḍī* as the dominant element. Similarly, in another case the husband divorced the wife by suspended *khulᶜ* by means of a letter (*jawāb*) in which it was said: "If my wife . . . repays all the money she has received from me, she will be a divorced woman"; the *qāḍī* said: "When we had read the letter to her, she paid all that was demanded of her and became a divorced woman," without in any way referring to the construction of a suspended repudiation. On the other hand, in a case in which the husband swore (*ḥalafa*) to divorce the wife by triple repudiation if the maid did not remain in the house, the *qāḍī* of Tripoli accepted the wife's allegation that the condition to which the divorce had been made subject (*muᶜallaq*) had been fulfilled and that the divorce had consequently become operative. He said that the period of four days for which the maid had remained in the house was required by her to pack her belongings and thus could not, as the husband contended, be regarded as proof of her continued stay in the

6. A:E104, p. 176 no. [305] 17 Feb. 53.

house. The Sharīʿa Court of Appeal, to which the husband applied, confirmed the *qāḍī*'s decision. In another case it had been laid down between the spouses as a stipulation (*sharṭ*) (in the marriage contract or during the marriage) that if the husband took back his divorced former wife the present wife would become a divorced woman. The divorced wife was reinstated, and the *qāḍī* of Derna granted the application of the new wife to confirm her divorce. It is not clear from the judgment whether we have to do here with suspended repudiation or with delegation to the wife of the power to divorce herself. The *qāḍī*s in Israel, too, have been vexed by various legal questions connected with suspended repudiation; they have been particularly divided over the legitimacy of applying it as a means to circumvent the prohibition of divorcing one's wife against her will.[7]

b. Divorce by Proxy or Letter

Delegated repudiation (*tafwīḍ al-ṭalāq*) is not common in Cyrenaica, and so the *qāḍī*s do not refer to it.[8] On the other hand, divorce through a *wakīl* or *nāʾib* is rather frequent. We have seen that a *wakīl* is appointed by the court by a formal process (*tawkīl sharʿī*). When the *wakāla* document has been presented, the *qāḍī* without further formality approves the acts the *wakīl* wishes to perform in the name or on behalf of his principal. Thus in one case an absent husband had appointed his brother as *wakīl*. The *wakīl* was summoned to court and confirmed the wife's story—that the husband had been absent for several years and had not sent her maintenance—and he then "divorced the wife on behalf (*biʾl-niyāba*) of his brother ... because he was his *wakīl*"; the court then decided that the marriage had been validly dissolved. In a case of a different kind a man had demanded that his wife, in obedience to his wish, follow him to another town. It emerged that the woman had redeemed herself from him by *khulʿ* through his brother, who had received a special mandate from him for this purpose; the woman had then married another man. The court was faced with the questions of the nature of that mandate and the standing of the woman's brother in the proceedings. The witnesses were at first divided in their statements; some said that the mandate was general (in which case the matter was not within the jurisdiction of the court), and some said that it was specific to the divorce. But in the end they agreed on the latter version, which the

7. A:E102, p. 357 no. 611 7 Aug. 54; and B2:KM38-43:T41-43, K7: p. 77 no. 203 1 Nov. 42, respectively; d'Emilia, pp. 37, 44-45, 49; Layish, *Women*, pp. 184-85, 189-90.
8. Cf., on the other hand, Layish, *Women*, pp. 197-98.

court adopted after examining the credibility (*tazkiya*) of the witnesses. The woman's first husband had contended that her brother had no standing in the proceedings; but the *qāḍī* decided—and the Court of Appeal confirmed his decision—that he had a standing and that it was his duty to protect the honor of his sister, who had meanwhile married another man. The *qāḍī* thus found that the mandate given to the first husband's brother to divorce the woman and the divorce performed by him were valid and that the woman's marriage to the second husband following that divorce was valid too.[9]

We have seen above that divorce by letter (*risāla*, *jawāb*) is rather frequent in Cyrenaica when the husband is in another locality or country. The court at first verifies the authenticity of the letter. It takes evidence of its contents from the person who drew it up if he is available, or from persons who were present when it was drawn up. It sometimes verifies (*taʾkīd*) the husband's signature, identifies the handwriting of the person who drew up the letter, and ascertains the identity of the witnesses. After all this the *qāḍī* reads the letter to the wife, explains its contents to her, and declares her divorced. If the divorce is conditional on the wife's renunciation of financial rights or on the payment of compensation to the husband, the *qāḍī* declares her divorced as soon as she has fulfilled the condition.[10]

c. Confirmation and Registration of Divorce

The Beduin resort to the *sharīʿa* court in matters of divorce for two purposes: confirmation followed by registration, and clarification of the financial rights involved. Unilateral divorces are effected by the husband and involve no legal proceedings, but reasons of legal security prompt those concerned to apply to the court for a declaratory judgment as to their new marital status. The registration of a divorce is a civil procedural matter and has no substantive *sharʿī* significance as to the validity of the divorce. Thus in one case a man who served as "adviser to the al-Maghāriba tribes in Ajdābiyya appeared in court and said: 'I appear in this court in order to register (*li-nusajjil*) the divorce of my wife, a member of the same *qabīla* and *ʿāʾila* [as myself].'" It is by no means certain that he meant only registration in the literal sense of the term; he probably meant also confirmation of the

9. B2:KM38-43:T41-43, K6: p. 84 no. 224 5 Jan. 43; and d'Emilia, pp. 31-32, 48.

10. E.g., B2:KM38-43:T41-43, K7: p. 77 no. 203 1 Nov. 42, K7: p. 94 no. 250 3 March 43, K7: p. 18 no. 55 14 Aug. 43; KD59-73, K48: p. 85 no. 166 25 April 61.

divorce.[11] On occasion it is the wife who initiates the issue of a declaratory judgment. Thus in one case the wife stated that four months before going away, "he released me by *khulʿ* in return for my dower and divorced me in the presence of...[two persons]." The latter confirmed her story exactly, and the *qāḍī* validated her divorce retroactively to the date of its occurrence. The question of the wife's consent to the divorce is irrelevant—although in this case the renunciation of the dower was equivalent to consent—and the *qāḍī* does not trouble to clarify it. In Israel, on the other hand, divorce against the wife's will is forbidden by criminal legislation, and that legislation is reflected to some extent in the *qāḍīs*' decisions.[12]

When confirming a divorce the *qāḍī* is usually careful to note that the spouses are legally competent to divorce and be divorced, respectively. The stereotypical formula is: "In reliance on the declaration of the parties that they are legally competent (*bi-ḥāla jāʾiza sharʿan*) [and on the fact] that this has been proved to his satisfaction, the *qāḍī* confirms the occurrence (*wuqūʿ*) of the *ṭalāq*" or "The husband has declared, willingly (*ṭāʾiʿan*) and of his own choice (*mukhtāran*), while enjoying the fullest qualifications relevant in legal respect (*wa-huwa bi-atamm al-awṣāf al-muʿtabara sharʿan*), that he is determined to divorce his wife."[13] The husband's statement that he has divorced the wife is sufficient for confirmation and registration unless the wife denies the divorce or is absent from court and cannot be examined; under these circumstances, or if the wife alleges that she has been divorced and the husband denies it, the *qāḍī* calls witnesses who were present at the time of the divorce.[14] But sometimes, surprisingly, he is satisfied with one witness. Thus in a case in which the wife alleged that the husband had divorced her by *ṭalāq* prior to going away, she had one witness to prove it. The witness confirmed her story and the *qāḍī* decided: "By virtue of this testimony, the woman has become divorced by one repudiation . . ." although religious law requires at least two male witnesses in order to prove an allegation.[15]

11. A:E102, p. 351 no. 601 26 July 54. On the meaning of *qabīla* and *ʿāʾila* see Behnke, p. 109; Colucci, *Tribù*, p. 25.
12. B2:KM38-43:T43, K7: p. 16 no. 46 16 July 43; Layish, *Women*, pp. 191ff., 195ff.
13. AP:E1, p. 145 no. 257 24 Nov. 52; and KD59-73, K50: p. 133 no. 296 12 Sep. 62, respectively.
14. E.g., B2: KM38-43:T43, K7: p. 16 no. 46 16 July 43.
15. B2:KM38-43:T43, K6: p. 6 no. 18 22 April 43. Cf. Linant, *Traité*, p. 382; Layish, *Women*, p. 193.

Where the wife denies having been divorced and the husband cannot produce witnesses, the court dismisses the husband's application for a declaratory judgment of divorce. Thus in one case the husband alleged that he had divorced the wife ten years previously and that this was why he "neglected (*muhmil*) her—that is, did not provide maintenance to her. The wife absolutely denied having been divorced, declaring that she "was still his wife" (*bāqiya ʿalā ʿiṣmatihi*). The *qāḍī* decided that since the husband "had not produced evidence [through witnesses] (*bayyina*) that he had paid her the delayed dower and that the *ṭalāq* had occurred on the date in question, it was established (*thabata*) to his satisfaction that she had not ceased to be his [legal] wife."[16] Sometimes under such circumstances, in the absence of the wife from the courtroom, the husband—for the second time, as he says—divorces the wife, and the *qāḍī* confirms the divorce performed in his presence. That is what happened in the aforesaid case, when the husband was unable to prove that he had divorced the wife ten years previously—which he probably claimed in order to avoid having to pay maintenance. In another case the husband came to court "to register his wife's divorce," alleging that he had already paid her all her dower and the waiting-period maintenance and owed her nothing more. The wife was not in court, and apparently for this reason the husband divorced her again. The *qāḍī* confirmed the divorce and ordered the wife to observe the waiting period "from the following day" (*min ghad*) (i.e., from the date of the divorce performed in court). The practice of an additional divorce in court, in the presence of the *qāḍī*, has been observed also in Israel.[17] The *qāḍī* does not examine the specific circumstances of each case beyond the question of the competence of the parties and the proof of the divorce. He does not concern himself with the reasons for the divorce, which aspect is not legally relevant. The *qāḍī* confirms the divorce, almost notarially, if it is valid according to the *sharīʿa*. Israeli *qāḍī*s proceed in the same way.[18]

For reasons of legal security, the parties apply to the court also for the clarification of financial rights and for the protection of such rights by *sharʿī* sanctions, and it seems that their expectations in this regard are fulfilled. Thus in one case the *qāḍī* confirmed the divorce of the wife

16. AP:E2, p. 19 no. 38 23 Aug. 51.
17. AP:E2, p. 19 no. 38 23 Aug. 51; and A:E102, p. 351 no. 601 26 July 54, respectively; Layish, *Women*, p. 193.
18. Layish, *Women*, p. 193.

performed in court in her absence and at the same time ordered the husband to produce "evidence (*ḥujja*) to him of the wife's [financial] claims that were to be validly established (*yuthbat lahā sharʿan*)." In another case, in which the wife was divorced by *khulʿ*, her brother said that she was pregnant and demanded that the husband be ordered to pay all her expenses (*kulfa*) for board (*maʾūna*) and clothing until she gave birth and thereafter the suckling wage. The court granted his request "and, for clarity's sake, we write it down and register it" (*fali-ajl bayānihi ḥarrarnāhu wa-sajjalnāhu*).[19]

d. Divorce by Consent

Divorce by consent is the form of dissolution most convenient to the *qāḍī*s, both ethically and legally: the divorce is, *prima facie*, not arbitrary; the *qāḍī*'s intervention for the prevention of divorce is not required—at any rate, not as it is in the case of ordinary *ṭalāq*; and the *qāḍī* is not required to exercise discretion, so that there is no risk of the *sharīʿa* being distorted by its application. In Nigeria under colonial rule the courts, when their efforts at reconciliation failed, sought to persuade the parties at least to dissolve their marriage by mutual consent. In Israel, in this kind of divorce, the *qāḍī*s are spared the embarrassment of a clash between the *sharʿī* and the secular norm owing to the prohibition, by criminal legislation, of divorce against the wife's will.[20] The *qāḍī*'s role is confined to the formal-technical aspects of the confirmation of divorce. He is careful to note that both parties to the divorce agreement are in full possession of their physical and mental faculties, which is a condition of the validity of the divorce, and that the agreement was reached voluntarily. The usual text under these circumstance is as follows: "Both of them [the parties] have declared, willingly and of their own choice, their intention to testify on their own behalf, while in perfect health, in full possession of their mental faculties, and competent from a *sharʿī* point of view" (*qarrarā ṭāʾiʿayn mukhtārayn bi-qaṣd al-ishhād ʿalā anfusihimā wa-humā bi-atamm ḥāl min ṣiḥḥatihimā wa-kamāl ʿaqlihimā wa-jawāz taṣarrufihimā al-sharʿī*).[21] A wife who upon divorce renounces any financial rights in favor of her husband is said to be

19. A:E102, p. 351 no. 601 26 July 54; and B2:KM38–43:EA, K49: no. [28] 28 Sep. 32, respectively.
20. Anderson, *Africa*, pp. 209–10; Layish, *Women*, p. 198.
21. AP:E4, p. 121 no. 118 9 April 47. See also AP:E2, p. 11 no. 22 6 Aug. 51; KD59–73, p. 104 no. 218 21 Dec. 61.

"in legal condition [i.e., legally competent] and in good health" (*bi-ḥāla jā᾿iza wa-ṣiḥḥa jayyida*).[22]

It seems that the *qāḍī*'s contribution to the substance of the agreement is rather modest. The spouses or their representatives generally lay down the terms of the renunciation and compensation between them out of court. The usual formula is: "They have agreed on dissolution by amicable settlement (*ṣulḥan*) [not involving judicial proceedings]." At the time of the divorce, the agreement is submitted to the *qāḍī* for confirmation for reasons of legal security. It is seldom suggested that he plays any part in its conclusion, and his role may be confined to being present at the negotiation of its terms. Thus in one case it was said in the *qāḍī*'s presence that the husband agreed with the wife's father—after the latter had renounced his daughter's financial rights in the husband's favor—on "dissolution by amicable settlement" (*al-firāq ṣulḥan*).[23]

The *qāḍī* sometimes notes that the wife consents to the divorce, but this should be taken to mean consent to the *terms* of a divorce by consent. Thus in one case the spouses had reached agreement that "divorce is the best solution." The wife demanded nothing but maintenance during her pregnancy, and the *qāḍī* stated: "Considering... the wife's consent (*muwāfaqa*) [given] to him [the husband] as to the *ṭalāq* and the husband's acceptance (*qabūl*) thereof and his consent [given] to her, he divorced her by one repudiation."[24] In fact the wife's consent does not relate to the divorce itself (such consent not being legally relevant); rather it should be interpreted as an "offer"—synonymous with *ījāb*—to renounce financial rights, which is accepted by the husband. A binding quasi-contractual engagement is thus created. When an agreement on the terms of the divorce has been reached, the *qāḍī* "permits" or confirms it and gives it *shar῾ī* effect. Thus in one case the spouses agreed on the release of the wife by *khul῾*—namely, in return for the deferred dower. The husband "accepted" (*qabila*) it and thereupon divorced her. The *qāḍī* "permitted" (*ajāza*) the arrangement and decided accordingly—that is, he gave *shar῾ī* effect to the *khul῾* agreement. Similarly, in another case a wife claimed maintenance from her absent husband and, after she had declared that she was not willing to live at his house without the marriage being

22. E.g., KD59–73, K45: p. 111 nos. 232–33, 15 March 62.
23. AP:E2, p. 178 no. 174 26 Nov. 47. Cf. Layish, *Women*, p. 198.
24. AP:E4, p. 71 no. 70 4 July 46.

consummated, the parties, at the appeal stage before the Sharʿī Supreme Court in Tripoli, agreed on dissolution by *khulʿ* and the court "confirmed the *ṣulḥ*." The expression *ajāza* stresses the modest part of the *qāḍī* in the proceedings. There is no judgment here in the usual sense, based on the application of material law at the *qāḍī*'s discretion, but a formal confirmation of a voluntary agreement reached by the parties without judicial proceedings; in fact that expression is common in the practice of the *qāḍīs* in the case of *ṣulḥ* agreements reached in civil disputes of various kinds.[25]

Similarly, the *qāḍīs* may order the parties to renounce various financial and other rights, even if they are anchored in the *sharīʿa*, because the renunciation is based on a voluntary agreement. Thus in one case the wife renounced the outstanding balance of the dower, which was a financial liability (*dhimma*) of the husband, and undertook to support herself during the waiting period. In another case the wife renounced also the custody of her son. In a further case the wife's father, in return for the divorce, renounced all his daughter's financial rights vis-à-vis her husband and undertook to pay "out of his own money" whatever she might demand from her husband and to maintain her during the waiting period. In all these cases the *qāḍī* debited (*alzama*) the wife (and her father, respectively) "with the obligations she had assumed by renouncing the rights she still had vis-à-vis the husband and with the provision of maintenance during the waiting period."[26] When agreement has been reached on the terms of the renunciation and the compensation, the husband divorces the wife and the *qāḍī* confirms the validity of the *khulʿī ṭalāq*;[27] he sometimes adds that "no more cause of action (*daʿwa*), claim (*ṭalab*), or marital [financial] right (*ḥaqq minaʾl-ḥuqūq al-zawjiyya*) exists between them."[28]

In a case heard in Tripoli the validity of enforced *khulʿ* was considered. In the marriage contract it had been stipulated that the bride must be a virgin. After the *zifāf* (the nuptial procession), but before the consummation

25. E.g., KAMD, p. 29 no. 11 16 Feb. 34; AP:E4, p. 97 no. 95 23 Oct. 46 (the honor—*ʿirḍ*—of the woman); AP:E3, p. 296 no. 496 8 Feb. 54 (injury following assault); d'Emilia, p. 43.

26. AP:E1, p. 153 no. 269 6 Jan. 53. See also A:E103, p. 160 no. 279 13 Jan. 53; A:E104, p. 204 no. 343 4 May 53.

27. E.g., B2:KM38-43:EA, K4a: no. [28] 28 Sep. 32; AP:E4, p. 105 no. 103 13 June 47; AP:E102, p. 347 no. 593 17 July 54.

28. E.g., KD59-73, p. 104 no. 218 21 Dec. 61, K45: p. 111 no. 232 15 March 62; KDP, K45: p. 12 no. 29 16 May 65.

of the marriage, disputes arose in connection with that stipulation, and the wife was divorced during the wedding night—after, according to the husband, she and her father had renounced the dower and other rights. In court the wife and her father—as a *walī mujbir*, a guardian authorized to marry off his ward compulsorily—demanded that the divorce be annulled on the ground that the renunciation of the dower and the other rights had been extorted (*ikrāh*) from them. The husband denied this allegation, declaring that the *khulʿ* had taken place with the full consent of the parties. The *qāḍī* believed it to be improbable that a wife would, on her wedding night, voluntarily renounce her honor (by consenting to be divorced on the ground that she was not a virgin) and her financial rights, and he decided that the renunciation was not operative (*ghayr nāfidh*). In this decision, he relied also on a *fatwā* of the *muftī* of Tripoli, who found that the marriage had not been dissolved by *khulʿ* but by unilateral *ṭalāq*. The *qāḍī* ordered the husband to make payment to her according to her "financial rights." His judgment was confirmed by the Sharīʿa Court of Appeal.[29]

e. Customary *Khulʿ*

Making the remarriage of a woman divorced by customary *khulʿ* dependent on the transfer of the dower from the new husband to the divorcing husband, especially if the transfer is made through her agnates without her being a party to the proceedings, is in glaring contradiction of the *sharīʿa*. How do the *qāḍī*s react to this contradiction? They seem to be totally unaware of it. They treat customary *khulʿ* as *khulʿ* in all respects. They do not interfere in voluntary agreements between the parties, which were probably reached out of court and included in the wife's *quṣṣa*, but honor and confirm them as part of the *sharʿī* judgment. They are content if it is proved to their satisfaction that the financial arrangement was made by the free consent of the parties and that they were legally competent to give up rights and assume financial obligations, and they order the woman (or her agnate) to fulfill her (or his) obligation upon her marriage to a third party. Thus in one case it was said in the judgment following a statement of the conditions of the customary *khulʿ*: "On the basis of what the parties have agreed between them of their own free will (*ṭawʿan*), at the session of the court ... the *qāḍī* awards a *khulʿī ṭalāq* and orders the wife and her father to pay the compensation, with which the latter redeems her by

29. d'Emilia, pp. 38-39.

virtue of a power of attorney from her." In other cases it is said: "On the basis of what has been agreed between them—they being competent from a *sharʿī* point of view—and on the basis of a financial arrangement held by him to be sound, the *qāḍī* awards a *khulʿī ṭalāq* and debits the wife's father with what he has renounced and has undertaken to pay on his daughter's marriage to another man."[30]

It seems that the *qāḍīs* regard customary *khulʿ* as a legitimate—since mutually agreed—deferment, prompted by financial distress of the woman or her agnates, of the payment of compensaton to the divorcing husband. We have mentioned a case in which the wife, who had initiated the *khulʿ*, requested a "deferment of the payment [of compensation] to the husband because of her poverty." The husband granted the request. The *qāḍī* tried to prevent the dissolution, and when he did not succeed, he declared that the *khulʿ* and the deferment were valid owing to the husband's consent. When it is agreed between the parties that the period of deferment shall end upon the woman's marriage to another man, the *qāḍī*'s are careful to note in the judgment that the debt shall be paid "in due time, without subterfuge or delay."[31] The *qāḍīs* confirm the customary *khulʿ* agreement even if it is found in the course of the proceedings that an explicit *sharʿī* norm has been ignored—namely, that the woman's father has undertaken to pay to the divorcer of his daughter, at the time of her marriage to another man, a certain amount of money which "he received out of her dower." The woman's father is ordered to fulfill his undertaking in disregard of the *sharʿī* norm that the dower is the property of the wife. Although the *qāḍīs* also order the wife's agnate or guardian to fulfill his obligation as regards her financial rights as a divorced woman, such as maintenance during the waiting period, they seem to be doing so not because these rights are anchored in the *sharīʿa* but because of the agreement between the parties or by virtue of a unilateral undertaking.[32]

The court confirms the security designed to ensure the implementation of the *khulʿ* agreements—for example, the guarantee (*kafāla*), anchored in customary law, by the wife's relatives for the payment of compensation to

30. AP:E2, p. 182 no. 178 8 Jan. 48; A:E102, p. 30 no. 58 21 Sep. 51, and p. 333 no. 567 23 June 54, respectively.
31. AP:E4, p. 121 no. 118 9 April 47, and p. 137 no. 127 23 May 47, respectively. See also p. 117 no. 114 20 March 47.
32. A:104, p. [197] no. [335] 8 April 53; A:E103, p. 96 no. 178 3 July 52.

the husband.[33] Moreover, the *qāḍī*s confirm such security even where, on the face of it, it is contrary to the *sharʿī* norm. We have seen that the *khulʿ* agreement frequently stipulates that the compensation to the divorcing husband shall be paid before the reading of *al-Fātiḥa*, and sometimes it is even stated expressly that the wife must not remarry before the compensation has been paid. A debt of a divorced woman to her first husband is not a *sharʿī* bar to her remarriage, but it may be a bar to it according to the customary concept of marriage, by which the woman is not a party to the contract.[34] Moreover, the court is instrumental in upholding customary *khulʿ* agreements contrary to the *sharīʿa*. We have seen that the parties resort to the court as a statutory judicial authority in the expectation that the compensation will be paid through it before the marriage contract is made, and they thereby turn the court into a full partner, in a deviation from the *sharīʿa*. In fact in one case it was held that if the marriage was performed before payment of the compensation into court, "the person who reads the *Fātiḥa* is a transgressor [and shall be ordered] to pay the amount."[35] The reader of the *Fātiḥa* may be the *maʾdhūn*, the person authorized on behalf of the *sharīʿa* court to perform marriages. The court thus gives *sharʿī* sanction to a customary punishment, although the *maʾdhūn* would be acting within the *sharīʿa* if he refused to postpone the remarriage of the divorced woman for non-*sharʿī* reasons.

Similarly, the *qāḍī*s lend a hand in enforcing customary *khulʿ* agreements involving a deviation from the *sharīʿa*. We have seen how a man who had divorced his wife by customary *khulʿ* empowered another man to receive a sum of money from her new husband and even to sue him before *sharʿī* and other authorities, as might be necessary. The *qāḍī* permitted (*ajāza*) this delegation of power (*tafwīḍ*) although the second husband was not a party to the *khulʿ* agreement and although the claim should have been addressed to the wife or her authorized representative. We have also seen how a woman contended against her husband that her former husband was claiming the dower from him. The *qāḍī* did not dismiss the action *in limine* on the grounds that there was no legal connection between the two cases, but rejected the woman's claim solely because she had not succeeded in

33. E.g., AP:E3, p. 342 no. 582 6 July 54.
34. See above, pp. 67ff.
35. KD59–73, p. 24 no. 56 4 Aug. 65. See also KD59–73, K50: p. 131 no. 270 11 July 62, K51: p. 203 no. 490 24 Aug. 64, K50: p. 18 no. 42 7 July 65.

proving her contention: "unless she brings [before the court] just, conclusive proof from [her first husband]...." We have already noted a feature observed on the Gold Coast: a wife who eloped with her lover might dissolve her marriage by paying compensation to the husband. But the court claimed the compensation from the *wife's father*, who, according to the customary concept, is a party to the marriage contract, and he in turn sought to recover it from the new husband. Some Nigerian *sharīʿa* courts prohibited a wife who obtained her freedom with the encouragement, and perhaps the financial assistance, of her lover from marrying him,[36] probably because adultery of the wife is a serious offense according to the *sharīʿa*.

All the foregoing leads to the conclusion that the *sharīʿa* court feels bound to confirm agreements reached outside it under the rules of customary law even if they conflict with the *sharīʿa*, provided they were reached by free choice: "The parties have become reconciled (*iṣṭalaḥā*) and the dispute (*shiqāq*) between them has ceased, and the *qāḍī* has permitted the reconciliation (*ṣulḥ*) arrangment."[37] In some other cases of customary *khulʿ*, in which the wife undertook to pay the husband a sum of money upon her marriage to another man, the court gave effect to the divorce and ordered the wife "to fulfill her undertaking upon her remarriage" or saw to it that the sum was entered in her *quṣṣa* and paid when she remarried. This attitude of the *qāḍī*s toward customary *khulʿ* is strikingly in line with the declared attitude of Muslim *qāḍī*s in Israel on the same issue, according to which the court does not interfere in voluntary agreements, holding that "mutual agreement is stronger than the *qāḍī*" (*al-tarāḍī yaghlib al-qāḍī*); the court treats the undertaking to compensate the first husband upon the marriage of the divorced wife to another man like a promissory note that has to be honored.[38]

The *qāḍī*s regard customary *khulʿ* as an ordinary *khulʿ* also as to the legal consequences of the dissolution. The divorce comes into force immediately and is not conditional on compensation to the husband. The *qāḍī*s pronounce dissolution and order the wife to observe the waiting period from the date of the judgment. Thus in one case when the parties had agreed

36. B2:KM38-43:T43, K6: p. 37 no. 111 28 Dec. 43, and B2:KM38-43:EA, K4a: no. 1 4 July 32, respectively; Anderson, *Africa*, pp. 210, 272.

37. AP:E3, p. 326 no. 555 29 May 54.

38. E.g., A:E103, p. 150 no. 265 13 Dec. 52; A:E104, p. 182 no. 314 28 Feb. 53; KD59-73, p. 217 no. 518 26 Dec. 64; Layish, *Women*, pp. 160-61, 198.

on the amount to be paid to the husband upon the wife's remarriage, the husband divorced her by one minor irrevocable repudiation entailing a short separation (*bānat baynūna ṣughrā*), after which the wife "is not legally permitted to him unless a new marriage contract is concluded and a new dower paid"; she was ordered to observe the waiting period (*iʿtidād*) from the date of the judgment. The *qāḍī*s serving among the Berbers of the Kabyle Mountains also sometimes—although not frequently—treated customary *khulʿ*, as to its legal consequences, like *sharʿī khulʿ*. This was true also in the French courts during the time of colonial rule in Algeria.[39]

3. JUDICIAL DIVORCE

a. Nonprovision of Maintenance by an Absent Husband

Nonprovision of maintenance by a husband who is far away but whose whereabouts are usually known is the principal ground for judicial divorce. On confirming a dissolution on this ground, the court is guided by the following considerations: that the husband is financially unable to provide maintenance (*iʿsār al-nafaqa*); that "he did not leave [to the wife] any thing [property] that might have been sold (*shayʾ yubāʿ*)" for the purpose of providing maintenance; that he did not appoint a proxy for the provision of maintenance (*wakīl yunfiq*); and that there was danger that hardship (or temptation (*ʿanat*)) would result for the wife.[40] If the husband leaves any property out of which maintenance may be collected, the court permits the wife to sell it for that purpose. In one such case the wife said that the husband had been absent for two years without supporting her or her children and that she had suffered injury in consequence. But, she said, he owned a *sāniya* (water scoop, well, or irrigated garden) in partnership with his brother and she wished to sell his share to the latter. After the *qāḍī* had established that she enjoyed maturity of mind (*rushd*), health (*ṣiḥḥa*), and freedom of choice (*ikhtiyār*), he permitted the sale and she in fact sold her husband's share to his brother. In Aden at the time of the British Protectorate, too, the *qāḍī*s permitted the sale of an absent husband's

39. KD59-73, K50 p. 10 no. 25 14 April 65. See also A:E104, p. 182 no. 314 28 Feb. 53, p. 197 no. 335 8 April 53; KDP, K45: p. [?] no. 136 26 Nov. 60; Bousquet, *Coutumes kabiles*, p. 75.

40. E.g., B2:KM38-43:T41-43, K5: p. 59 no. 143 1 June 42, K7: p. 85 no. 226 6 Jan. 43, K6: p. 93 no. 248 27 Feb. 43.

property to provide maintenance to his wife, but they did not do so in Nigeria.[41]

The usual court procedure for dissolution on the ground of nonprovision of maintenance by an absent husband is as follows: The wife appears in court and declares that the husband "went away without my permission" (*lā adhintu lahu fī*ʾ*l-safar*), that he has been absent for a long time (she usually states the number of years), does not support her, left her nothing or has no salable property and has not appointed a *wakīl* to support her, that "she has suffered injury through her complete destitution" (*taḍarrarat mina*ʾ*l-iḥtiyāj al-kullī*), and that she fears hardship (or temptation). For all these reasons, she asks to be divorced from her husband and applies to the court to act accordingly: "The matter is entrusted (*munawwaṭ*) to your honors."

The court asks her to prove the validity of her contentions by witnesses (*bayyina tashhad bi-ṣiḥḥat* or *tu*ʾ*ayyid thubūt da*ʿ*wāhā*). She produces honest (ʿ*adl*) witnesses, and the court examines their credibility by the usual identification (*ta*ʿ*rīf*) proceedings. If the witnesses confirm the wife's story in full, which they usually do, the court adjourns the proceedings for a month "allowing time for the absent [husband] to return; [if he does not return,] a notice will be issued if he cannot be reached" (*irjā*[ʾ*an*] *lil-ghāyib* [*ghā*ʾ*ib*] *iblāghan fī*ʾ*l-i*ʿ*dhār ilayhi*). In Israel too the *qāḍī*s will, under similar circumstances, dissolve the marriage on the application of the wife thirty days after publication of a notice in the press; some even waive publication and content themselves with the declaration of the wife, supported by witnesses, that the husband has absented himself without leaving maintenance. In the Gambia, the marriage of a wife left without maintenance by an absent husband was dissolved either at once or after a month's adjournment.[42] If by the end of the period of adjournment the husband has not provided maintenance, the wife appears again in court, asking for her application for dissolution to be studied once more (*im*ʿ*ān al-naẓar*), and the court has her swear on the Qurʾān, as follows: "By Allāh, beside whom there is no god, and by the genuineness of this copy of the Qurʾān (*wa-ḥaqq hādhā al-maṣḥaf al-sharīf*), I did not permit my husband to leave." She then quotes her original application and winds up by again asking the court to dissolve her marriage. This oath is known as *yamīn*

41. B2:KM38–43:T41–43, K7: p. 71 no. 175 29 Aug. 42; Anderson, *Africa*, pp. 21, 211.

42. Layish, *Women*, p. 203; Anderson, *Africa*, p. 241.

al-istiẓhār (oath of disclosure). The wife must swear that her husband has not left or sent to her any maintenance, that she is not rebellious (and therefore deprived of the right to maintenance), and that to the best of her knowlege she has not yet been divorced. Only then will the court grant dissolution *ex parte*. In one case the Sharīʿa Court of Appeal, on the ground of procedural defects, quashed the judgment of the court of first instance dissolving a marriage by reason of absence (*ghayba*) of the husband and nonprovision of maintenance to the wife. The appellate court held that the lower court should have clarified whether the husband absented himself before or after the consummation (*bināʾ*) of the marriage and whether he left for a place near to or far from the place where the wife was. It should also have clarified in what economic circumstances he left the wife. A retrial was held in the lower court in which those points were clarified and in which it was proved that injury had been caused to the wife by the absence of the husband, who had left for a place not more than a ten-day journey (*masāfa*) away. The *qāḍī* ordered the husband to return to his wife or to divorce her within a specific time. When that time passed and the husband "had not appeared in order to maintain marital relations with the wife" and had also not divorced the wife, the *qāḍī* declared the wife divorced.[43]

However, as far as can be judged from Cyrenaican *sijill*s, the court does not itself dissolve the marriage but gives the wife "an option to continue the marriage or to divorce herself" (*khayyarhā tabqā ʿalā ʿiṣmat zawjihā aw tuṭalliq nafsahā minhu* or, in a different version, *khayyarahā . . . al-baqāʾ baynaʾl-ṭalāq wa-fakk ʿiṣmatihā minhu aw al-baqāʾ maʿahu ʿalā hāt al-ḥāla*). She may then opt for divorce (*ikhtārat al-ṭalāq*), declaring: "I divorce myself (*ṭallaqtu nafsī*) from my husband . . . ," whereupon the court decides that the wife "has thereby [by the divorce formula] acquired control of herself from him [from the husband] and their marriage has been dissolved" (*malakat bihā amr nafsihā wa-infaṣalat baynahumā ʿuqdat al-nikāḥ*). The court then orders the wife to observe the waiting period from the date of the decision, "hoping that the absent [husband] will return [during that period, when he will still be able to reinstate her]; if he [does not return and] cannot be reached, a notice will be issued." The court sometimes declares that it "permits her to divorce herself, by single repudiation, which will entitle [the husband] to reinstate her if he returns with sufficient means to

43. Anderson, *Africa*, p. 379; d'Emilia, pp. 42–43, 49. Cf. Fluehr-Lobban, p. 162.

maintain her during the waiting period" (*adhina lahā fī ṭalqa wāḥida yamlik bihā raj^catahā in qadima mūsiran fī ʿiddatihā*). The dissolution procedure described here is strikingly similar to the one set forth by Milliot, which relates to cases of nonprovision of maintenance by a husband whose whereabouts are unknown or who—where he is not technically "absent" or "missing"—is far away.[44]

However, dissolution by the wife does not fit the concept of judicial divorce according to the Mālikī doctrine, under which by way of a legal device the court exercises the husband's power of divorce. In Egypt, on the other hand, judicial divorce under similar circumstances is effected in the proper sense of the term—that is, by the *qāḍī*, not by the wife. There is no explanation in Cyrenaican decisions for the transfer of the option of divorce to the wife. The *sharʿī* basis of this practice is not clear. The grant to the wife of the choice (*khiyār*) between continuing the marriage or divorcing herself is technically similar to delegated repudiation (*tafwīḍ al-ṭalāq*). Earlier a distinction was pointed out between two kinds of delegation to the wife: the first kind grants her the exclusive choice between continuance and dissolution of the marriage; if she chooses the latter alternative, the divorce is irrevocable, although the husband may stipulate that it shall be revocable. The second kind of delegation consists in the husband's renunciation of his right of divorce in favor of the wife; in this case the divorce is revocable.[45] The *qāḍī*s may combine the mechanism of judicial divorce on the ground of nonprovision of maintenance by an absent husband with that of delegated repudiation of the first-mentioned kind.

Confirmation of this assumption may be obtained from other places where delegated repudiation is used as a remedy for the problem of the absent husband. We have seen that in Algeria under French rule the wife, where the husband was absent beyond the period agreed between them, would ensure dissolution by means of delegated repudiation provided for in the marriage contract. If the husband infringed his undertaking not to be absent beyond the agreed period, the wife swore, in the presence of

44. E.g., B2:KM38-43:T41-43, K5: p. 8 no. 19 14 June 41, K8: p. 11 no. 26 27 June 41, K7: p. 85 no. 226 6 Jan. 43; AP:E2, p. [159] no. [153] [? Aug. 47]; A:E102, p. [27] no. [53] 9 Sep. 51; KD59-73, K51: p. 24 no. 47 21 Dec. 59, K47: p. 41 no. 78 9 May 60, K47: p. 27 no. 53 17 Feb. 61, K51: p. 146 no. 321 27 Nov. 62; Milliot, pp. 328-29. Cf. Fluehr-Lobban, p. 164. See above, p. 82. Cf. Milliot, pp. 382-83.

45. Hill, pp. 81-82, 91, 99 n. 7; Linant, *Traité*, pp. 330-33; Anderson, *Africa*, p. 377. See above, pp. 35-37.

witnesses, that he had done so, and she also swore that she had not permitted him to be so absent (this form of oath occurs in the Cyrenaican decisions before us). She then divorced herself instantly by irrevocable repudiation, probably because the husband had not stipulated that the repudiation should be revocable.[46] Milliot reports that in North African judicial practice it was usual for dissolution by the wife to be effected by suspended repudiation, which is in fact delegated repudiation, if the husband infringed an obligation imposed by the marriage contract—such as not to take a second wife, to pay at an agreed date part of the prompt dower the payment of which had been delayed, to live in a particular town, not to move to another town without the wife's consent, or not to force her to go with him. In the last-mentioned case, which is similar to the one under consideration (the husband's departure for another place for an extended period being like a change of residence), the wife might refuse to go with him and, if he insisted that she do so, might dissolve the marriage. We have seen that Milliot regards the infringement of a condition of the marriage contract by the husband as a ground for dissolution by the *qāḍī*. In other words, we have to do here with another instance of a combination of judicial and delegated repudiation. Milliot notes that if the condition conflicts with a *sharʿī* right of the husband, he is not required to fulfill it, even though it is strongly recommended that he should.[47]

In one case, nonprovision of maintenance by the absent husband was combined with nonpayment of the dower. The wife, on applying for dissolution, said that she had not waived the dower—"not a single dirhem"—and the *qāḍī* held that "maintenance-related distress had been proved to his satisfaction, since [the husband] had not paid anything to her [the wife] and not left anything to her that might be sold." It seems that the nonpayment of the dower is mentioned here only as an illustration of the lack of maintenance and not as an independent ground for dissolution, which is valid only if the marriage has not been consummated, and even then only if a year's grace is allowed for payment. In the present case the marriage was dissolved by the procedure usual in cases of nonprovision of maintenance (i.e., after a month's delay), and the *qāḍī* awarded a revocable divorce, which is peculiar to the latter ground for dissolution.[48] In another

46. Bousquet, *Précis*, pp. 190–91. See above, p. 89.
47. Milliot, pp. 383–84. See above, IV1f.
48. B2:KM38–43:T41–43, K8: p. 11 no. 26 27 June 41. See above, IV1c.

case, in which the husband was absent for four months to escape blood vengeance following a homicide, the *qāḍī* permitted the wife to divorce herself on the ground of nonprovision of maintenance after she had sworn that the husband had left her nothing and had no salable property. Four months is the shortest period for dissolution encountered by the author in the *sijill*s in a case of nonprovision of maintenance, and it is also the minimum time that in the opinion of Mālikī jurists must pass before a marriage may be dissolved on the ground of absence of the husband.[49]

Nonprovision of maintenance by an absent husband, whether or not his whereabouts are known, is a ground for dissolution by judicial divorce in several places in Africa and other regions. In northern Nigeria, the Alkalai requested the absent husband, if he had been located, to provide maintenance to the wife and, if he did not comply within a month, treated him as if he were present and recalcitrant, and dissolved the marriage. If the husband's whereabouts were not known, his relatives were asked to locate him, and if they did not succeed, the wife was called upon to take an *istiẓhār* oath and the court dissolved the marriage. In the days of the Aden Protectorate, jurists held that, in the case of an absent husband whose whereabouts were unknown, two months' grace should be given before the marriage was dissolved. In Israel, too, nonprovision of maintenance by an absent husband is the principal ground for dissolution by legal proceedings even where the husband's whereabouts are known, provided that it is proved to the satisfaction of the *qāḍī* that he has no property from which maintenance might be collected (*māl min jins al-nafaqa*). Some *qāḍī*s shrink from applying this ground, which is anchored in the Ottoman Family Rights Law and based on the Mālikī doctrine, because it does not agree with the position of the Ḥanafī school.[50]

As stated, the author has not, in the Cyrenaican *sijill*s, found instances of dissolution on the ground of nonprovision of maintenance by a present husband owing to poverty. This ground for dissolution appeared in other places. In Nigeria, the Alkalai usually dissolved the marriage, at the wife's request, after a month's grace; some held that the period of grace should be two months. In the Aden Protectorate the court usually dissolved

49. B2:KM38-43:T41-43, K7: p. 7 no. 204 1 Nov. 42. See above, IV1a.
50. Anderson, *Africa*, pp. 211 and 29, respectively; Anderson, *Nigeria*, p. 25; Layish, *Women*, pp. 200–204.

the marriage on that ground, provided the husband had no property elsewhere; if he had, he was given a period of grace for its realization.[51]

b. Fear for the Wife's Chastity

We have seen that nonprovision of maintenance by an absent husband as a ground for dissolution is often accompanied by another ground: fear of harm to the wife's chastity (owing to the husband's physical remoteness), which is one of the conditions for dissolution on the ground of the husband's absence according to the Mālikī school.[52] The decisions frequently mention circumstances relevant in this connection: the wife's youthful age, the long duration of the husband's absence, fear that the wife may be lured into sin by "wily Satan," and the like.[53] On the face of it the *qāḍī*s are impressed by these grievances, which they write down in detail and sometimes describe as injury (*ḍarar*), which in turn is an independent ground for dissolution. However, in these cases too the court grants dissolution on the ground of nonprovision of maintenance, which apparently in its opinion is the principal ground, and decides that the divorce is revocable, enabling the absent husband to reinstate the wife if he returns and proves within the waiting period that he is able and willing to provide maintenance to her.[54] In Nigeria most jurists recognized the wife's right to dissolution on the ground of injury caused to her by the denial of the husband's physical companionship as a result of his absence, and of the fear that she might go morally astray. Most were prepared—at least so they said—to enable reliance on this ground for dissolution after a month's separation or delay, and some were even prepared to dissolve the marriage at once if the wife was in danger of lapsing into adultery. A similar position existed in the Gambia: here too the *qāḍī*s were prepared to dissolve a marriage within less than the one year required by the Mālikī school; Anderson regards this as a concession to customary law. Some dissolved a marriage only if the absent husband refused to return or to have his wife join him at the request of the court. Some were prepared to dissolve it

51. Anderson, *Africa*, pp. 210 and 21, respectively. For the Gambia see p. 232.
52. See above, IV1a.
53. See above, IV2b.
54. E.g., KD59-73, K48: p. 33 no. 64 4 April 60, K47: p. 43 no. 81 15 May 60, K51: p. 146 no. 321 27 Nov. 62.

without monetary compensation even where the husband was present but persistently refused to cohabit.[55]

In Egypt too the *sharīʿa* courts (abolished in 1956), in reliance on modern legislation anchored in the Mālikī school, were wont to dissolve a marriage on the ground of fear for the wife's chastity. Thus in one case in which the wife applied for dissolution on the ground that the husband had not cohabited with her (*hajruhu iyyāhā fī maḍjaʿihā*) for seven years, the *qāḍī* said: "The aforementioned allegation has been proved. It appears that the plaintiff is a young woman who fears temptation (*takhshā ʿalā nafsihā al-fitna*), and her husband has kept away from her (*hajarahā*) without a *sharʿī* reason and has abandoned her, weak and young (*ʿalā jadhaʿ*), complaining of loneliness (*tataʾallam minaʾl-waḥsha*) and harassed by pain." Moreover, he has been sentenced to four years' imprisonment (which by itself is a ground for dissolution). "It is unjust that a woman should be kept in suspense without being able to contact her husband and without his divorcing her so that she might marry another man. . . . Throughout all that time she has found it difficult to preserve her chastity (*ʿiffa*) and honor (*sharaf*), which is something human nature cannot bear because woman was created in order to be loved." The court further considered that nothing harms a wife more than the husband's keeping away (*hajr*) from her, and that in the present case it had been proved to its satisfaction that injury (*ḍarar*) had been caused to the wife by the husband's keeping away. For all these reasons the court dissolved the marriage.[56] In Israel some *qāḍī*s stress the injury caused to the wife by the husband's absence even more, or at any rate not less, than that caused to her by nonprovision of maintenance. Some hold that the wife is entitled to dissolution if the husband has been absent for one year, even if he has left maintenance, because loneliness is contrary to human nature. The plea of injury arises also where the husband is in prison; it is regarded as a ground similar in weight to nonprovision of maintenance by an absent husband.[57]

c. Injury

According to the Mālikī school, injury to the wife is a ground for dissolution by court-appointed arbitrators. In addition to the divorce, the latter also determine the financial consequences, having regard to the responsibility of

55. Anderson, *Africa*, pp. 212, 232, 241.
56. *MSH*, vol. 4, no. 4 (1932), pp. 328ff., no. 105 of 8 Oct. 1932. Cf. Rosen, pp. 236–37.
57. Layish, *Women*, pp. 203–4.

each of the parties for the dissolution. However, although there have been several cases of dissolution on grounds clearly definable as injury to the wife, the court, without any explanation, did not resort to the arbitration procedure. This seems strange because the arbitration mechanism is anchored in the Mālikī school more than in any other and is closer to the tradition of a tribal society than to that of a settled urban or rural one. In one case the husband showed cruelty to the wife by habitually beating and humiliating her in public, in addition to not providing appropriate housing to her, which is one of the components of maintenance. The court, "in view of the serious, painful injury (*ḍarar*) convincingly proved," gave the wife the option between continuance and dissolution of the marriage. The wife opted for dissolution; "she was given permission for it" (*udhina lahā bihi*) and "she divorced herself from her husband on the ground of evident injury . . . and a judgment was awarded (*ḥukima*) accordingly"—that is, her divorce was confirmed by the court. If injury was indeed the ground for the dissolution, one would have expected the court to apply the arbitration mechanism intended for this purpose; but since the wife dissolved the marriage herself, it seems that the *qāḍī*'s decision was prompted by the nonprovision of maintenance. Similarly, the *qāḍī* of Tobruk and the Sharīʿa Court of Appeal regard "repeated beating" (*takarrur al-ḍarb*) of the wife as cruel treatment, which in turn is a ground for dissolution. They use arbitration only to prove the beating; dissolution (*firāq*) is left to the wife as an option by the side of continuing (*baqāʾ*) the marriage. In one such case the wife opted (*ikhtārat*) for dissolution. On the other hand, the question of damage to the wife's property (*ḍarar mālī*)—having regard to the fact that Islamic law provides for separation of the property of the spouses—as a ground for dissolution is controversial with the *qāḍī*s. Thus in one case the *qāḍī* of Derna awarded dissolution on this ground whereas the Sharīʿa Court of Appeal quashed that award and held that the marriage was still valid. The court relied in its decision on the Mālikī jurists Ibn ʿĀṣim, the author of *al-Tuḥfa*, and his commentator al-Tasūlī, although they were divided on the issue. In the opinion of the former, where there is no express contractual agreement between the spouses, only recurrent (*takarrur*) infliction of damage is a ground for dissolution; according to the latter, there is under these circumstances no ground for dissolution even in the case of recurrent damage. The Court of Appeal did not address the matter of recurrence at all, which indicates that it inclined toward the view of al-Tasūlī. Moreover, it relied also on local custom, noting that injury to the property (or person) of the wife was not taken into account the first time either in Tripoli or elsewhere.[58]

A further case of injury to the wife was even more serious than the preceding ones. The husband beat the wife several times so that she had to be hospitalized, and when she was discharged from hospital she found refuge at her father's house for many months without her husband—who was imprisoned for several weeks because of the beatings—providing maintenance to her. Her father, as her *wakīl*, demanded her divorce (*taṭlīq*) from the husband in view of what he had done to her, whereupon "the husband was ordered [by the court] to divorce his wife." But the husband refused to divorce her before he received back the dower he had paid to her father. The court, in view of the husband's refusal to divorce the wife although he admitted beating her very severely, and in conformity with religious-legal literature (*Ḥāshiyat al-Ṣāwī ʿalā al-Sharḥ al-ṣaghīr*), according to which "severe beating is prohibited" (*lā yajūz al-ḍarb al-mubarriḥ*), gave judgment in accordance with the *wakīl*'s demand; an infringement of that prohibition constitutes injury (*ḍarar*) and creates a ground for dissolution on the wife's initiative (*lahā al-taṭlīq*). Religious-legal literature further lays down: "The divorce is effected by the judge (*bi-yad al-ḥākim*); he assumes (*yatawallā*) [the power of divorce] if the wife requests it of him and the husband refrains from using it." The *qāḍī* in fact "assumed (*tawallā*) the power to divorce the wife himself (*taṭlīq bi-nafsihi*) and divorced her by one irrevocable (*bāʾin*) repudiation, [which entails] a minor period of separation (*baynūna ṣughrā*), after which she is again [legally] permitted (*taḥill*) to him by means of a new dower and a new marriage tie (*ʿaqd*)." Even in this case the *qāḍī* refrained from applying the arbitration procedure, although he stressed the element of injury.[59] Milliot, too, finds that where a ground for judicial divorce exists the *qāḍī* usually orders the husband to divorce the wife and that he probably effects the divorce himself, on behalf of the husband, only if the latter refuses to dissolve it; the dissolution seldom takes the form of a judgment.[60]

During colonial rule in Nigeria, the Gambia, Zanzibar, and the Aden Protectorate, *qāḍī*s also dissolved marriages on the ground of cruelty to the

58. AP:E4, p. 135 no. [126] n.d. (the last page, which indicates the type of repudiation, is missing; a revocable repudiation would confirm our assumption); and d'Emilia, pp. 40ff., 49, respectively.

59. A:E102, p. 345 no. 589 12 July 54 and the reference to Ibn ʿĀṣim, p. 305.

60. Milliot, pp. 375–76.

wife—such as recurrent beatings, accusations of adultery, and the like. It is interesting to note that Israeli *qāḍī*s, the most veteran of whom are adherents of the Ḥanafī school—which does not empower arbitrators to dissolve a marriage without prior authorization by the parties—have turned arbitration into an efficient mechanism for dissolution in cases of cruelty or injury to the wife, nonprovision of maintenance to her and her children, conflicts arising out of exchange marriages, social or cultural incompatibility of the spouses, and the like. In other words, they give an extremely wide interpretation to the term "dispute and discord" (*nizāʿ wa-shiqāq*) as circumstances justifying the appointment of arbitrators and to their power to dissolve marriages—far beyond the expectations of the Ottoman legislator, in the spirit of the modern legislation of Arab countries.[61]

d. Marriage of a Minor Girl

The marriage of a minor girl, even though she cannot consummate the marriage, is not a ground for dissolution by legal proceedings, as there is no *sharʿī* limitation on the age of marriage. The *qāḍī* did not think so in a case in which such a marriage was a source of constant conflict between the spouses. The *qāḍī* ascertained that the wife had been married at the age of twelve while she had fraudulently been registered in court as seventeen. She was unable to consummate the marriage because of her age, and the husband's relatives regarded themselves as cheated. The wife's father asked them to give her time until she was physically mature, but they refused, being inclined to settle the matter in court. After the facts had been established, "the court dissolved the marriage against everybody's will" (*fāraqathā al-maḥkama jabran ʿanhum jamīʿan*). But later it was said that, with the consent of the parties, the divorce had been performed by the husband's father by virtue of an official power of attorney (*wakāla*) from his son. If the court had been requested to dissolve the marriage on the ground of injury caused to the wife by being married while sexually immature, it would have had to apply the arbitration mechanism. But the wife was the defendant here, and in any case the court's intervention was by-passed when the parties agreed to dissolve the marriage themselves.[62] In Israel it has been provided that the marriage of a girl under seventeen

61. Anderson, *Africa*, pp. 20–21, 73, 212, 232, 241; Layish, *Women*, pp. 198, 206–8.
62. KD59–73, K50: p. 3 no. 12 11 Feb. 65.

years of age shall not only be a criminal offense (which, however, does not detract from the substantive religious law of marriage) but also creates a statutory ground for divorce. However, the *qāḍī*s do not apply that ground—although the phenomenon of marriage to a sexually immature girl is known—for the reason that it is contrary to the *sharīʿa* and that its application may harm society.[63]

The author has not, in the Cyrenaican *sijill*s, come across a divorce by the court on the ground of a defect or disease of the husband, or a conditional delegation for repudiation. What was noted earlier, however, was a combination of delegation with judicial divorce on the ground of nonprovision of maintenance by an absent husband.[64]

4. CONSEQUENCES OF DIVORCE

a. Legal Consequences

(1) **Revocable divorce.** Revocable divorce is frequent but, as far as the position is reflected in the *sijill*s, not dominant, and it seems that the *qāḍī*s are not particularly concerned with it. As the Mālikī school has no special term for it, it cannot be identified on the basis of the general divorce formula unless it is expressly described as such; where the divorce is not accompanied by a term indicating finality or triple repudiation, the first and second repudiations are regarded as revocable provided that the marriage was consummated, and it seems that the *qāḍī*s in fact apply this criterion. In divorces otherwise than by consent they tend to be lenient—that is, to assume revocability as a first resort unless it is submitted and proved by one of the parties that the wife was divorced irrevocably. Thus in some cases the husband declared that he had divorced the wife and made payment, or expressed willingness to make payment, in accordance with her financial rights, and the *qāḍī* decided that she was revocably divorced (*ṭalāq rajʿī*, *ṭalqa wāḥida rajʿiyya*).[65] At the same time the author has not encountered the phenomenon (observed in Israel) of a *qāḍī* trying to mitigate the legal consequences of divorce, even where it was expressly described as irrevocable, in reliance on the absence of intent

63. Layish, *Women*, p. 209.
64. See above, pp. 140–41.
65. E.g., A:E102, p. 10 no. 20 6 Aug. 51; A:E104, p. 162 no. [282] 21 Jan. 53, p. [211] no. [254] 18 June 53; KD59-73, K50: p. 133 no. 296 12 Sep. 62. See above, pp. 97–98, 101ff.

(*niyya*) on the part of the husband, who might plead that he had blurted out the divorce formula in a fit of anger; the Cyrenaican *qāḍī* made no such attempt, although the moralistic Mālikī school attaches importance to the element of intent.[66]

In some cases in which the wife was divorced by consent, the *qāḍī*s awarded a revocable divorce. As stated, this is possible according to the Mālikī school provided that the parties have so agreed and the wife has not paid compensation. Thus in one case the spouses agreed on dissolution following a dispute over the balance of the dower. The husband divorced the wife and the *qāḍī* awarded a revocable divorce, ordering the husband to pay the waiting-period maintenance.[67] But revocability seems surprising where the wife renounces various financial rights or even compensates the husband for her release—not only because it is contrary to the religious-legal norm which prescribes that divorce by consent under these circumstances shall be irrevocable, but also because it is contrary to the wife's interest, since the husband may reinstate her during the waiting period. It seems that the spouses had so agreed between themselves and that the *qāḍī*s acquiesced in this custom and gave it *sharʿī* legitimacy.[68]

Occasionally, the *qāḍī*s decide that the wife is divorced by a single revocable (*rajʿiyya*) repudiation through which she "acquires control of herself and the marriage between them is dissolved" (*malakat bihā amr nafsihā wa-infaṣalat baynahumā ʿuqdat al-nikāḥ*).[69] This combination is somewhat strange as regards the legal consequences, since the latter part of the passage suggests irrevocable divorce; in revocable divorce the wife does not become free and the marriage remains valid, since the husband can reinstate the wife at will without a new marriage and dower during the waiting period. Thus in one case in which the husband divorced the wife by one express revocable repudiation, the *qāḍī* correctly awarded "a revocable (*rajʿī*) divorce . . . and he retains matrimonial authority over her (*yamlik bihā ʿiṣmatahā*) as long as the waiting period has not ended." It therefore seems that the words *malakat bihā amr nafsihā* . . . should be regarded as a cliché appropriate only in the context of an irrevocable divorce, but that

66. Cf. Layish, *Women*, p. 211.

67. A:E103, p. 154 no. 270 7 Jan. 53.

68. E.g., KD59–73, K50: p. 133 no. 273 25 July 62, K43: p. 139 no. 306 18 Oct. 62, K50: p. 142 no. 314 7 Nov. 62, K44: p. 215 no. 515 22 Dec. 64.

69. E.g., KD59–73, p. 103 no. 216 13 Dec. 61, p. 123 no. 261 23 June 62, K43: p. 139 no. 306 18 Oct. 62, K50: p. 142 no. 314 7 Nov. 62, K44: p. 215 no. 515 22 Dec. 64.

their legal significance is not taken note of by the *qāḍī*s. Similarly, among the Berbers of the Kabyle Mountains it was usual to state upon dissolution on the ground of nonprovision of maintenance (and prolonged absence of the husband) that the wife "acquiert la libre disposition de sa personne."[70]

According to the Mālikī doctrine, the judicial divorce of the wife of an absent husband on the ground of nonprovision of maintenance is likewise revocable: the husband may reinstate the wife if he proves in the waiting period that he is able and willing to provide maintenance to her. It seems that this rule indeed guides the *qāḍī* in determining the legal consequences of divorce under these circumstances, although it is the wife and not the *qāḍī* who dissolves the marriage. The *qāḍī* decides that the wife "has opted for" (*ikhtārat*), and divorced herself by, one repudiation, through which "he [the husband] retains matrimonial authority over her (*yamlik bihā ʿiṣmatahā*)" or "retains [the right] to reinstate her if he turns up as a man of means (*yamlik bihā rajʿatahā in qadima yāsiran*) during her waiting period." In so deciding, the *qāḍī* hopes that the husband will return during the waiting period; if he does not return and cannot be reached a notice is to be issued.[71] The court awards a revocable divorce also where nonprovision of maintenance is accompanied by fear for the wife's chastity and morals in view of the husband's many years of absence. Thus in a case mentioned earlier, in which the wife said: "I am a young woman and Satan is cunning" (*waʾl-shayṭān shāṭir*) and stated that she could not bear the separation from her husband ("that is the limit of my endurance [*iṣtibārī*]"), the *qāḍī*, relying on the element of nonprovision of maintenance, held that the absent husband might reinstate the wife "if he appears as a person of means in her waiting period."[72]

The author has come across only one instance of reinstatement in the waiting period in the presence of the *qāḍī*. The husband reinstated (*rājaʿa*) the wife in the session (*majlis*) of the court "and he [the *qāḍī*] required us to attest (*ashhadanā*) it [the reinstatement]." This was apparently done to remove all doubt as to its legitimacy. The *qāḍī* treated the reinstatement as a part of the amicable settlement—not involving application of the

70. AP:E2, p. 158 no. 152 11 Aug. 47; Bousquet, *Coutumes kabiles*, p. 80.

71. E.g., B2:KM38-43:T41-43, K8: p. 11 no. 26 27 June 41, K5: p. 18 no. 41 2 Aug. 41, K6: p. 93 no. 248 27 Feb. 43; AP:E2, p. [159] no. [153] [?] Aug. 47; A:E102, p. 27 no. 53 9 Sep. 51; KD59-73, K48: p. 7 no. 14 28 July 59, K51: p. 146 no. 321 27 Nov. 62; KDP, K45: p. 13 no. 32 21 June 65. See above, pp. 137ff. Cf. Layish, *Women*, p. 211.

72. KD59-73, K51: p. 146 no. 321 27 Nov. 62. Cf. on the other hand Rosen, p. 237.

sharīʿa—of the dispute between the spouses. Other elements of the settlement were an undertaking by the husband to placate the wife with new clothes and to treat her and her co-wife equally. The *qāḍī* "permitted the settlement to be carried out amicably" (*ajāza al-ṣulḥ*). In other words, he did not state positively that the reinstatement had been validly effected, perhaps because the court was unable to check the nature of the divorce. It is possible that the spouses conspired to represent an irrevocable (and perhaps triple) divorce as a revocable one in order to facilitate the restoration of their marriage.[73]

The author has come across one instance of reinstatement subsequent to the waiting period. The woman stated that when several years after the divorce she visited her son, who was in the custody of his father, her ex-husband, the latter "reinstated me (*rājaʿanī*)...and we cohabited for twenty days, whereupon he again divorced me by *ṭalāq*." The man confirmed her story. The end of the document, containing the *qāḍī*'s decision, is not in the author's possession, so it is not known how the *qāḍī* reacted to that un-*sharʿī* reinstatement.[74]

(2) **Minor irrevocable divorce.** Minor irrevocable divorce is the dominant form of divorce reflected in the *sijill*s. It is seldom identifiable by the divorce formula, as when it is said that the husband divorces the wife by *ṭalāq bātt* (i.e., definite or irrevocable repudiation) or *ṭalāq bāʾin* (i.e., a repudiation entailing separation between the spouses).[75] The divorce formula is usually neutral, suitable for both irrevocable and revocable divorce—for example, the man "launched one repudiation against her, whereby she acquired control of herself and the marriage between them was dissolved" (*wa-qad arsala ʿalayhā ṭalqa wāḥida malakat bihā amr nafsihā minhu wa-infaṣalat baynahumā ʿuqdat al-nikāḥ*) or "he divorced her by one repudiation, whereby she acquired her freedom (*malakat bihā ḥuriyyatahā*)."[76] Under these circumstances minor irrevocable divorce is identifiable only by the legal consequences, as formulated by the *qāḍī*. After the divorce formula he adds that the wife "is separated [from the husband] for a minor period of

73. AP:E3, p. 328 no. 558 2 June 54.
74. A:E104, p. 222 no. 369 [?] July 53.
75. E.g., KD59–73, K45: p. 118 no. 247/2 6 April 62, and K45: p. 112 no. 235 21 March 62, respectively.
76. KD59–73, K47: p. 42 no. 78 29 Sep. 66, and K50: p. 133 no. 274 end of Aug. 62, respectively.

separation" (*bānat baynūna ṣughrā*) and that "she is not legally permitted to him except by a new marriage that meets all the conditions and basic principles" (*fa-lā taḥill lahu illā bi-ʿaqd jadīd mustawfin biʾl-shurūṭ waʾl-arkān*)—that is, the payment of a new dower, the consent of the woman or her guardian, and the like, as is usual in the case of an ordinary marriage contract.[77] The *qāḍī* sometimes states expressly that the wife "shall not be lawfully permitted to him [the husband] without a new marriage and a new dower (*ṣadāq*)."[78] To remove all doubt, the *qāḍī* is sometimes careful to note that the husband "has no right to reassert his matrimonial authority over her under the existing marriage (*fa-lā yamlik irjāʿahā li-ʿiṣmatihi*) but only under a new marriage." This practice was also observed in Algeria. The *qāḍī*s stressed the irrevocability of the divorce, thus reflecting, in Charnay's opinion, society's concern that the divorced spouses might "live in sin" (i.e., continue to cohabit in disregard of the divorce).[79]

Most of the evidence in the *sijill*s relates to the restoration of a marriage by a new marriage, although the *qāḍī* sometimes uses the term "reinstatement," borrowed from the context of revocable divorce. Thus in one case the *qāḍī*, relying on the consent of all concerned as to "the reinstatement (*tarjīʿ*) of the wife to married life (*muʿāshara*) with her husband [she had been divorced only four days after her marriage and the divorce had been proved to his satisfaction and both sides had been in lawful condition at the time of the divorce]..., decided upon the wife's return (*rujūʿ*) to the matrimonial authority (*ʿiṣma*) of her husband..., and the *Fātiḥa* [chapter] of the Qurʾān was read to them for the purpose of benediction (*wa-quriʾat baynahumā fātiḥat al-kitāb lil-tabarruk*)"; this shows that we have to do here with a new marriage and not with the reinstatement of a divorced woman during the waiting period.[80] Sometimes the *qāḍī*, in the case of the "reinstatement" of a woman, notes that she is "free from *sharʿī* impediments and from marriage ties" (*khāliya minaʾl-mawāniʿ al-sharʿiyya waʾl-ʿalāʾiq al-zawjiyya*) and gives permission (*idhn*) for the contraction of the marriage (*ʿaqd*), and the marriage is contracted on

77. E.g., KD59-73, p. 103 no. 217 18 Dec. 61, p. 104 no. 219 20 Dec. 61, K43: p. 218 no. 1 23 Dec. 64; KDP, K47: p. [?] File 2/68 2 June 68.
78. E.g., KD59-73, p. 220 no. 5 26 Dec. 64, K48: p. 47 no. 88 9 Dec. 65.
79. E.g., KD59-73, K43: p. 218 no. 1 23 Dec. 64; Charnay, p. 285. Cf. Bousquet, *Précis*, pp. 157ff.
80. AP:E1, p. 143 no. 254 19 Nov. 52.

the basis thereof.[81] The payment, upon reinstatement of the wife, of a dower equal to the first dower (*rajaʿahā ʿalā ṣadāqihā al-awwal*) and the wife's consent to the reinstatement likewise suggest that we have to do with a new marriage and not with the reinstatement of a woman divorced by revocable repudiation.[82]

As one may expect, the *qāḍī* awards minor irrevocable divorce in the case of divorce on the husband's initiative or by consent (*ṭalāq khulʿī*)[83] and in the case of judicial divorce, provided it is not on the ground of nonprovision of maintenance to the wife.[84] In one case the husband was absent for several years and did not provide maintenance. But he appointed his brother as *wakīl*; the brother divorced the wife on the husband's behalf, and the *qāḍī* decided that their "marriage is dissolved and they are separated (*iftaraqā*)." It seems that the reference is to minor irrevocable divorce, because the marriage was dissolved by ordinary *ṭalāq* and not by judicial divorce. There is no instance in the *sijill*s of the application of Law No. 76, according to which the character of a judicial divorce on the ground of injury depends on who is the plaintiff: if it is the wife, the divorce is irrevocable; if it is the husband, it is revocable.[85]

(3) **Major irrevocable divorce.** We have seen above that a husband divorcing his wife often states the number of the divorces in court: "one *khulʿī* divorce, which corresponds to a first divorce launched against her" or "one divorce preceded by a divorce, so that she has two divorces from him [in all] (*taqaddamahā ṭalqa qablahā ṣāra lahā minhu ṭalaqatān*)."[86] The number of the divorces is of course important with regard to the legal consequences, since after the third divorce an intermediate marriage is necessary before the woman may remarry the man who divorced her. From the counting of the divorces one might gain the impression that Cyrenaican society is aware of this vital matter. It is more probable, however, that the counting is the *qāḍī*'s contribution to the enforcement of the *sharʿī* norm in court and that the husband's statement as to the number of the divorces,

81. E.g., AMR42-44, A3: p. 76 no. 76 24 Aug. 43, A3: p. 82 no. 82 12 Sep. 43.
82. KD59-73, K50: p. 19 no. 45 7 Sep. 65.
83. E.g., AP:E4, p. 107 no. 105 18 Jan. 47; KD59-73, K43: p. 218 no. 1 23 Dec. 64. Cf. Bousquet, *Précis*, pp. 157ff.
84. E.g., A:E102, p. 345 no. 589 12 July 54 (*ḍarar*).
85. B2: KM38-43 T41-43, K6: p. 84 no. 224 5 Jan. 43. See above, p. 99.
86. E.g., KAMD, p. 29 no. 11 16 Feb. 34; AP:E2, p. 170 no. 164 22 Sep. 47; AP:E1, p. 145 no. 257 24 Nov. 52.

especially if it is made in the third person, is in fact "put into his mouth" by the *qāḍī*. The *qāḍī*'s ability to count the divorces is very limited, especially if they take place in strict privacy. The measure of his success depends on the degree of people's piety. In the absence of piety, it is doubtful whether the reports as to the number of divorces reflect reality, since people do not as a rule get themselves into trouble unnecessarily.

The *qāḍī*s' attitude as to three separate divorces or a triple divorce does not deviate from orthodox doctrine. They make a technical, not a normative, value-related distinction between three cumulative divorces performed at different sessions and a triple divorce performed at one session, while explaining the legal consequences involved. Thus, for instance, when the husband divorces the wife by a divorce that is established in court as the third ("corresponds to the third divorce I launched against her" or "I divorced her by one divorce preceded by two divorces"), the *qāḍī* is careful to point out that the wife "is separated from him [her husband]" (*bānat* or *ṣārat mubtūta*) or is divorced from him by a "repudiation entailing separation between the spouses" (*ṭalāq bāʾin*), which entails a "major period of separation (*baynūna kubrā*) and [by which] the ties of marriage and cohabitation between them are dissolved (*wa-infaṣalat baynahumā ʿuqdat al-nikāḥ waʾl-ʿalāʾiq al-zawjiyya*)."[87] This implies that if the husband wishes to reinstate the wife he can do so only after she has gone through an intermediate marriage. When the husband divorces the wife by a triple divorce, the *qāḍī* points this out, adding that the divorce was "by a single word" (*fī kalima wāḥida*) and that the wife is "cut off from him" (*mabtūta ʿalayhi*); the *qāḍī* then stresses that "she is not legally permitted to him from now on until she has been married to another man" (*lā taḥill lahu min baʿdi ḥattā tankaḥ zawjan ghayrahu*).[88] The *qāḍī* sometimes adds sternly that the intermediate marriage must "meet all the conditions and basic principles" (*yastawfī biʾl-shurūṭ waʾl-arkān*)—meaning, apparently, that the marriage and the divorce must be in good faith (including consummation of the marriage) and not, as held by the Ḥanafī

87. E.g., A:E104, p. 164 no. 286 28 Jan. 53, p. 170 no. 297 8 Feb. 53, p. 176 no. [305] 17 Feb. 53; KD59–73, K45: p. 89 no. 174 15 May 61, p. 220 no. 6 29 Dec. 64.

88. E.g., B2:KM38–43:T41–43, K9: p. 3 no. 8 14 May 41, K5: p. 33 no. 84 1 Jan. 42; KD59–73, K51: p. 9 no. 18 17 Aug. 59, K47: p. 54 no. 104 16 Aug. 60, p. 56 no. 107 24 Aug. 60. Cf. d'Emilia, pp. 37, 49.

school, "with intent to render [the woman] permitted [again to her former husband]" (*bi-qaṣd al-taḥlīl*).[89]

In one case the *qāḍī* ordered an intermediate marriage without indicating that two earlier divorces had taken place or that the divorce had been triple. The spouses "agreed upon dissolution (*firāq*)," and the husband consented to divorce the wife by a "definite [i.e., irrevocable] (*bātta*) divorce" and indeed "launched an irrevocable divorce against her," and the *qāḍī* decided that she "is not permitted to him before she has been married to another man." No explanation is given for this decision. The parties may have agreed on triple divorce coupled with renunciation of financial rights or with compensation paid to the husband in return for the release of the wife, which would mean that they were determined not to restore their marriage; or the present divorce may have been preceded by two other divorces without this being indicated in the decision.[90] In one case the husband divorced the wife for the third time and the *qāḍī* decided that she "had become forbidden (*ḥārima*) to him until she had been married [by an intermediate marriage] to another man." In the view of most jurists a *ḥarām* oath (to abstain from the wife) is by itself equivalent to a triple divorce; but it is not indicated that the husband took that oath, and perhaps we should understand the word *ḥārima* in its plain sense. In Nigeria during colonial rule the Alkalai were divided as to the legal consequences of a *ḥarām* oath: some dissolved the marriage with the consequences prescribed for triple divorce; others disregarded the divorce completely if the wife or the husband affirmed that the divorce had been unintentional.[91]

The author has not come across attempts by *qāḍī*s to mitigate the legal consequences of triple divorce—in view of the damage likely to be caused to the spouses and their children—by assigning the divorce to a lower degree of gravity, one not requiring an intermediate marriage. In the Mālikī school such mitigation is comparatively easy, because that school attaches importance to the element of intent (*niyya*). In one case mitigation is perhaps referred to. The wife claimed that the husband had divorced her by

89. KD59-73, K44: p. [131] no. 291 20 Aug. 62; Layish, *Women*, p. 211.
90. KD59-73, K51: p. 145 no. 319 7 Nov. 62.
91. KD59-73, K44: p. 210 no. 505 17 Oct. 64; Anderson, *Africa*, p. 213.

triple divorce and not, as had been recorded in the original judgment a month before, by double divorce, although she had described the situation to the *qāḍī* correctly. It is not clear whether the latter (well-meaningly) disregarded the triple divorce on purpose at the prompting of the husband, or whether he did so in good faith. At any rate, when the wife's witnesses confirmed her version that she had been divorced three times in their presence, the *qāḍī* had no choice but to quash the original decision and grant a triple divorce with all its implications. In one case the *qāḍī* of Tripoli rejected the wife's contention that she had been divorced by triple repudiation because one of the witnesses, a religious *shaykh*, was blind. The husband had consulted that *shaykh* as to the possibility of reinstating the wife without an intermediate marriage, and the *shaykh* had responded in the negative. In court, the *shaykh* confirmed that someone who claimed to be the husband had called on him, but that because of his blindness he could not be sure that he was indeed the husband. The *qāḍī* decided that the wife had not proved by witnesses that she had been divorced and that her marriage was therefore to be regarded as valid. The Court of Appeal confirmed that decision but directed that the woman should be given another opportunity to prove, by other witnesses, that she had been divorced. On the other hand, in a case in which a man claimed that his wife, after leaving his house, had married another man while still married to him, the second husband proved that before marrying him she had been divorced by triple repudiation after renouncing various rights. Witnesses testified to the truth of his statement; moreover, he produced a divorce certificate (*ḥujja*) from the tax office setting out the terms of the *khulʿ* agreement. The *qāḍī* of Tarhuna confirmed that before her second marriage she had been divorced by triple repudiaton; he relied on the witnesses, who had passed a credibility test (*tazkiya*), disregarding the written document—which was an innovation introduced by the colonial law. Prior this the *qāḍī* had ordered that the woman should be placed in the charge of a third party pending the completion of the proceedings. In another case the *qāḍī* confirmed the validity of the triple divorce with effect from the date of the man's acknowledgment (*iqrār*) of it in court. In Israel the *qāḍī*s have contributed to the abatement of the serious consequences of triple divorce not by its invalidation (the element of intent is of no importance in the Ḥanafī school) but by legalizing the fictitious intermediate marriage by means of "the one who renders [the divorced wife] lawful [to her ex-husband]... with intent to permitting [the woman again to her first husband] (*bi-qaṣd al-taḥlīl*)."[92] No such practice has been encountered in the Cyrenaican *sijill*s.

In Algeria a *qāḍī* decided that a triple divorce had the effect of only one divorce and that, according to the provisions of the Qurʾān, three divorces performed on separate occasions might be accumulated. Under reformist legislation of several Arab countries adhering to other schools, every double or triple divorce is considered one revocable divorce.[93]

In one case the *qāḍī*, in a matter of dissolution on the ground of nonprovision of maintenance by an absent husband, decided that the wife had been divorced for the third time and was liable to an intermediate marriage. It is true that a judicial divorce on that ground is considered a revocable divorce; but since in judicial divorce the *qāḍī* is deemed to stand in the husband's shoes, and since the divorce under reference had been preceded by two other divorces, the *qāḍī* correctly decided that the wife was forbidden to the husband save after an intermediate marriage.[94]

Three cases have been mentioned in which the husband divorced the wife more than three times—four, seven, or even a hundred. This was assumed to be a manner of speaking, probably based on custom, intended to demonstrate the husband's determination to sever his ties with the wife. In two of these cases the *qāḍī*s' approach was purely technical, oblivious of the deviation from the *sharʿī* norm, which recognizes only three divorces at one session. The *qāḍī* recorded the number of divorces, noting, as was his wont, that the wife "is cut off from the husband (*mabtūta ʿalayhi*) and is not permitted to him until she has been married to another man."[95] The third case is exceptional in that it represents an attempt to cope with custom by bringing it within the orbit of the *sharīʿa*. The husband divorced the wife "by four repudiations" immediately after a first repudiation, and the *qāḍī* declared: "As the divorcer combined (*awṣala*) the four repudiations with the first repudiation and there was no interval between them," the wife has been divorced "by five repudiations at one session; three of them were debited to his account, and two made a mockery of qurʾānic verses" (*khams ṭalaqāt fī dafʿa wāḥida thalātha marra minhā ʿalayhi wa-ithnān*

92. A:E102, p. 361 no. 617 22 Aug. 54; d'Emilia, pp. 33–37; Layish, *Women*, pp. 210–11.
93. Charnay, p. 290; Anderson, *Reform*, p. 124; Coulson, *History*, p. 195. Cf. Layish, *Women*, p. 210.
94. B2:KM38-43:T41-43, K7: p. 77 no. 204 1 Nov. 42.
95. KD59-73, K44: p. 136 no. 301 14 Oct. 62 (seven times), p. 37 no. 71 24 April 60 (a hundred times).

uttukhidha bihimā āyāt allāh huzu'an). In other words, three out of the five divorces exhausted the *shar'ī* quota to which the man was entitled, while the other two were contrary to the *sharī'a*.[96]

(4) **Waiting period.** Underlying the waiting period (*'idda*) is the concept of the sanctity of natural paternity in the event of the divorced woman being pregnant, and of its identity with legal paternity, in addition to the purpose of enabling the husband who revocably divorces his wife to reinstate her before the divorce becomes irrevocable. From these two points of view the institution of the waiting period is completely alien to customary law; it represents a departure rather than continuity, unlike most matters of personal status and succession, as to which the *sharī'a* has adopted the concepts of customary law as basic while mitigating them by means of religious-ethical norms. This may account for the uncompromising insistence of the *qāḍī*s on observance of the waiting period. It seems that in this matter the exponents of the *sharī'a* are not prepared to make the slightest concession to custom. Immediately after the confirmation of divorce, "the court orders the woman to observe the waiting period from the day following the date of the divorce" (*wa-ta'mur al-maḥkama al-mar'a bi'l-i'tidād min ghad ta'rīkh al-ṭalāq*) or "from the date thereof"—that is to say, retroactively from the moment the divorce came into force and not from the moment of its confirmation by the court.[97] In one case the husband stated that he had divorced the wife "before the month of Ramaḍān last year," and the wife's brother confirmed this. The *qāḍī* decided that the wife was to be considered divorced "from the time of the occurrence of the divorce" (*ḥasb zamān tawqī' al-ṭalāq*)—that is, from the day of the actual divorce and not from the day, one year later, of the passing of the declaratory judgment as to the validity of the divorce. In a case of a different kind, it was not proved in the court of first instance that there had been an irrevocable divorce. The parties agreed in the course of the litigation on dissolution by *khul'*, apparently in reliance on an earlier divorce, and the *qāḍī* applied the opinion of the Mālikī jurist Khalīl that in the case of an acknowledgment (*iqrār*) of an earlier divorce the waiting

96. A:E102, p. 28 no. 54 9 Sep. 51. For *āyāt allāh* see Lane, p. 135.
97. E.g., A:E102, p. 361 no. 617 22 Aug. 54; KD59–73, K48: p. 47 no. 88 9 Dec. 65. Cf. Layish, *Women*, p. 212.

period should begin at the time of the acknowledgment. The Court of Appeal confirmed the *qāḍī*'s decision.[98]

The commencement date of the waiting period has of course additional importance in the case of revocable divorce, when the husband may reinstate the wife without a new marriage and dower.[99] In the case in which the wife was divorced "before the month of Ramaḍān last year," the *qāḍī* decided that the wife had become "separated [by irrevocable divorce] upon the termination of her waiting period" (*bānat... bi-intihāʾ ʿiddatihā*)—that is to say, the divorce had become irrevocable because the option of reinstating the wife in the waiting period had not been exercised. Where the divorced woman is pregnant, the court points out to her that "her waiting period ends upon her delivery" (*intihāʾ ʿiddatihā huwa waḍʿ ḥamlihā*).[100] If the woman is not in court when the validity of the divorce is confirmed, the *qāḍī* orders that the duty of observing the waiting period shall be explained to her by her agnates—her father and her germane brothers[101]—and sometimes by her cognates, such as a maternal uncle (*khāl*), who represent her in the divorce proceedings. In one case the court instructed the husband to explain the matter to the woman; that case involved a revocable divorce, which as we know does not actually sever the marriage tie, so that the woman continues to live in the husband's house.[102]

In some cases the court releases the woman from the requirement of the waiting period. The reason is always nonconsummation of the marriage. In one such case the man "renounced his betrothed and divorced her before the consummation (*bināʾ*) of the marriage." In another case the parties stated that consummation (*dukhūl*) had not taken place, and the *qāḍī*, in reliance on these statements and after confirming the validity of the divorce, decided that "the requirement of the waiting period does not apply to her."[103] In some similar cases, the *qāḍī* noted that the divorce had taken place before the consummation of the marriage but did not say that the woman was exempt from the requirement of the waiting period; it seems, however, that this was merely an omission and that he really intended to

98. AP:E104, p. 162 no. [282] 21 Jan. 53; and d'Emilia, p. 40, respectively.
99. E.g., A:E103, p. 154 no. 270 7 Jan. 53; KD59–73, K50: p. 142 no. 314 7 Nov. 62.
100. A:E104, p. 162 no. [282] 21 Jan. 53; and KD59–73, p. 218 no. 1 23 Dec. 64, respectively.
101. E.g., AP:E4, p. 139 no. 129 2 June 47; A:E104, p. 201 no. [340] 20 April 53.
102. A:E104, p. 164 no. 286 28 Jan. 53; and A:E102, p. 351 no. 601 26 July 54, respectively.
103. AP:E3, p. 348 no. 595 5 July 54; and A:E104, p. 168 no. 294 4 Feb. 53, respectively.

exempt her from that requirement.[104] Only in one case did the *qāḍī* permit the remarriage of a woman divorced after a consummated marriage without insisting on observance of the waiting period; she stated that she had been divorced four days after her marriage and that some two weeks later she had remarried her former husband. The *qāḍī* "decided upon the return (*rujūʿ*) of the woman to the matrimonial authority (*ʿiṣma*) of her husband...and they read the *Fātiḥa* of the Book [the Qurʾān] between them for the purpose of benediction." We thus have to do here with a new marriage and not with the reinstatement of a divorced woman in the waiting period. The reason for noninsistence on the waiting period in this particular case was that the woman remarried her former husband; under these circumstances the waiting period is dispensed with according to the *sharīʿa*, even in the case of a minor irrevocable divorce; if the woman is pregnant at the time of the divorce, the question of paternity will not arise. Nonobservance of the waiting period for considerations of public interest (*maṣlaḥa*) has been observed in a Druze court even in grave cases of adultery. In an exceptional case of a different kind, in which the wife was divorced by her husband's brother, who had received a special mandate for that purpose, and married another man while the first husband denied the divorce, the *qāḍī* of Msellata decided that both the divorce and the second marriage were valid but ordered the second husband not to consummate the marriage before the woman had menstruated and become purified (*istibrāʾ*).[105]

b. Financial Consequences

(1) **Waiting-period maintenance.** As we have seen, the husband owes waiting-period maintenance only in the case of revocable divorce and, in the case of irrevocable divorce, if the wife is pregnant; if she is not pregnant, she is entitled only to living accommodation. It seems that the *qāḍī*s do not deviate from the orthodox norm. Where the husband divorces the wife by revocable divorce, the *qāḍī* confirms the divorce and orders the husband to pay maintenance until the end of the waiting period. Sometimes an undertaking to pay waiting-period maintenance is given by the husband

104. E.g., A:E102, p. 16 no. 31 16 Aug. 51; KD59-73, K43: p. 60 no. 116 5 Oct. 60.

105. AP:E1, p. 143 no. 254 19 Nov. 52. See above, p. 98; Layish, *Druze*, pp. 235-36; d'Emilia, pp. 31-33, 48. For *istabraʾa* see Lane, p. 179.

following a revocable divorce, and the *qāḍī* in turn orders the husband to pay it on confirming the divorce.[106]

Where the woman alleges that she is pregnant, her allegation is not considered unless it is proved that she is in fact pregnant, whereupon she is entitled to full maintenance—not only in the case of revocable divorce but also in the case of irrevocable divorce. It seems that the *qāḍī*s' decisions conform with the *sharīʿa* in this respect as well. Thus in one case the *qāḍī* ordered the husband to pay waiting-period maintenance, adding: "If it is found that she is pregnant (*wa-in tabayyana anna lahā ḥaml* or *wa-idhā tabayyana anna lahā ʿayyil*), he shall have to provide maintenance to her [throughout the period of her pregnancy]."[107] In one case the court ordered a man to pay "pregnancy maintenance (*nafaqa ʿalā ḥamlihā*) for six months... and to support the child during the *sharʿī* custody period"; it seems that the wife's appearance, in the third month of her pregnancy, convinced the *qāḍī* that she was indeed pregnant. The judgment does not refer to "past maintenance" (*nafaqat al-māḍī*), to which the wife is entitled—that is, for the first three months of her pregnancy up to the time when it was proved.[108] In one case the wife alleged that upon her divorce she had a "sleeping embryo" (*ḥaml nāʾim*); a month later, the embryo had woken up and begun to move. She demanded that the court order the husband to pay maintenance until she gave birth. The husband confirmed her story in full, and the *qāḍī* ordered him to pay waiting-period maintenance and maintenance for the child from the date of the divorce. It thus seems that the concept "sleeping pregnancy" is accepted also by the court. Mayer encountered several Libyan Appeal Court judgments dealing with paternity and showing that the court was ready to recognize a maximum pregnancy period of twelve years, so that a child born many years after the termination of the marriage by divorce or by the death of the husband could be considered the husband's legitimate offspring. It thus seems that we have to regard "sleeping pregnancy" as a device intended to save a woman from distress when she has become pregnant out of wedlock. This device is rooted both in the Mālikī school, which recognizes a

106. AP:E2, p. 19 no. 38 23 Aug. 51; A:E103, p. 124 no. 219 8 Sep. 52, p. 154 no. 270 7 Jan. 53. See above, V2a.

107. B2:KM38-43:EA, K10: no. 21 8 March 33; and KD59-73, p. 102 no. 215 16 Dec. 61, respectively.

108. KD59-73, K43: p. 218 no. 1 23 Dec. 64; Pesle, p. 169.

pregnancy period of several years, and in custom. The purpose is probably the same. The Italian administration did not like this device. It did not give effect to *sharʿī* judgments concerning a period of pregnancy extended under Mālikī norms and the determination of the paternity of a child born in the period of the extension, on the ground that such judgments were contrary to public policy.[109]

Only where the wife renounces the waiting-period maintenance, which happens in the case of divorce by consent, does the *qāḍī* exempt the husband from the payment of that maintenance—or, more exactly, from the provision of living accommodation—and require the wife "to fulfill her undertaking to provide her own maintenance in the waiting period." In one case the wife renounced the pregnancy maintenance, and the *qāḍī* ordered her to observe the waiting period "until her delivery," regardless of the pregnancy maintenance to which she would have been entitled but for the renunciation.[110] The author has come across no instance of the court ordering a divorcing husband to provide his ex-wife with living accommodation. The reason seems to be that the woman has renounced all her financial rights. Nor has the author come across an instance of the court awarding a divorced woman maintenance beyond the waiting period—for life or until remarriage—or a one-time compensation to ensure her subsistence. Such phenomena have been observed in Israel, where the *qāḍīs* use various devices to give them *sharʿī* backing. One or two years' maintenance for a divorced woman has been introduced in several Arab states by means of statutory legislation.[111] It seems that in traditional Cyrenaican society a divorced woman returns to the house of her agnates or, if still young, soon remarries, so that the question of maintenance is not relevant.

The author has come across only one case in which the *qāḍī*, on dissolving the marriage, ordered the husband to pay maintenance accumulated during its existence. Following the husband's acknowledgment that he had beaten the wife with a stick so that she had had to be hospitalized and that she had then gone to live at her father's house, the *qāḍī* dissolved the marriage himself and ordered the husband to pay to the

109. A:E102, p. 8 no. 15 1 Aug. 51; Mayer, *Sexual mores*, p. 291; d'Emilia, p. 16 n. 2. See above, p. 112 and the sources indicated in n. 47.
110. A:E103, p. 150 no. 265 13 Dec. 52; and KD59-73, K50: p. 4 no. 13 15 Feb. 65, respectively.
111. Layish, *Women*, pp. 212-17; Anderson, *Reform*, pp. 124-25; Layish, *Mahkama*, xiii, p. 40.

wife, *inter alia*, maintenance for the eighteen months that he had "neglected" (*ahmala*) her at her father's house (i.e., had not paid maintenance to her). According to the Mālikī (as distinct from the Ḥanafī) doctrine, a woman is entitled to marital maintenance retroactively to the date on which she was transferred to her husband; her right to maintenance for the period preceding the filing of her claim is like a debt due from her husband.[112]

(2) **Suckling wages and custody maintenance.** Upon divorce, the wages for suckling (*raḍāᶜ*) the child and the renumeration for the custody (*ḥaḍāna*) of the child by his divorced mother are regulated along with the waiting-period and pregnancy maintenance. Upon divorce by consent, the woman is disadvantaged as to realizing her rights in this respect as well; but the court, which prefers agreement to the application of *sharᶜī* law, confirms the agreement in all its details and gives it the effect of a judgment. Thus in one case the court decided that the man should pay the woman suckling wages. The man complained that owing to his straitened circumstances and having a family (possibly by another wife) to provide for he was unable to pay the amount fixed by the court. The woman's father "took pity on him" and expressed willingness to be satisfied with a smaller amount on condition that payment was not delayed. The woman concurred with this proposal, and the *qāḍī* sanctioned the agreement. In another case it was agreed between the spouses, upon their divorce, that the man should pay the woman pregnancy maintenance, suckling wages from the child's birth to its weaning (*fiṭām*), and maintenance for the child (*ᶜayyil*) "until the age of five, when he [the father] would take over his son." The *qāḍī* gave effect to the agreement (*hādhā mā ṣāra ᶜalayhi al-ḥukm waʾl-ittifāq*). In northern Nigeria the Alkalai removed children from the custody of their mother on reaching the age of two years. Coulson ascribes this practice to custom; for according to the Mālikī school, the period of custody lasts till the child reaches maturity.[113] Even where a woman, under the divorce agreement, renounces custody maintenance completely, the court confirms the renunciation (*tanāzul*) without substantively relating to it, although such a renunciation is of no effect according to the Mālikī school.[114] Only in

112. A:E102, p. 345 no. 589 12 July 54; Linant, *Traité*, pp. 276–77.

113. A:E103, p. [115] no. 205 11 Aug. 52; and B2:KM38–43:EA, K10: no. 23 12 April 33, respectively; Coulson, *History*, p. 138.

114. E.g., AP:E3, p. 302 no. 507 25 Feb. 54. See above, pp. 51–52.

the absence of agreement between the parties does the *qāḍī* note the woman's rights in this sphere: he orders the husband to pay suckling wages and custody fee to her until the end of the *sharʿī* periods.[115]

(3) **Dower.** On confirming a divorce, the *qāḍī*s sometimes expressly refer to the deferred dower. Thus in one case described above the court dissolved a marriage on the ground of wife beating and in view of the husband's refusal to divorce the wife until the dower he had paid to her father was returned to him, and it ordered the husband to pay the wife the deferred dower.[116] At the same time, it is not certain that the reference is to deferred dower in the conventional sense of the term—that is, the part of the dower to which the wife is entitled following divorce or death. It seems that what is meant is customary deferred dower—that is, the part of the prompt dower the payment of which has been deferred by consent of the parties to some date during the existence of the marriage. Thus in one case the *qāḍī*, on confirming a divorce, held that since it had not been proved that the husband during the existence of the marriage had paid the deferred (*muʾajjal*) dower to the wife, his financial liability (*dhimma*) continued to exist—that is to say, he had to pay that part of the dower after the divorce. In another case the wife, who had received only part of the specified dower, claimed a bracelet "which had remained due from him on account of the dower," and the *qāḍī* awarded revocable divorce "in the expectation that the wife would prove her right to the bracelet." In this case there is no doubt that the reference is not to deferred dower in the usual sense, since in revocable divorce the marriage tie remains in existence.[117]

This concept of deferred dower is confirmed by decisions of the Sharīʿa Court of Appeal, although the latter is at variance on this issue with the courts of Tripoli and Derna. The *qāḍī*s of the courts of first instance have decided on several occasions that in irrevocable divorce the husband must pay the deferred dower forthwith, without waiting until the end of the period indicated in the marriage contract ("the deferred dower is due at the time of the divorce [*yaḥull biʾl-ṭalāq*]"), while the Court of Appeal, to which the husbands applied, quashed those decisions and held that even in cases

115. E.g., A:104, p, [169] no. [296] 8 Feb. 53; A:E102, p, 361 no. 617 22 Aug. 54; KD59-73, K45: p. 89 no. 174 15 May 61.
116. A:E102, p. 345 no. 589 12 July 54.
117. AP:E2, p. 19 no. 38 23 Aug. 51; and A:E103, p. 154 no. 270 7 Jan. 53, respectively. On the customary deferred dower see above, pp. 48–49.

of irrevocable divorce the deferred dower must be paid at the original date of payment ("the deferred dower must be paid at the appointed time [*dafʿuhu ilā ḥulūl ajlihi*]" or "when the period of deferment ends" [*ʿinda inqiḍāʾ muddat al-taʾjīl*]); until then "it remains pending" (*yabqā mūqifan*). In one case a husband who had divorced his wife by triple repudiation was prepared to pay her the deferred dower if she proved that the time for its payment had come. The marriage contract mentioned the amount of the dower but apparently did not mention the time of payment, and the *qāḍī* said that one must distinguish between prompt dower and deferred dower (although this distinction is a matter of custom and not of law), without taking a stand as to the time for the payment of the deferred dower.[118]

If the wife is divorced before consummation of the marriage she is entitled to one-half of her dower. There is one express testimony to the court's acting in accordance with this rule. After the husband had acknowledged that he had divorced the wife before consummation (*bināʾ*) of the marriage, the *qāḍī*, in reliance on his acknowledgment, which was made "while he was in a legally fit condition," decided that the wife was divorced by "one repudiation before consummation of the marriage and has acquired control of herself...and that she is entitled to one-half of the specified [dower] (*tastaḥiqq niṣf musammāhā*) if it is proved that he has not consummated the marriage (*in thabata annahu lam yadkhul bihā*)." In a further case, in which the husband acknowledged nonconsummation two months after the marriage, it was agreed between the spouses that the husband should pay the wife a certain amount in addition to the amount that, as he had already proved by witnesses, he had paid as part of the dower; and the *qāḍī* sanctioned the agreement without referring at all to the question whether the aggregate of the two amounts constituted the half of the dower to which she was entitled by law. The *qāḍī*s of other regions of Libya and also the Sharīʿa Court of Appeal likewise decide in cases of divorce before consummation that the woman is entitled to half of the dower.[119]

(4) **Financial rights of a divorced woman.** It seems that the *qāḍī*s are as a rule aware of a divorced woman's financial rights under the *sharīʿa* and are careful to note them in the judgment on confirming the divorce,

118. d'Emilia, pp. 36–37, 43–45, 49.
119. A:E102 p. 16 no. 31 16 Aug. 51; and A:E104, p. 168 no. 294 4 Feb. 53, respectively; d'Emilia, p. 38 n. 3, p. 39 n. 4, p. 43.

provided the woman duly proves her rights. Even where the husband alleges that he has fulfilled all his financial obligations toward her, the *qāḍī* gives her an opportunity to plead and prove her rights. Thus in one case a man appeared in court "to register" his wife's divorce, saying: "I have given her the whole of her dower and the waiting-period maintenance, and she has no more claim against me," and immediately afterward he divorced her (in her absence). The *qāḍī* decided that the wife was divorced by revocable repudiation, "giving her time (*murjiʾan*) to submit evidence (*ḥujja*) as to what she claims [as her financial rights] and what is duly proved (*wa-yuthbat lahā sharʿan*)." The *qāḍī* proceeded similarly in another case in which a man came "to register the divorce" of his wife and expressed willingness "to pay what is due to her before and after the divorce." Here, too, "the *qāḍī* gave her time to present evidence (*arjaʾa al-ḥujja*) as to her claims from him in the matter of her rights."[120] Sometimes, in the absence of agreement between the parties, the court is expected to be instrumental in settling financial claims. Thus in one case the husband released the wife by *khulʿ* in return for her dower; but the parties did not reach agreement as to items (*shurūṭ*) accompanying the dower—clothing, bedding, etc.—and therefore applied to the *qāḍī* to decide (*yafṣil*) between them and to pronounce judgment (*yaqḍī*) in the dispute (*nizāʿ*) as to the value of those items.[121]

After the woman's financial rights have been determined, the court, when ordering the man to pay accordingly, sometimes states that they have been fixed at a level befitting the status of the couple; this seems to mean the economic status. The decisions do not indicate the procedure by which the rates of the various kinds of maintenance are fixed (in Israel, this is done by *mukhbirūn*, specialists or experts). But it is hinted that the criterion is the economic position of the man (not the living standard of the woman before the marriage). Thus in one case, in which the woman claimed pregnancy maintenance, the *qāḍī* assessed it "as befitted their [the couple's] status" (*talīq bi-mithlayhimā*) but actually decided that it should be "in accordance with his [the man's] ability" (*ḥasb maqdaratihi wa-wusʿihi*). In another case, in which the man undertook to pay the woman a sum of money, to give her a she-camel, to divide the household effects (*athāth*) between them, and to pay maintenance to her daughters "as the

120. A:E102, p. 351 no. 601 26 July 74; and A:E104, p. 170 no. 297 8 Feb. 53, respectively.
121. KD59–73, K42: p. 158 no. 333 14 March 63.

court may decide," the court confirmed the validity of the divorce and "his undertaking to pay to her in accordance with what is due to women of her status from men of his status (*mā huwa ʿāʾid li-zawjāt mithlihā min amthālihi*)."[122] At the same time it seems that the *qāḍī*s are also guided by social considerations, taking account of the special circumstances of each case. Thus in a case of divorce by consent in which the wife claimed only pregnancy maintenance, the *qāḍī* awarded maintenance (probably at a high rate) "in the knowledge that a pregnant woman has greater expenses than another"; this may be regarded as a humane gesture toward the divorced woman. As against this, in another case the *qāḍī* awarded pregnancy maintenance at a lower rate, having regard to the situation of the husband, "a poor wretch deprived of his eyesight."[123]

The court denies the woman her financial rights if she has committed adultery. Thus in one case the husband alleged that the wife "commits adultery and leads an immoral life" (*ʿāhir ghayr maḍbūṭa*) and his accusation was proved. The *qāḍī* dissolved the marriage and decided that "she has no [financial] right against him since moral corruption (*fasād*) has been proved against her." This practice conforms with the *sharʿī* norm that in cases of adultery the husband is entitled to get back the dower. The sanctions of dissolution of the marriage and denial of financial rights for adultery are moderate compared with both the *sharʿī* and customary sanctions in such cases. Of course the *qāḍī*s' decision solves only the problem of the deceived husband, who wishes to get rid of a financial burden; restoration of the family honor sullied by the adultery is, under customary law, the concern of the wife's agnates.[124] When, upon divorce, the financial claims have been settled between the parties, either by actual payment or by mutual renunciation, the court declares: "No plea, claim, or marital [financial] right is left between them"(*wa-lā baqiya baynahumā daʿwa wa-lā ṭalab wa-lā ḥaqq minaʾl-ḥuqūq al-zawjiyya*).[125]

We have seen that the wife's agnates or guardians who represent her in the negotiations on the divorce and its terms often renounce various financial rights in her name. In case the woman should not recognize the

122. AP:E4, p. 71 no. 70 4 July 46; and AP:E4, p. [128] no. [123] 26 April 47, respectively. Cf. Layish, *Women*, p. 177.

123. AP:E4, p. 71 no. 70 4 July 46; and KD59–73, p. 220 no. 5 26 Dec. 64, respectively.

124. B2:KM38–43:T41–43, K5: p. 33 no. 84 1 Jan. 42; Milliot, p. 381; Layish, *Judaean Desert*; Kressel, pp. 144–45.

125. E.g., KD59–73, K44: p. 1 no. 1 7 June 59.

renunciation and still claim the financial rights concerned from her former husband, the agnate occasionally undertakes to cover any such claim out of his own money, and the *qāḍīs*, apparently in correct appraisal of the situation, incorporate the undertaking in the judgment. Thus in one case the woman's germane brother confirmed the man's statement that he had divorced her and "paid her everything due to her before or after the divorce." But it seems that this was a cliché not necessarily reflecting the facts; for immediately afterward "he [the brother] took upon himself to pay out of his own money whatever his sister might demand that could be proved to be due to her," and the *qāḍī* "required (*alzama*) the brother to pay what he had undertaken to pay—whatever could be proved [to be due to his sister by law]." In another case the guardian of an orphaned girl renounced all her financial rights "and everything to which she is entitled under the *sharīʿa*" and undertook that if she claimed any right from her divorcing husband in the future he would pay the amount out of his own money. The *qāḍī* confirmed the divorce and ordered the guardian "to do everything he has taken upon himself as to the payment of any amount which his ward (*rabība*) might demand and which proved to be due in accordance with the *sharīʿa*." In another case it was the wife's maternal uncle (*khāl*) who laid down the terms of the divorce with the husband and "undertook that if she claimed any right from the husband contrary to what had been mentioned [agreed between them], he would pay the amount out of his own money, provided she was entitled to it and proved her right validly." The *qāḍī*, as usual, required the uncle to fulfill his undertaking.[126]

These undertakings by relatives in respect of possible claims of the woman are not in keeping with the customary concept of marriage, according to which the woman is not a party to the contract, since they appear to reflect an awareness of the woman's rights under the *sharīʿa*. It is not certain that such an awareness in fact exists; the *qāḍī* probably deems it his duty to draw the attention of the relatives to the woman's *sharʿī* rights, by which he contributes to the *sharʿī* indoctrination of the population resorting to the court. Similarly, we should treat with caution the picture emerging from the *sijill*s according to which the woman and her agnate jointly conduct negotiations with the husband for the achievement

126. A:E104, p. 162 no. [282] 21 Jan. 53; A:E104, p. 208 no. 349 20 May 53; and A:E104, p. 164 no. 286 28 Jan. 53, respectively.

of a divorce, renouncing rights, or granting compensation for his consent to it. The judgment sometimes states that the woman "redeems herself" from her husband in return for certain financial rights while the agnate either pays the amounts involved or assumes responsibility toward the court for any future financial claim of the woman against her former husband. Again, the assignment of release by *khulʿ* to the woman is apparently a contribution by the court, which seeks to formulate social custom in *sharʿī* terms and thereby to naturalize it in the *sharīʿa*. But it seems that the court's practice is not consistent; hence the strange, anomalous combination in divorce proceedings of the wife and her agnate—a compromise between the demands of custom and the *sharīʿa*.[127]

127. See above, III5a, and below, VII3b.

CHAPTER VII

Sharīʿa and Custom in the Cyrenaican Family

The institution of divorce, as reflected in the *sijill*s, is a true mirror of the complex of relations between *sharīʿa* and custom in the Cyrenaican family and of the role of the *qāḍī* in shaping the pattern of the tensions between two legal norms: the *sharīʿa*, which derives its authority from sanctions rooted in a revelation interpreted by its competent exponents, and custom, which draws its strength from social tradition. There are several reasons for this: divorce is central to the complex of relations between spouses; divorce is an inseparable part of the legal and social concept of marriage, the two being one integrative whole; and divorce terminates the state of matrimony—although in Islam the transition from that state to what follows is not always clear-cut. Thus, for instance, revocable divorce does not mean immediate dissolution, with all the attendant legal implications; it leaves the husband an option, throughout the waiting period, to reinstate the wife. The *sijill*s faithfully reflect the increasing resort of the Cyrenaican tribal population, which has largely become sedentary, to *sharʿī* jurisdiction; the latter, in turn, contributes greatly to the Islamization of that population; and the decisive role of the *qāḍī* in that jurisdiction enables him to influence considerably the consequences of the encounter between the *sharīʿa* in its Mālikī version, which confers on divorce a special character unparalleled in other schools, and tribal custom.

As known, normative Islam, with its system of beliefs, institutions, and laws, plays no central part in the shaping of a nomadic society or its philosophy or way of life. Although customary law was one of the sources of inspiration of Islamic law in the formative period, its absorption into Islam involved softening and refining by the religious-ethical and social norms inherent in an urban community. These norms in many cases created a new legal entity, and in this sense one may say that Islam is an urban religion that encountered difficulties in adjusting to a tribal society. Folk religion, including the worship of saints and intercession, still predominates. Moreover, in Cyrenaica vestiges of the Sanūsiyya—another instance of a folk religion adapted to the institutional and normative system of a tribal society—remain, although the Sanūsī establishment ceased to exist after the Italian conquest. Custom survived even when its followers had nominally adopted Islam. Evans-Pritchard comments that although the Beduin of Cyrenaica were considered Muslims, their knowledge of Islamic doctrine, worship, and ethics was modest even after the Sanūsī revivalist movement had become established in their midst. Thus they were negligent in fulfilling the practical commandments, and customary law had the upper hand in its encounter with Islamic law. Similarly, Colucci notes that the reception of Islamic law by the Cyrenaican Beduin had been partial and slow and was not yet complete. Milliot distinguishes—apparently on the pattern of the distinction between *dār al-ḥarb* and *dār al-islām*—between *le pays de ʿorf* and *le pays de sharʿ*. He notes that the Berbers had adopted Islam in a distorted form and quotes Edmond Douté to the effect that Maraboutism is "la revanche de l'anthropolâtrie berbère sur le monothéisme du Coran." Although the process of Islamization of the Beduin has lasted for centuries it is not yet complete in every respect. The Beduin are not fully aware of it. Oweidi, for example, who is himself of Beduin origin, attests that Jordanian Beduin identify themselves as Muslims in every respect and are proud of their identity. They believe in Allāh in word and deed, and ask for his help in various circumstances. According to Oweidi, they regard tribal law (*ʿawāʾid*) as part of their Islamic heritage, although he admits that some of those customs are inconsistent with normative Islam. The fact that they have become sedentary brings them closer to normative Islam, which is gradually becoming a binding life style as regards worship, practical religious duties, and law in those fields in which they resort to the *sharʿī* judicial system and to the exponents of the *sharīʿa*—that is, in matters of personal status and succession.[1]

1. Gellner, p. 100; Evans-Pritchard, p. 62; Colucci, *Tribù*, p. 24; Milliot, pp. 157, 166; Oweidi, pp. 121, 134–37, 149, 321–22; Coulson, *History*, pp. 135–36; Layish & Shmueli, p. 31 and the sources indicated there.

Indeed, in the complex of relations between *sharīʿa* and custom reflected in the Cyrenaican *sijill*s, we may distinguish a wide range of grades corresponding to stages of the transition from a tribal to a sedentary society. That complex of relations may be divided into two main categories: one in which custom reigns almost absolutely, outside the control of the *sharīʿa*, with slight concessions in deference to the venue where the cases are heard, and one prominently displaying the impact of the *sharīʿa*, which wields assimilative power over custom. In the latter category, the *qāḍī*s play a decisive role. This is of course a schematic division; the differences between the two categories are sometimes blurred, as is to be expected in a transitional period.[2]

1. SUPREMACY OF CUSTOM OUTSIDE THE CONTROL OF THE *SHARĪʿA*

Custom is outside the scope of the sanctions of an institutionalized judicial system; it does not rely on the coercive power and execution proceedings of any authority. It relies on the consent of the parties and on social pressure, which exercises a kind of moral coercion. The *sharīʿa* is enforceable by an authority, but on the other hand it is perceived as an eternal revelation imposed on society from above and theoretically immutable. As against this, the legal norms of custom grow from the bottom upward and are therefore flexible, adaptable to the requirements of positive law according to changes in the environment and to social pressures. Milliot notes that in certain mountainous regions of North Africa custom was the only mechanism for the development of legal norms, and where the *sharīʿa* did not adapt itself with the necessary speed its place was taken by custom. Bousquet estimates that the Arabic-speaking population of North Africa, although in principle faithful to the *sharīʿa*, frequently adhered to customs conflicting with it and not recognized by the *sharīʿa* courts. In the Kabyle Mountains, custom was at times stronger than both the *sharīʿa* and French law, especially as the French courts did not enforce their judgments. The population preferred to litigate before tribal arbitrators and only turned to the *sharʿī qāḍī* as a last resort. The Beduin of the Judean Desert, who have largely become sedentary, still prefer tribal arbitration to the *sharīʿa* court. Moreover, even after proceedings before the *sharīʿa* court have begun, the

2. Cf. Layish & Shmueli, p. 31.

parties occasionally resort to tribal arbitration because of the efficiency of its proceedings, its sensitivity to justice in terms of a tribal society, and its intimate character. The *sharīʿa* court applies the *sharīʿa* too rigidly and strictly for their taste. The Jordanian Beduin, according to Oweidi, regard appearance before the state courts (civil as well as *sharʿī*) not only as too time-consuming but also as degrading. In their view, the judges represent an arbitrary authority opposed to their egalitarian philosophy.[3]

In fact, the Cyrenaican *sijill*s contain many and variegated instances of the supremacy of custom in divorce. Especially where the divorce does not involve legal proceedings, most of the causes are anchored in social custom: nonconsummation (either because of refusal by the wife or impotence of the husband); incompatibility due to differences in age, temper, social background, etc.; disobedience; adultery or suspected adultery of the wife; disputes between the spouses due to incitement or harassment by relatives; nonpayment of the dower and nondelivery of items connected with it such as clothing; and fears or defamatory reports about the wife's chastity in cases of the husband's absence. Common to all these factors is that they can be explained in terms of a traditional society in which the concepts of customary marriage, the primacy of agnates, and the chastity of women are basic. Thus, for instance, the wife's refusal to consummate the marriage or the nonpayment of the dower to the wife's agnate negates the *raison d'être* of the marriage transaction, in which the bride is the object and not a party. Support for some of those causes may be found in the *sharīʿa*, but it is doubtful whether the parties are aware of this. Divorce by *ṭalāq* out of court may be another manifestation of the supremacy of custom. Although even under the *sharīʿa* a *ṭalāq* divorce does not require legal proceedings for its validity, it should be borne in mind that this institution was adopted into the *sharīʿa* from custom and that sometimes many years elapse between the date of the divorce and its confirmation by a court, especially where a customary divorce formula or a *ẓihār* oath is used. This oath has indeed been incorporated into the *sharīʿa*; but, again, it is doubtful whether the Beduin are aware of this.

It seems that the terms of divorce by consent, which is the prevailing form of divorce, are usually determined out of court—that is to say, outside

3. Milliot, pp. 157–59, 165–66; Bousquet, *Islamic & customary law*, pp. 59–60; Bousquet, *Coutumes kabiles*, p. 125; Layish & Shmueli, p. 35; Oweidi, p. 181.

its control—although the court is resorted to *ex post facto* for reasons of legal security. Under such circumstances a divorce is part of an amicable settlement (*ṣulḥ*)—that is, a settlement not involving legal proceedings—and such settlements are negotiated according to the rules of customary law. Moreover, it is at times expressly stated that the settlement was reached without the intervention of the *qāḍī* or even that it was necessary to "overcome" his desperate attempts to reconcile the parties. One is impressed by the dominant position of the wife's agnates in divorce-by-consent proceedings. They initiate the divorce, negotiate the conditions of renunciation and compensation, undertake to compensate the husband out of their own pockets, and accept the divorce from his hands. They may even act against the wife's will as to the divorce itself or its conditions and may be guided by consideratons that have nothing to do with the wife. Even where it is noted that the wife herself conducted the negotiations on her redemption by *khulᶜ*, the role of the agnate in the proceedings and in financing the compensation points to his central position in those proceedings. As we shall see, the presentation of the wife as a party to the divorce proceedings may have to be interpreted as an attempt by the *qāḍī* to formulate custom in *sharᶜī* terms. True, the functions and liability of agnates in divorce by consent are formally anchored in a power of attorney or other *sharᶜī* document and reflect the coercive power (*jabr*) of the guardian according to the Mālikī school (in cases where the woman is a minor as to the disposal of property and especially where the marriage has not been consummated). Nevertheless, in substance and style they reflect the concept of marriage as a contract to which the bride is not a party; vestiges of that concept survive in the Mālikī school, although the general tendency in Islam is to discard that concept and make the wife a party to the marriage contract and the divorce proceedings. We have seen that in divorce by consent the parties occasionally seek to protect themselves against future claims of financial rights by stipulating that whichever of them raises such a claim shall be regarded as a *ẓālim*—not in the ethical-religious sense the term has taken on in Islam (sinner) but in a legal-customary sense (offender); that is to say that a ground for legal proceedings against that party shall be created. Similarly, some *khulᶜ* agreements, in the best tradition of customary agreements, require a guarantee (*kafāla*) by a person of means as security for the payment of compensation to the divorced woman's former husband upon her marriage to another man.

In Islamic law, too, the division of dower into prompt and deferred is a matter of practice, not of law. But such a division is regarded as "normative" provided that the deferred dower is paid at the time of the divorce or at death, whereas the deferred dower reflected in the *sijill*s is the part of the prompt dower that by advance agreement is to be paid at a later date while the marriage is still in existence and is anchored in "the custom of the people of the desert." This and similar expressions are frequent, especially in marriage contracts; there, too, they appear in connection with the dower. Thus in one case it was said that the son of a *faqīh* wished to marry a certain girl and paid a specified sum to her as dower: half of it was to be paid in two years and the remainder in ten years, "according to the custom of the desert dwellers, in the case of shame or absence (*ʿalā ʿayb aw ghayb*)." In another case it was said that the deferred part of the dower was to be paid "in the event of expiration [of the deadline] or death (*ʿalā fawt am mawt*)... which is one of their customs (*wa-dhālika min ʿawāʾidihim*)." In other words, the source of inspiration here is not the *sharīʿa*. In another case it was said that the deferred dower is "in accordance with the custom of the tribe" (*ka-ʿādat al-qabīla*).[4] In a case of a different kind the husband claimed the dower from the wife on the ground that "according to the custom prevailing in the desert (*al-ʿāda waʾl-ʿurf al-jārī fīʾl-bādiya*) the nearest kinsman takes it in order to protect it [from predatory attacks]."[5] "The custom of the desert" may appear also in other contexts than dower. Thus in one case a girl was affianced to a blood relation, who "spent what he spent [on her] in accordance with the custom of the desert (*ʿalā ʿādat*

4. AMR42–44, A5. p. 129 no. 129 10 Feb. 44, A3: p. 110 no. 110 30 Nov. 43, and A17: p. 94 no. 138 [?] Oct. 43, respectively. See also A5: p. 101 no. 101 16 Nov. 43 (*ʿādatuhum*) and A12: p. [?] no. 27/5 6 April 50 (*ka-ʿādat ahl al-balad*). On the possible meanings of the expression *ʿalā ʿayb aw ghayb* see p. 49, n. 25. Shaykh Mūsā Ḥasan al-ʿAṭāwna, of the Negev Beduin, knows the expression *ʿalā fawt am mawt* in connection with the payment of debts: a debt must be paid at the appointed time or, if the debtor dies earlier, upon his death, when it is paid out of his estate; the author is beholden to Dr. C. Bailey for this information. A similar rule exists in Islamic law: the normative deferred dower is payable upon divorce or death, "whichever is the earlier" (*li-aqrab al-ajalayn*). Analogously, the deferred dower in the customary sense is payable *during* the marriage, at the time agreed between the parties, unless the husband dies earlier, in which case it is payable out of his estate. Another possibility, suggested by the rhyme, is that one of the two terms is a dummy word—i.e., a meaningless word merely intended to supply the rhyme; in this case, the meaningful word would seem to be *mawt*. The author is indebted to Professor M. Piamenta for drawing his attention to this possibility.
5. A:E103, p. 94 no. 175 30 June 52.

al-bādiya) viz. the animals slaughtered for the wedding feast, etc." In another, similar case it was agreed between the spouses, upon divorce, that their nursling child should remain with his mother while his father should provide maintenance for him in a specified amount "according to the custom of the village dwellers" (*ka-ʿādat ahl al-balad*) until he was weaned. It is apparent that we have to do here with a matter of custom, not of religious law.[6]

Occasionally, custom is not only outside the control of the *sharīʿa* but in express opposition to it. The most impressive and most frequent instance is customary *khulʿ*—that is, compensation to the husband out of the dower received by the divorced wife upon her remarriage or (which is more serious from a *sharʿī* point of view) prohibition of remarriage so long as the dower has not been returned to the first husband, with the threat of sanctions (these, too, under customary law) against the person performing the marriage before compensation is paid. According to the *sharīʿa*, the freedom of remarriage of an irrevocably divorced woman is unlimited; her remarriage cannot be made conditional on the payment of a debt to her former husband. The source of inspiration of the linkage between remarriage and the payment of a debt is custom. This linkage is anchored in the concept of marriage as a contract to which the woman is not a party. Customary *khulʿ* is probably a structural solution in cases where the wife's guardian is in straitened circumstances, unable to compensate the husband forthwith for the annulment of the transaction (i.e., for the divorce); he undertakes to compensate the husband when things are easier—that is to say, when the woman, in a new transaction, is delivered to another husband. As a matter of fact, the *sharīʿa*, which adopted customary *khulʿ*, deviated from it by adapting the *khulʿ* mechanism to the norms resulting from the conversion of the woman into a party to the marriage contract: she is no longer an object of the transaction, and the dower is her property.

Other instances of custom conflicting with the *sharīʿa* are divorce by more than triple repudiation on a single occasion—which is, in a way, an expression of "rebellion" against the *sharīʿa*; the assignment of a woman's financial rights to her agnates rather than to herself as is required by the *sharīʿa* (this practice reflects the survival of the customary concept of

6. AP:E4, p. 73 no. 73 end of July 46; and KD59-73, K47: p. 182 no. 431 27 Jan. 64, respectively. Cf. *ḍarāʾib* among Awlād ʿAlī in Mohsen, *Conflict*, p. 18; Colucci, *Tribù*, pp. 24-25.

marriage); and finally—although this is a rare phenomenon—the reinstatement after the expiration of the waiting period, without a new marriage, of a woman divorced by revocable repudiation.

2. IMPACT OF THE *SHARĪʿA* ON SEDENTARY BEDUIN

a. Interaction of *Sharīʿa* and Custom

As stated, sedentarization brings the Beduin closer to normative Islam. The reasons for this transformation are numerous: the strengthening of the central government, which in turn strengthens the orthodox Muslim establishment; the enforcement of *sharʿī* jurisdiction on the Beduin, along with the abolition of institutionalized, statutory tribal jurisdiction; the spread of religious education (for instance, Jordanian Beduin *shaykh*s bring urban teachers of religion to their tribes and send their sons to town for religious studies); the geographical proximity to urban, religious, administrative, and economic centers; the contacts with pilgrims traversing Beduin centers on their way to holy places; and the modern means of communication (radio, TV). The decline of tribal organization entails an increased importance of the extended family as an economic unit and a framework for socialization. Islam adopted the pre-Islamic patrilineal, patriarchal, and patrilocal Arab family. These characteristics are given exact expression in Muslim personal status law while softened and refined by religious-ethical norms. The sedentarization of the Beduin thus narrows the gap between custom and *sharīʿa* in the family.[7]

In fact, alongside instances of the supremacy of custom, the *sijill*s contain instances of the impact of the *sharīʿa* on sedentary tribal society. These instances cover a wide gamut of degrees: from a compromise between *sharīʿa* and custom (i.e., the adjustment of custom to *sharʿī* norms by various devices) to the enforcement of *sharʿī* norms, with all their effect and validity. Customary *khulʿ* in some of its manifestations strikingly illustrates various nuances of interaction between *sharīʿa* and custom. Slight concessions by custom to the *sharīʿa* may be seen in cases where a father guarantees possible financial claims of his daughter against her husband. According to custom the wife is not a party to the divorce proceedings; but since, according to the *sharīʿa*, she may demand her rights as a divorced woman in

7. Layish & Shmueli, pp. 31, 41; Layish, *Sharīʿa u-minhag*, pp. 377–78 and the sources indicated there; Layish, *Challenges*, p. 220; Oweidi, p. 149.

court, perhaps under the guidance of the *qāḍī*, her father is required to secure her claims. Similarly, those cases in which it is said that the dower is delivered to the wife and her father together may be regarded as a compromise between *sharīʿa* and custom, reflecting a combination of two legally and socially opposed philosophies. The obligation to compensate the divorcer before the reading of the *Fātiḥa* introduces a Muslim element into a customary context. The reading of the *Fātiḥa* is usual also in customary marriages, and the application of the Muslim sanction is designed to validate them in *sharʿī* respect.[8]

Cases in which a woman makes her marriage to another man conditional on compensation being paid to her first husband reflect a somewhat bizarre coexistence of two legal norms: the substance (the compensation arrangement) reflects a custom anchored in the concept of marriage as a contract to which the woman is not a party, whereas the woman's being an apparently full-fledged party to the arrangement reflects the *sharʿī khulʿ*, anchored in the view that the woman is a party to the marriage contract. The same applies also in cases in which the woman includes an agnate in the *khulʿ* agreement, either because of difficulties in putting up the compensation or for some other reason; again, the financial arrangement is purely customary, but it is apparently the woman and not the agnate who conducts the negotiations and who alone, in the legal-technical respect, is responsible for the husband's compensation. These cases, and all the more cases in which cognates appear beside the woman, may be said to represent a transitional stage between customary *khulʿ* and *sharʿī khulʿ*. This stage preserves authentic vestiges of the customary institution, by which the first husband is compensated with the dower of the second, even after the *sharʿī* concept, according to which the woman is a party to the marriage contract, has been adopted. When the woman exercises her competance to own property under the *sharīʿa*, one might expect the application of *sharʿī khulʿ* in the full sense of the term. But the many instances of *khulʿ* in the *sijill*s do not indicate the woman's competence to own property. We have to do here with *sharʿī khulʿ* in a technical sense only. One may conclude only that the wife's agnates are capable of compensating the husband on the spot and do not have to resort to the mechanism of customary *khulʿ*.

A further instance of coexistence are the numerous *khulʿ* agreements that stereotypically give as the reason for the divorce that "no intimate

8. Cf. Layish & Shmueli, p. 33.

association, such as is expected between spouses, was established" (*wa-lam tanṭaẓim baynahumā al-ʿishra* [or: *al-muʿāshara*] *al-maṭlūba baynaʾl-azwāj sharʿan wa-ʿādatan*).[9] Sometimes—and typically in the 1960s—the customary norm (*ʿādatan*) is dispensed with; that is to say, the *sharīʿa* reigns supreme, at least in the view of the *qāḍī* who formulates the decision.[10]

The *sijill*s indicate various mechanisms designed to facilitate the absorption of customary practices into the *sharʿī* framework. The application of suspended *khulʿ* on the husband's initiative, especially where the spouses are far apart, is designed to encourage the wife, or more exactly her agnates, to waive financial rights and compensate the husband for the grant of the wife's freedom. This mechanism gives formal, institutionalized expression to a practice prevailing in such cases. It is further usual under such circumstances to apply the *sharʿī* mechanism of divorce by means of a letter (*risāla, jawāb*); the Mālikī school is the most liberal in permitting this technique. Similarly, the appointment of a proxy (*wakīl*) or representative (*nāʾib*) by the court to represent the wife for the purposes of the divorce and the regulation of her financial claims, sometimes against her will, institutionalizes and validates in the *sharʿī* context a tendency anchored in custom to deny women status in the relevant proceedings. Mohsen notes that the marriage customs (*darāʾib*) of the Awlād ʿAlī in the Western Desert are based on the *sharīʿa*, with slight variations intended to adapt them to the requirements of the local way of life.[11] Whether this appraisal of the situation reflects the actual reality or whether it is more correct to say that the marriage is based on custom with slight concessions to the *sharīʿa* in order to preserve the latter's nominal supremacy, at any rate we have to do here with interaction, or a compromise between *sharīʿa* and custom.

b. Supremacy of the *Sharīʿa*

Express manifestations of the impact of the *sharīʿa* may be seen in the application of various legal institutions that in part were adopted from custom but have long since assumed a pronounced *sharʿī* character and in part are *sharʿī* innovations without any basis in custom, or even reflect norms expressly opposed to customary practice. These manifestations

9. E.g., KAMD, p. 29 no. 11 16 Feb. 34; KD59–73, K44: p. 2 no. 4 21 June 59.
10. E.g., KD59–73, p. 105 nos. 220–21 5 Jan. 62.
11. Mohsen, *Conflict*, p. 83. Cf. Colucci, *Tribù*, p. 24.

consist in grounds for dissolution by legal proceedings (such as nonprovision of maintenance; absence of the husband and the resulting fear for the wife's chastity; the application—although to no great extent—of sophisticated *sharʿī* mechanisms for dissolution on the wife's initiative in unilateral *ṭalāq* divorces, and especially suspended repudiation (*taʿlīq al-ṭalāq*) and delegated repudiation (*tafwīḍ al-ṭalāq*). Although the *ṭalāq* is a customary institution adopted by the *sharīʿa*, the sophistication intended to give status to the wife in this proceeding is probably inspired by the *sharīʿa* alone. The resort, to a significant extent, to judicial divorce—which has achieved refinement in the Mālikī school but is not recognized at all in customary law—is another expression of the supremacy of the *sharīʿa*. Although that school, too, assumes that this mechanism is based on the husband's right of *ṭalāq* (which has been vested in the court), the deviation from customary practice consists in the very resort to legal proceedings, even if the distinction between the different grounds for the application of that mechanism is frequently blurred. The only customary element left over is the dissolution by arbitrators on the ground of injury to the wife; but surprisingly enough it is precisely this mechanism that is not applied in court.

Perhaps the most impressive manifestation of the impact of the *sharīʿa*—qualitatively if not quantitatively—is the application of the legal consequences of the divorce. Some of their more important expressions are explicit departures from the customary norm: revocable divorce is frequent and fairly common though not preponderant (even if it may actually be more frequent than would appear from the *sijill*s); it is applied not only in *ṭalāq* divorces, but also in judicial divorce on the ground of nonprovision of maintenance. At the same time, there are only a few isolated instances of reinstatement during the waiting period, which is the principal *raison d'être* and purpose of revocable divorce. Moreover, revocable divorce is sometimes applied in distorted fashion—namely, after the expiration of the waiting period. In everyday reality, minor irrevocable divorce predominates in unilateral *ṭalāq* divorces; revocable divorce sometimes becomes irrevocable because the husband's right of reinstatement during the waiting period has not been exercised. In the case of irrevocable divorce, the marriage is usually rehabilitated by a new marriage tie and a new dower (as required by the *sharīʿa*), although financial accounts are sometimes carried forward from one marriage to the other. Major irrevocable divorce is common though not particularly frequent. The counting of divorces up to the third, and the triple divorce "in one word" (although the latter is reprehensible—*ṭalāq al-bidʿa*—according to religious-legal literature), are notable evidence of the enforcement of the *sharʿī* norm in court—or at least of an awareness of the matter. The lack of any reference to an intermediate marriage with intent to render the divorced wife permitted again to her first husband (*bi-qaṣd al-taḥlīl*)—if indeed the lack of such a reference reflects the actual state of things—suggests that there is no attempt to adapt this mechanism to customary practice. Such attempts are known to have been made in regions where the Ḥanafī school prevails. The reason for the absence of such attempts may be the moralistic attitude of the Mālikī school, which attaches importance to the element of intent (*niyya*).

It seems that, as a rule, the population resorting to the court strictly observes the waiting period (the *sijill*s mention only one exception, but there may in fact be more). At any rate, even if the rules of the *sharīʿa* relating to the legal consequences of divorce are applied in distorted fashion and the rules of *ṭalāq al-sunna* are not strictly adhered to, the very resort to the *sharīʿa* in this matter is extremely significant in the context of our study. Thus, for instance, even in those cases in which a woman is divorced by more than triple repudiation, the very reference to the number of repudiations is significant in appraising the impact of the *sharīʿa* on a tribal society in process of sedentarization.

The impact of the *sharīʿa* reveals itself also in the field of the financial rights of the divorced woman. It seems that, as a rule, she enjoys the right to maintenance during (but not beyond) the waiting period in revocable divorce, whether or not she is pregnant, and in irrevocable divorce if it is found *ex post facto* that she is pregnant, provided that the divorce is initiated by the husband. The same also applies to the woman's *sharʿī* right to suckling wages and to the maintenance of minor children during the custody period, although the latter right may have a basis in customary law as well; even where she redeems herself by *khulʿ* in return for financial rights, she does not give up her right to suckling wages. One also finds, to a significant extent, that the woman realizes her *sharʿī* right to the dower or, where she received part of it during the marriage, the balance thereof; but again, this applies only if the divorce was initiated by the husband. Moreover, even in divorce by consent—which is the prevailing form of divorce and one in which the wife and her agnates bear the main burden of the financial consequences—it is not impossible that the husband pays all or part of what the wife is entitled to according to the *sharīʿa*.

Other instances of the impact of the *sharīʿa* may be seen in resort to the *sharīʿa* court where the matter in dispute has in fact been settled out of court by agreement between the parties—not in accordance with the *sharīʿa* and sometimes in diametrical opposition to it, although the parties may not be aware of this. Thus occasionally when a customary *khulʿ* agreement is submitted for the *qāḍī*'s approval, the wife's father undertakes that if she should claim something contrary to what has been agreed between him and her husband, he will be responsible "to the esteemed court" (*amām al-sharʿ al-sharīf*) as to that claim. In view of the possibility that the wife rejects the custom-based agreement and claims from her husband her *sharʿī* rights as a divorced woman, her father is prepared to assume the obligation to indemnify the husband as to any claim likely to upset the agreement between them. In other words, he is prepared to retreat from custom to the *sharīʿa*. The very resort to the court in these circumstances attests to the desire of the parties to rely on the judicial competence of the *qāḍī* in order to support the customary compensation agreement by *sharʿī* and statutory sanctions. In the absence of agreement between the parties, the court is sometimes expected to assist in settling financial claims between them, and there is no reason to assume that the parties are not aware of the court's being guided by *sharʿī* norms.

Although the sacral aura enveloping the court and the religious sanctions of its judgments should not be underestimated,[12] it seems that the Beduin are not attracted to the court by reflection and careful consideration or by their formal subordination to it; they apply to it for practical reasons and owing to civil exigencies. A declaratory judgment as to a divorce out of court is required for reasons of legal security; a formal change of marital status is needed, especially by a divorced woman who wishes to remarry; and financial claims between spouses must be settled upon confirmation of the divorce to prevent future claims and to enable the enforcement of the terms of the divorce agreement upon the party neglecting to do his or her part. Paradoxically, it is precisely constraints unconnected with the *sharīʿa* that play an important role in the *sharʿī* indoctrination of the Beduin—a situation of which perhaps not everybody is aware. Colucci notes that the Beduin of Cyrenaica treat the *sharīʿa* as an auxilary source of law, to which they resort in the absence of a customary norm fitting the circumstances of

12. Cf. Milliot, p. 159.

the case or where customs conflict with each other and a decision must be taken between them.[13]

It is characteristic of this transition stage in the sedentarization of the Beduin that they resort simultaneously to the customary and the *sharʿī* mechanism. It thus seems that the various kinds of divorce by consent are performed out of court, probably with the assistance of mediators and arbitrators familiar with customary law, and that when consent has been achieved the husband repudiates the wife and thereafter appears with her in court, where he again repudiates her in the presence of the *qāḍī*, who confirms the divorce and the financial conditions connected with it. It is interesting to note that in the Judean Desert the parties occasionally appoint arbitrators for the express purpose of preparing the ground (*tamhīdan*) for the settlement of the dispute before the *sharīʿa* court. The arbitrators propose the desired arrangement, expecting the court to give it the legitimacy of a *sharʿī* judgment. At times, there is even cooperation for this purpose between the customary arbitrator and the *qāḍī*.[14] Moreover, the arbitrators sometimes on their own initiative refer the parties to the *sharīʿa* court to complete the legal process. The Beduin resort to a *sharʿī* decision for reasons of legal security. An arbitral award is not a judgment in the conventional sense but an opinion supported by the personal authority and prestige of the arbitrator. It is of course fortified by guarantees and fines, but it is not enforceable by an official authority. The authority of the arbitrators arises from the consent of the parties, without which the award will not be given effect. At any rate, it binds only the parties, not any third party. A *sharʿī qāḍī* can set aside an arbitral award if it is not consistent with the *sharīʿa* as interpreted by him. In other words, the ability of the arbitrator to compete with the institutionalized *qāḍī* is diminishing because the latter relies on statute and has at his disposal various kinds of sanctions to enforce his judgments. This is of course the main source of the *qāḍī*'s power of attraction and the source of the arbitrator's weakness in the eyes of present-day Beduin. In northern Nigeria customary arbitration with all its characteristics, including the imposition of fines, was common in the preindependence period. District officers did not consider that institution legal in the sense of "native law and custom" but were unable to uproot it. In preponderantly pagan areas

13. Colucci, *Tribù*, p. 24. Cf. Layish, *Islamization*, pp. 39–40.
14. Layish & Shmueli, p. 44.

there was sometimes, for reasons of administrative convenience, a strange combination of a *qāḍī* and pagan assessors on one bench. In the Western Desert, tribal arbitrators and civil courts operate side by side; sometimes the same matter is heard by both kinds of courts concurrently, and the offender is punished twice for the same offence.[15]

An instance of a different kind of the impact of the *sharīʿa* may perhaps be seen in the use of the term *jawāb* to denote a letter by which a husband who is far away divorces his wife. This term may indeed be found in the ordinary meaning of "answer"—for example, where someone, in court, asks another a question concerning a marriage and the latter answers (*ajāba*) it. But it is not impossible that the letter is called *jawāb* in the sense of *fatwā*, in accordance with popular usage in tribal society, the reason being that, as noted earlier, it was probably drawn up by a *faqīh*.[16] There is no evidence that the parties resort to the religious-legal opinion of a *muftī*, who is also of course an essential agent of *sharʿī* indoctrination; but the *sijill*s are probably not an appropriate source of such evidence. On the other hand the documents of the Beduin of the Judean Desert contain evidence of resort to Shāfiʿī *muftī*s, who are to extricate them from difficulties caused by triple repudiation. The Beduin asks the *muftī* to find a way to release his wife from the duty of intermediate marriage as a means to render her again permitted to him, and the *muftī* does so in reliance on the element of intent and other devices. The regional *sharīʿa* court cannot help in this matter because it is bound by the Ḥanafī school, which attaches no importance to the element of intent.[17] The moralistic Mālikī school, which prevails in Cyrenaican *sharīʿa* courts, attaches importance to that element; but there is no evidence that the *qāḍī*s use it to neutralize the harshness of triple repudiation, and it is therefore to be expected that people adversely affected by such a repudiation will seek relief in the opinion of a Mālikī *muftī*.

What is the impact of modern Libyan statutory legislation, ostensibly anchored in the *sharīʿa*, upon a population resorting to the court? Such legislation is not particularly extensive compared with that of other North African or Middle Eastern countries; but some of its innovations are rather

15. Layish & Shmueli, pp. 44–45 and the sources indicated there; Schacht, *Nigeria*, pp. 126–28; Schacht, *Report*, p. 9; Mohsen, *Conflict*, pp. 15–16, 31–35.
16. AP:E4, p. 73 no. 73 end of July 46. See above, p. 41.
17. Layish, *Islamization*, pp. 50ff.

far-reaching. As far as can be judged from the documents of the period up to the abolition of the *sharīʿa* courts in November 1973, those innovations have made no impact, probably because the public has not yet become aware of them or has found them difficult to digest. From what happens in other Arab countries, one may gain the impression that the population tends to ignore reforms in matters of personal status insofar as they are inconsistent with everyday practice—in other words, that custom is stronger not only than the *sharīʿa* but also than statutory legislation. According to Schacht, Nigerian *ʿulamāʾ* wondered how *qāḍī*s in Egypt and other countries could be willing to apply statutory legislation superseding the *sharīʿa*; a *qāḍī* would rarely agree to impose restrictions on a man's right to repudiate his wife. The Nigerian *ʿulamāʾ* were zealous adherents of the Mālikī school and were not prepared to adopt elements of other schools. They also opposed moderate administrative measures, on the ground that they conflicted with the pure *sharīʿa*. In Israel, Knesset legislation has contributed to a significant improvement in the status of women—especially by means of penal sanctions but also through substantive provisions—although such legislation has not been the only reason for the improvement of women's status.[18]

3. ROLE OF THE *QĀḌĪ* IN ISLAMIZATION

The role of the *qāḍī* is decisive in the Islamization of a Beduin population resorting to the *sharīʿa* court. The *qāḍī*, unlike the *muftī* entrenched in the ivory tower of the religious-legal establishment, is directly and constantly confronted with such a population; his ability to display a tolerant attitude toward custom, to compromise with it while adopting and absorbing it into the *sharīʿa*, may create a favourable climate for the resort of a custom-bound population to a *sharʿī* judicial authority and ultimately bring it within the orbit of the *sharīʿa*. On the other hand a *qāḍī*'s uncompromising effort to enforce the *sharīʿa* in letter and spirit, regardless of the modest Islamic equipment of those applying to the court, may turn the Beduin population away from its jurisdiction. There is ample evidence that when the *sharīʿa*, represented by its exponents, proved unable to join forces with Berber particularism and adapt itself to changing social circumstances, it met with insurmountable opposition in its practical application. In

18. Schacht, *Nigeria*, p. 139; Layish, *Maḥkama*, xiii, pp. 40ff.; Layish, *Women*, pp. 327-31.

northern Nigeria the *qāḍīs*' disregard of local custom was found to cause real hardship. Their attempt to enforce the *sharīʿa* strictly on population groups whose Islamization was merely nominal and who were attached to local custom led to the rejection of court decisions and sometimes even to avoidance of the courts. In other words, the population accepted the decisions only insofar as such decisions agreed with the customary norm. Similarly, the Jordanian Beduin have found ways to circumvent the judgments of the *sharʿī* (and civil) courts when these do not come up to their custom-inspired expectations; the authorities have in fact used administrative devices to bridge the gap between the *sharīʿa* and those expectations. The *qāḍīs* to whom the Beduin of the Judean Desert are amenable are aware that a strict, uncompromising application of the *sharīʿa* sometimes inflicts unendurable hardship on the community.[19] How do the Cyrenaican *qāḍīs* react to the challenging task of winning for the *sharīʿa* the Beduin in process of sedentarization? Several tendencies can be distinguished here.[20]

a. Reconciliation with Custom

Although it is inconceivable that the *qāḍīs* should not be aware of the fundamental distinction between *sharīʿa* and custom, they do not always give expression to this awareness, and a distant observer may wonder why this is so. Thus, for instance, the dependence of the remarriage of a woman divorced by customary *khulʿ* on compensation to the first husband out of the dower received by her agnate from the second husband, let alone the prohibition of remarriage so long as such compensation has not been paid, are in flagrant contradiction to the *sharīʿa*, since nonpayment of the compensation is not a *sharʿī* impediment to remarriage. Moreover, the commercial-legal connection between the two husbands makes sense only under customary law, which involves the concept of marriage as a contract to which the bride is not a party; the court confirms the security safeguarding the implementation of the customary *khulʿ* agreement, including the guarantee (*kafāla*) anchored in customary law. On the face of it, the *qāḍīs* are not aware that the customary *khulʿ* contradicts the *sharīʿa*; they refer to it as a *khulʿ* in all respects and treat the agreement making

19. Milliot, p. 166; Schacht, *Report*, p. 9; Schacht, *Nigeria*, p. 128; Oweidi, pp. 88–89; Layish, *Challenges*, p. 221; Layish, *Women*, p. 334; Layish, *Sharīʿa u-minhag*, pp. 407ff.
20. Cf. Layish, *Challenges*, p. 218.

the remarriage conditional on the payment of compensation as part of the *sharʿī* judgment.

It seems that the *qāḍīs*, in their practice, are guided by the principle that the agreement between the parties validates custom. Thus, for instance, they have adopted the "customary" deferred dower—that part of the prompt dower the payment of which is deferred by consent of the parties to some date during the marriage, although the normative prompt dower is expected to be paid before the consummation of the marriage, since non-payment in this case is a ground for disobedience of the wife to the husband without her losing the right to maintenance. But it seems that the rule guiding the *qāḍīs* is that the dower is a matter of custom, not of law, and that custom in turn relies on the consent of the parties. The *qāḍīs* adapt their decisions to differences in custom from one place to another. Thus the court in Tripoli relied on local custom when declaring that in that town (and in other places) no account was to be taken of injury (*ḍarar*) caused to the property or person of the wife for the first time or of rebelliousness (*nushūz*) of the wife as a ground for divorce. We have also seen that the concept of "sleeping embryo," anchored in custom (and in the Mālikī school), is accepted by the *qāḍīs*. The reference to local custom is sometimes anchored in law. The Muslim Court of Appeal (Chambre de révision musulmane) in Algeria frequently quashed *sharʿī* judgments because they were based on local custom rather than on the *sharīʿa*.[21]

It seems that the *qāḍīs* respect the agreement even if the custom in which it is anchored conflicts with the *sharīʿa*. This is the probable explanation of their practice of confirming the customary *khulʿ* agreement even if it appears in the proceedings that an express *sharʿī* norm has been disregarded—for example, that upon a woman's marriage to another man her father intends to take her dower, which is her property according to the *sharīʿa*, and to compensate her first husband with it. Sometimes the court is instrumental in executing agreements contrary to the *sharīʿa*. Thus, for instance, it confirms a power of attorney given by a person to his proxy to collect compensation from the husband of his former wife who was divorced by customary *khulʿ*, and even to sue him for it, although the husband is not a party to the *khulʿ* agreement and the suit should have been brought against the woman. Similarly, the court volunteers its statutory judicial power to enable the execution of a customary *khulʿ*

21. d'Emilia, p. 42 n. 1, p. 50; Charnay, p. 286.

agreement by prescribing, as part of the conditions of the agreement, that the compensation shall be paid "by means of the *sharīʿa* court before the reading of the *Fātiḥa*"—that is to say, before the remarriage of the divorced woman. The court thereby becomes a full partner in a deviation from the *sharīʿa*; it even uses its power to impose sanctions on the marriage solemnizer, although nonpayment of the compensation is no bar to the remarriage.

It thus seems that the *qāḍī*s' concept is that the mutual agreement, anchored by the nature of things in customary practice, is stronger then any other, even a *sharʿī* legal norm. Indeed, their principal concern when about to confirm agreements is that these agreements shall have been achieved voluntarily. A fitting expression of this concept is given by Israeli *qāḍī*s in the context of customary *khulʿ*: "The mutual agreement prevails over the *qāḍī*" (*al-tarāḍi yaghlib al-qāḍī*). Analyzing the secret of the strength of custom unsupported by legal sanctions in the conventional sense or by enforcement through an institutionalized legal system, Milliot explains that the consent on which custom is based creates a moral-psychological constraint even before being given material expression. Legal consent consists not only in contractual consent; customary consent, too, is a form of legal consent. The tribal arbitrators in the Judean Desert, whose judicial status is not anchored in statute, derive their authority solely from the consent of the parties.[22] It seems that this concept of mutual consent underlies also the *qāḍī*s' efforts to end disputes between parties by an amicable settlement (*ṣulḥ*) not involving legal proceedings; they sometimes invoke religious sanctions (*sammāhu allāh khayran*) for this purpose. It is interesting to note in this connection that the *qāḍī* of Bethlehem, who has jurisdiction over the Beduin of the Judean Desert, holds that "reconciliation is stronger than the *qāḍī*" (*al-ṣulḥ aqwā minaʾl-qāḍī*). In fact, a settlement is frequently reached by the mediation of tribal *shaykh*s. Moreover, the *qāḍī* sometimes refers the parties to an arbitrator and gives *sharʿī* effect to the arbitral award. The arbitrator supplies the substance and the *qāḍī* the form (*ṣīgha*). Davis describes a case among the Zuwaya tribes of Cyrenaica in which agreement was reached concerning compensation for assault. Afterward all the people involved recited the *Fātiḥa* together, under the direction of a *sharīf* (descendant of Muḥammad), and on Friday they met in the mosque and demanded the amount of the compensation from the family

22. Milliot, p. 159; Layish & Shmueli, p. 44.

of the assailant. In northern Nigeria, Schacht came across an instance of Muslim-pagan syncretism: an attempt by *qāḍīs* to reinforce a qurʾānic sanction by a pagan one. As the Muslims, whose Islamization had not yet been completed, would perjure themselves on the Qurʾān, the chief *qāḍī* would, immediately after they were sworn on the Qurʾān, swear them on the Chain of Tsoede, which has been sacred to them since the pagan period that preceded the Muslim Fulani movement.[23]

In Cyrenaica, instances can still be found of attempts to enlist sanctions accompanying saint worship to discover the truth in a judicial proceeding that was in part conducted outside the control of the court, although probably with its knowledge and tacit consent. Thus a woman with the status of a *zaʿlāna* (an ill-tempered woman) alleged that her pregnancy was not by her husband although she admitted having had relations with him even while not at his house. To establish the truth, a middleman familiar with custom and the Sanūsī *ṭarīqa* (order) was instructed to investigate the matter. He summoned the woman to his house, pointed out some object to her that belonged to the saint (*sīdī*) Jibrīl and warned her to tell nothing but the truth. It seems that the saint's sanction had the desired effect: three days later the woman admitted that she was pregnant by her husband. The enlistment of saints' sanctions is, as one would expect, usual in other parts of Africa as well. The Awlād ʿAlī, who also are adherents of the Sanūsiyya, are still convinced of the ability of the *murābiṭūn biʾl-baraka*, whom they believe to be in direct communion with supernatural powers, to harm those who offend them. Therefore, and because of their neutral position among the tribes, they play an important role in mediation and the settlement of disputes. Mohsen describes a case of homicide heard before a *shaykh* of the *murābiṭūn* whom everyone treated with reverence and fear, believing that after his death he would be a saint (*walī*). In another case the devotees of a certain saint gathered round his grave for the administration of an oath. According to tribal custom in the area concerned, where a person required to take an oath refuses to appear at the saint's grave, the case is automatically decided against him, and collective oaths of compurgation are taken at saints' graves in cases of murder, with a view to benefiting from their sanctions. The cult of saints and attempts to benefit from their blessings (*baraka*) were also observed in northern

23. Layish, *Challenges*, p. 218; Layish, *Shariʿa u-minhag*, pp. 400–401; Layish, *Women*, pp. 198, 333; Davis, *Politics*, pp. 225–26; Schacht, *Nigeria*, p. 129; Schacht, *Report*, p. 9.

Nigeria, although the object of the Fulani movement was to eradicate customs conflicting with pure, normative Islam.[24]

We have seen that conciliation is guided by a longstanding tradition of arbitration and mediation rooted in customary law and perhaps also by a desire to avoid the application of the *sharīʿa* as much as possible lest it be distorted. The question of a possible contradiction between *sharīʿa* and custom obviously does not arise in the case of conciliation efforts aimed at avoiding dissolution. It may arise in a divorce case. But when a divorce agreement has been reached the *qāḍī*s do not interfere with its substance even if its particulars are inconsistent with, or downright contrary to, the *sharʿī* norm. Thus, for instance, the court will give the effect of a *sharʿī* judgment to a divorce agreement that deprives the wife by denying her financial rights under the *sharīʿa* and by confirming her renunciation of the maintenance of minor children in her custody—although this renunciation is ineffective according to the Mālikī school. Only in the absence of an agreement between the parties does the *qāḍī* take care to specify the rights of the divorced woman, which indicates that an agreement is stronger than the *sharīʿa*.

It is significant in this context that the *qāḍī* uses the term *ajāza* (permit), common in cases of *ṣulḥ* agreements in civil disputes, to confirm agreements in matters of divorce. Such agreements are generally achieved out of court, without the intervention of the *qāḍī*; and, as is to be expected, they are anchored in customary practice. The court uses the *ṣulḥ* mechanism also where it experiences difficulty in controlling the application of the *sharʿī* norm. Thus, for instance, where it is not possible to verify the plea that the wife has been divorced by revocable repudiation, the *qāḍī* has the husband testify to that effect and confirms the reinstatement of the wife without a new marriage tie—as if this were part of an amicable settlement of the dispute. All the *qāḍī* seems to have to do is to permit such settlement, as in fact he does (*ajāza al-ṣulḥ*). Sometimes, one may even gain the impression that the *qāḍī* upholds the *sharʿī* norm by virtue of the mutual consent and not by its own right. Thus, for instance, in renunciation divorces he requires the divorcing husband and the representative of the wife to grant or return, as the case may be, financial rights of the wife—not because they are anchored in the *sharīʿa* but by

24. AP:E2, p. [189] no. [186/7] 16 Feb. 48; Mohsen, *Conflict*, pp. 25-26, 58-59, 131-32, 136-37; Schacht, *Nigeria*, pp. 135-36. Cf. Coulson, *History*, pp. 93-94.

virtue of the agreement between the parties. Charnay notes that the Algerian *qāḍī* was engaged in mediation rather than in adjudication: "facilite une transaction plus qu'il n'impose sa décision (jugement: *ḥukm*)." Bousquet, too, notes the readiness of North African *qāḍī*s to put up with instances of the supremacy of custom in the *sharīʿa* court although theoretically they are supposed to apply the *sharīʿa* strictly. This phenomenon is universal and has been observed in other regions as well.[25]

b. Absorption of Custom into the *Sharīʿa*

Besides passive reconciliation of the *qāḍī*s with custom, there is evidence of attempts by them to contend with it—from efforts to adapt it to the *sharʿī* venue whilst compromising with it, to its complete absorption into the *sharīʿa*. There is evidence of *qāḍī*s being alive to the contradiction between custom and *sharīʿa* and seeking a way to blur that contradiction by couching custom in *sharʿī* terms. Thus in *khulʿ* divorces, and especially in customary *khulʿ*, it is not certain that the wife is a full-fledged party to the proceedings in the sense that she conducts the negotiations herself and compensates the husband personally, as would seem to appear from the *sijill*s. It is more probable that her agnate is concerned with these proceedings. It seems therefore that the attribution of the *khulʿ* to the wife is the share of the *qāḍī*, who wishes to formulate the divorce proceedings in a manner compatible with the *sharīʿa*. His intervention consists in smoothing and polishing custom so as to adapt it as much as possible to the *sharʿī* norm. But as noted earlier, this practice is not followed consistently, so that divorce proceedings sometimes present an odd combination of the wife and her agnate as a compromise between the requirements of the *sharīʿa* and custom, although it is not inconceivable that these cases in fact reflect a transition stage between customary and *sharʿī khulʿ*.

Similarly, it is not certain that the agnates in fact renounce various financial rights and compensate the husband *in the wife's name* or undertake to cover any possible claim *by her* out of their pocket. This practice agrees with the *sharʿī* norm, but it is doubtful whether a tribal population is aware of this norm. In a society amenable to customary law, agnates operate by their own right and not by the right of the woman. Financial claims of the wife, who according to the customary concept of marriage is not a party to the contract but rather its object, are not

25. Charnay, p. 276; Bousquet, *Islamic & customary law*, pp. 59–60. Cf. Rosen, pp. 232ff.

relevant at all in this context. The *qāḍī*, who is aware of the true situation, probably wishes to validate the customary proceedings by couching them in terms fitting the *sharīʿa*, under which the woman is a party to the marriage contract. It is significant in this context that in the case of customary *khulʿ* the *qāḍī* instructs the agnate to settle out of his own pocket any financial claim to which the wife will be "entitled to make under the *sharīʿa*" (*tastaḥiqquhu sharʿan*), or which "will be validly proved" (*yuthbat lahā sharʿan*), if such a claim is made in spite of the agreement between the parties. Similarly the *qāḍī*, under an agreement between the parties, will anchor the wife's financial rights in a *sharʿī* sanction. The *qāḍī* will direct that proof (*ḥujja*) of the wife's financial claims be produced before he confirms them and will require the divorcer to settle them "so long as she is legally (*sharʿan*) entitled to make them." The frequent references to the *sharʿī* norm, even where the substance is purely customary, may be regarded as *sharʿī* indoctrination.

In several cases in which a wife was divorced by more than triple repudiation at one session, apparently by way of a *façon de parler*, the *qāḍī* disregarded the deviation from the *sharʿī* norm, which recognizes an upper limit of three repudiations at one session; he mechanically recorded the number of repudiations, adding the earlier repudiations, and decided that the woman had to undergo an intermediate marriage before being legally permitted again to her former husband. These cases are evidence that the *qāḍī*s are prepared to put up with customs based on deviations from the norm so long as it is possible to preserve the nominal supremacy of the *sharīʿa*. Bousquet notes that in some North African regions, such as the Kabyle Mountains, where it was not possible to enforce the *sharīʿa* and reject custom, the *qāḍī*s were faced with the alternative of yielding to local particularism or achieving a practical compromise between the two legal norms, and it seems that a compromise was reached with the object of preserving some of the supremacy of the *sharīʿa*. This phenomenon has also been observed by Anderson. He found that in regions in which the *sharīʿa* enjoyed a comparatively firm position, making its strict application possible, an attempt was sometimes made at a reconciliation, though a superficial one, between the *sharīʿa* and custom by means of some device (*ḥīla*) the main purpose of which was to preserve the nominal supremacy of the *sharīʿa*.[26]

26. Bousquet, *Islamic & customary law*, p. 65; Anderson, *Africa*, p. 378; Schacht, *Introduction*, pp. 78ff.

c. Adjustment of the *Sharīʿa* to Social Reality

Besides the adjustment of custom to the *sharʿī* ambience, the decisions of the *qāḍī*s contain instances of the application of social considerations. Thus there can be no doubt that the *qāḍī*s' attempts at reconciliation between the spouses following disputes threatening to break up the marriage are guided by concern for the welfare of the parties. When about to confirm dissolution because of nonprovision of maintenance by an absent husband, the *qāḍī* is guided, *inter alia*, by social considerations that indeed have been institutionalized as *sharʿī* grounds: economic distress and fear for the wife's chastity. The marriage of a minor girl who cannot consummate the marriage is, in the eyes of the *qāḍī*, a ground for dissolution, although the *sharīʿa* does not recognize an age limit for marriage (perhaps the *qāḍī* is impressed by the complaint of the husband's relatives, who regard themselves as cheated).

Where the term expressing divorce is not accompanied by a term expressing finality or triplicity, the *qāḍī*s—unless otherwise agreed between the parties—regard the first and the second divorce as revocable; and although this practice finds some support in the *sharīʿa*, it seems that their inclination toward leniency is guided by the interest of the parties. In one exceptional case the *qāḍī* approved the remarriage of a divorced woman without—as was his wont—insisting on observance of the waiting period; but this was done because the woman wished to remarry the man who had divorced her. As already stated, this is permitted even in the case of a minor irrevocable divorce.

Clearer evidence of the *qāḍī*s' openness to social considerations is provided by cases where the rate of the maintenance of a divorced woman was fixed with reference to her pregnancy or to her husband's difficult economic position. Occasionally, the *qāḍī* orders the husband to pay maintenance to the wife even for the period that he "neglected" (*ahmala*) her at her father's house *before* the divorce, although she is not entitled to maintenance retroactively.

It must of course be borne in mind that the social considerations guiding the Cyrenaican *qāḍī*s do not necessarily conflict with the *sharīʿa* and are sometimes even supported by it, and that they may at times be justified by a traditional motive, such as the desire to preserve the integrity of the marriage and the chastity of the wife. At the same time these reservations, as far as the *qāḍī*s are aware of them, do not detract from their efforts to adjust the *sharīʿa* to the changing requirements of society.

Israeli *qāḍī*s declare that they are guided by humane considerations, and especially by the *maṣlaḥa* (public interest) principle, as long as their decisions do not explicitly conflict with the textual sources. Their judgments in fact reflect attempts to Islamize custom, both traditional and modern, taking into account social considerations. There is, as is well known, a close connection between custom and the social motivation underlying the *maṣlaḥa* principle.[27] The *qāḍī*s' contest with custom in preindependence Cyrenaica went on under comparatively favorable conditions because the Italian regime preserved the situation that had prevailed at the end of Ottoman rule, interfering in the judicial system only to ensure that the *sharīʿa* courts did not exceed their powers or deviate from the accepted European norm ("public policy"). It did not relegate the *sharīʿa* to the status of "native law and custom" as the British administration did in several African countries. In those countries, adjustment of the *sharīʿa* to changing requirements and circumstances depended on the degree of openness, and of willingness to cut loose from conservative orthodoxy, evinced by the *qāḍī*s, the rulers, and the population resorting to the courts. In northern Nigeria, for instance, the courts made concessions to customary law on a wide gamut of subjects, and the British gave them formal cover under the umbrella of "native law and custom"—although from a *sharʿī* point of view, the *sharīʿa* should not be identified with custom. Moreover, the colonial regime imposed normative restrictions on the application of Islamic and customary law, with the aim of preventing infringements of the principles of natural justice, morality, equity, and good conscience as conceived by Western law; more specifically, the purpose was to prevent corporal punishment.[28]

d. Rejection of Custom and Enforcement of the *Sharīʿa*

Besides the tendency to maintain coexistence between *sharīʿa* and custom, with mutual concessions, one finds among the *qāḍī*s an inclination to reject custom *in limine* and enforce the *sharīʿa*. This inclination appears especially where there is no agreement between the parties, in which case the *qāḍī*s apply the *sharīʿa* strictly and uncompromisingly, although

27. Layish, *Women*, pp. 332–34. Cf. Rosen, pp. 234–35.
28. Anderson, *Nigeria*, pp. 22–23, 27; Anderson, *Conflict*, pp. 443, 447; Anderson, *Future*, p. 626; Schacht, *Report*, pp. 4, 6, 9, 12–13.

perhaps without much enthusiasm.[29] The purely *shar'ī* decisions usually show a technical-formalistic approach. Thus the court—quasi-notarially—confirms the divorce, retroactively to the date of its performance, as far as it is valid according to *shar'ī* law, provided it is satisfactorily proved that the spouses were competent to be parties to the divorce proceedings. If the husband denies the divorce, the *qāḍī*, before confirming it, hears witnesses who were present at the act. Although the husband sometimes divorces the wife twice, once out of court and once in court, the *qāḍī* relates only to the divorce performed in his presence; but this is due merely to the difficulty of supervising divorces performed out of court. The *qāḍī* may suspect that the "external" divorce was effected by use of customary divorce formulas not meeting the requirements of the *sharī'a*. Similarly the court confirms divorces by proxy, and any acts (financial arrangements and the like) a proxy is authorized to perform on behalf of the principal, provided the proxy was appointed by a valid proceeding (e.g., a *tawkīl shar'ī*). The same applies also to a divorce by letter: the *qāḍī* first verifies the authenticity of the letter; he then takes evidence of its contents from the persons who drew it up or were present when it was written; and once these proceedings have been completed to his satisfaction, he reads the letter to the wife and declares her divorced. Where the divorce is conditional on the wife's renunciation of any financial rights or on compensation to the husband, the *qāḍī* declares the validity of the divorce when the condition has been fulfilled.

The *qāḍī*s' decisions express almost no normative preference as to the substance of the case. The specific causes of divorces not involving legal proceedings are not examined, as they are not relevant from a *shar'ī* point of view. No distinction (such as is usual in religious-legal literature) is made between *ṭalāq al-sunna* and *ṭalāq al-bid'a*; an arbitrary divorce is not reproved, in the words of a *ḥadīth* attributed to the Prophet, as "the most detested act permitted by Allāh," and there are certainly no signs of a progressive social philosophy. Attempts to reconcile the spouses, though prompted by considerations of *maṣlaḥa*, are probably based on a traditional philosophy that discriminates against women and even finds a justification in nature for doing so. The legal system that grants the husband a unilateral right to divorce the wife is not contested, while the Mālikī judicial divorce, which enables the wife to obtain her release by legal

29. Cf. Layish, *Challenges*, p. 218; Layish, *Islamization*, pp. 43ff.

proceedings on *shar*ʿ*ī* grounds, is anchored in the same system; no attempt is made to mitigate the harsh consequences of divorce so as to adapt them to a philosophy suited to a changing reality. The *qāḍī*s make a technical, not a value-related, normative distinction between three cumulative divorces at different sessions and a triple repudiation at one session; no effort is made—by assigning the divorce, in reliance on the moralistic character of the Mālikī school, to a lower degree of gravity—to mitigate the legal consequences of a minor or major irrevocable divorce from the point of view of the injury likely to be caused to the spouses and their children. The only value judgment the author came across in the *sijill*s concerned dissolution by reason of adultery of the wife. The *qāḍī* dissolved the marriage and deprived the wife of her financial rights on the ground that she was guilty of immorality (*fasād*). Although the denial of rights under these circumstances fits the *shar*ʿ*ī* norm, one cannot avoid the impression that the *qāḍī* was guided by a traditional social philosophy.

The *qāḍī*s take care to enforce the *shar*ʿ*ī* norm as to everything relating to the legal consequences of divorce and, where the divorce was not by consent of the parties, also as to the financial consequences. It seems that the husband's declaration as to the number of repudiations is not so much a testimony to his awareness of the legal norm as result of instruction by the *qāḍī*, who wishes to enforce it strictly. The *qāḍī*s find it difficult to verify the number of repudiations, especially in the case of revocable divorce performed without witnesses. The measure of a *qāḍī*'s success in enforcing the *shar*ʿ*ī* norm depends on the degree of the husband's piety. But the husband's declaration as to the type and number of repudiations is in itself indicative of the objective pursued by *qāḍī*s in this matter—namely, *shar*ʿ*ī* indoctrination. After the third or the triple repudiation, the *qāḍī* is careful to point out that the wife is forbidden to the husband and is not permitted to him again until after an intermediate marriage to another man. The same importance is attached by the *qāḍī*s to the waiting period following an irrevocable divorce. They instruct the woman—personally or, if she is not in court, through another person—to observe it carefully; they dispense her from it only, in accordance with the *sharī*ʿ*a*, if the marriage has not been consummated. The legal consequences of Islamic divorce are its main features; although it is ultimately anchored in customary law, its consequences embody Islamic ethico-religious and social concepts that distinguish it from its early sources of inspiration. This may account for the absolute unwillingness of the *qāḍī*s to compromise with custom in this matter. The legal consequences of divorce are, at any rate, outside the sphere of bargaining and the agreement between the parties.

The position is different with regard to the financial consequences. Here the *qāḍī*s are willing to deviate from the religious-legal norm, provided the parties agree upon the deviation; in the absence of agreement, they strictly enforce the *sharʿī* norm. It seems that as a rule the *qāḍī*s are aware of the woman's financial rights and are careful to note these in their decisions, provided she has validly proved them. Thus, for instance, they award a revocably divorced woman full maintenance during (but not beyond) the waiting period and disregard the assertion of an irrevocably divorced woman that she is pregnant for the purposes of maintenance unless her assertion is proved *ex post facto*, in which case they award her full maintenance (and not only residential accommodation), as required by religious law. Similarly, they decide that a woman is entitled to the whole of her dower if she has not yet received it, or to the balance of her dower if she has received only part of it. Where the marriage has not been consummated, they decide—again in accordance with religious law—that the wife is entitled to half the specified dower.

Other instances of *sharʿī* indoctrination are the recitation of the *shahāda*, the administration of oaths on the Qurʾān, and the quoting of passages from the Qurʾān in giving judgment. Thus, for instance, in proceedings for dissolution for nonprovision of maintenance by an absent husband, the wife is called upon to recite the *shahāda*, and to swear on the Qurʾān (*yamīn al-istiẓhār*) that she did not permit her husband to go, that he did not leave or send her maintenance, that she is not rebellious, and that she has not yet been repudiated.[30] Oaths on the Qurʾān (*kitāb allāh* or *al-maṣḥaf al-sharīf*) are usual also in disputes on various matters of personal status other than divorce—such as a demand by the wife's father, who was unable to prove by witnesses the existence outside the marriage contract of an agreement with his son-in-law concerning the amount of the dower, that his son-in-law swear there was no such agreement; a witness's statement, on the husband's initiative, that the latter was poor and therefore unable to install the wife in a "fair dwelling" (*maskan ʿadl*); and a demand by a husband, following an appeal to an administrative committee from a declaration of rebelliousness (*nushūz*) against the wife, that the wife swear

30. E.g., B2:KM38-43:T41-43, K5: p. 8 no. 19 14 June 41, K8: p. 38 no. 98 1 April 42, K7: p. 77 no. 204 1 Nov. 42; KD59-73, K48: p. 7 no. 14 28 July 59.

on the Qurʾān that her refusal to return to his house was due to her revulsion from him and not to incitement by her parents. At the same time, Colucci notes that the oath on the Qurʾān (and on al-Bukhārī's collection of *ḥadīths*, common among the Beduin of Cyrenaica) shows the characteristics of a popular Marabout ceremony.[31] In other words, customary Ṣūfī ceremonies are translated into Islamic terms. Sometimes, though rarely, the *qāḍī*, in stating the legal norm concerning a particular matter, quotes passages from the Qurʾān in support of the norm.

At times the *qāḍī* opens the judgment with the *basmala* or some other religious formula, such as "May God bless and grant salvation to our lord Muḥammad and his family and companions" (*wa-ṣallā allāh ʿalā sayyidinā Muḥammad wa-ālihi wa-ṣaḥbihi wa-sallama*) or "In the reign of the glorious Muḥammad Idrīs the First, King of the United Libyan Kingdom and Amīr of Barqa, may God protect him (*ḥafiẓahu allāh*), amen!"; or "In the *sharīʿa* court of Ajdābiyya, in the presence of the *qāḍī*..., may Allāh prosper his condition (*aṣlaḥa allāh aḥwālahu*), amen!."[32] Similarly, the *qāḍīs* conclude their judgments with religious formulas and invoke religious sanctions in many different ways so as to educate the people to behave in accordance with the appropriate norms. Thus in an action against a man who had insulted a woman by using profane language, the *qāḍī* instructed him to keep his tongue in check, to refrain from speech forbidden by the *sharīʿa*, and not to indulge in vicious habits, lest Allāh chide and punish him. The case ended with an amicable settlement (*ṣulḥ*), the judge saying: "May Allāh reconcile all people; may Allāh and his messenger be pleased with it [the settlement]; He [Allāh] has power to bring this about, and He is worthy of all praise" (*waffaqa allāh al-jamīʿ fīhi raḍiya allāh wa-rasūluhu innahu ʿalā dhālika qadīr wabi-kull faḍl jadīr*).[33]

Similarly, one finds religious elements also in the settling of disputes among the Awlād ʿAlī in the Western Desert: the recitation of the *basmala*, the reading of the *Fātiḥa*, the attribution of everything evil to "Satan, who found his way to the souls of men, while now, thank God, they have come to their senses." The tribal arbitrators in the Judean Desert likewise seek

31. A:E103, p. 94 no. 174 28 June 52; AP:E4, p. 133 no. [126] n.d.; and KD59-73, p. 57 no. 109 10 Sep. 60, respectively; Colucci, *Tribù*, pp. 26, 36-37.
32. E.g., AP:E2, p. 15 no. 31 15 Aug. 51; KM63DP:EP, p. 50 no. 95 6 July 60; AP:E1, p. 143 no. 254 19 Nov. 52.
33. AP:E4, p. 97 no. 95 23 Oct. 46.

to enlist *sharʿī* sanctions in support of their judicial proceedings: they use formulas intended to stress the belief in the oneness of Allāh and in his messenger Muḥammad; they have the parties swear oaths of compurgation on the Qurʾān and in holy places such as mosques; they insert qurʾānic verses in their judgments; and, humbly and modestly, they ascribe the art of arbitration to Allāh (*allāh khayr al-ḥākimīn*).[34] Instances of *sharʿī* indoctrination of a not yet fully Islamized Muslim population were also observed in northern Nigeria among *qāḍī*s with a good *sharʿī* education. In Algeria, an inclination was observed among *qāḍī*s to apply Islamic law very strictly in their decisions so as to obviate Westernizing tendencies engendered by the French legal system, to which the Muslim population was subject at the upper judicial levels. In this sense, we may regard those *qāḍī*s as the guardians of Islamic ethics against the influence of Western culture. The wide discretion left to Middle Eastern *qāḍī*s under Western-inspired reformist legislation has made them, too, guardians of public ethics, although it is still too early to estimate how they exercise that discretion.[35]

e. The Religious-Legal Power of the *Qāḍī*

Needless to say, the religious-legal power of the *qāḍī*s is of great importance to the discharge of their functions in the Islamizaton of the Beduin. The *sijill*s contain instances of deviations from the *sharīʿa* in the course of its application. For example, where the husband denies the divorce, the court may confirm it on the evidence of one witness although at least two are required. Similarly, it was observed in Algeria that a *qāḍī* would confirm marriages on the testimony of one witness; this too is, *sharīʿa*-wise, a mistake for which there is no apparent explanation.[36] It is not certain that the *qāḍī*s are fully aware of the mechanism of suspended repudiation, even where the husband has made express use thereof; at any rate they do not refer to its legal consequences. It seems that the *qāḍī*s combine grounds for judicial divorce, especially absence of the husband and nonprovision of maintenance, although each of them has an independent existence and

34. Mohsen, *Conflict*, pp. 27-28, 45-46, 101-2; Layish & Shmueli, pp. 41-42; Layish, *Challenges*, pp. 213-14 and the sources indicated in n. 42; Layish, *Judaean Desert*. Cf. Rosen, p. 226 and the source indicated in n. 7.

35. Schacht, *Nigeria*, p. 129; Charnay, pp. 283-84, 286; Coulson, *Conflict*, pp. 108ff.; Layish, *Maḥkama*, xiii, p. 41.

36. Charnay, p. 286.

separate legal consequences. Moreover, even under these circumstances the court does not, as required in judicial divorce according to the Mālikī school, itself dissolve the marriage but gives the wife the option to divorce herself and awards a revocable divorce when she has done so. This practice, which was observed also in other places in North Africa, resembles delegated repudiation, and one cannot but gain the impression that the *qāḍī*s here combine, without apparent cause, two quite unconnected dissolution mechanisms. Moreover, even in the few cases that can clearly be defined as causing injury to the wife, the court did not resort to the procedure, reserved for such circumstances, of appointing arbitrators for dissolution, but again gave the wife the option to divorce herself, which in fact she did. This is strange, especially in the case of the Mālikī school, which more than any other school resorts to arbitrators and grants them discretion to dissolve marriages even without prior authorization by the spouses. In some cases in which the wife compensated the husband for her *khulʿ* release, the *qāḍī*, contrary to the position of the Mālikī school and without giving any reason, awarded a revocable divorce. The only possible explanation seems to be that the parties had so agreed.

Occasionally the *qāḍī*s apply legal terms without regard for their significance. For instance, they declare that a woman is divorced by a "single revocable repudiation through which she acquires control of herself and the marriage tie is dissolved," thus combining two mutually contradictory elements; or they use terms actually relating to the reinstatement of the wife after revocable repudiation to designate the rehabilitation of a marriage by a new marriage tie. Such phenomena, which are somewhat puzzling, may account for the *qāḍī*s' eagerness to settle disputes by reconciliation or agreement not involving application of the *sharīʿa*.

The decisions of the *qāḍī*s are very concisely worded, stereotyped and without references to legal literature, commentaries or codifications (the last of which, in Libya, have the status of statutory law). Only in one case did a *qāḍī* deviate from this pattern. The circumstances were exceptional: a husband who had beaten his wife so severely that she had to be hospitalized refused to divorce her on the demand of her father. The court referred to authoritative literature (*Ḥāshiyat al-Ṣāwī ʿalā al-Sharḥ al-ṣaghīr* and Ibn ʿĀṣim) to support its decision that wife beating is a cause for dissolution on the ground of injury (*ḍarar*) and that, if the husband refuses to divorce the wife, the *qāḍī* is competent to do it for him. The *qāḍī* in this case in fact did so.[37] The scanty use of Mālikī literature by the *qāḍī*s of Ajdābiyya and Kufra is notable compared with the relatively extensive reliance of *qāḍī*s elsewhere in Libya, especially in the Sharīʿa Court of Appeal in Tripoli, on Mālikī jurists such as Khalīl, Saḥnūn, Ibn ʿĀṣim, Ibn al-Qāsim, al-Dasūqī, al-Tasūlī, and al-Dardīr in matters relating to divorce and other matters.[38] The latter *qāḍī*s are also more aware of sophisticated *sharʿī* mechanisms relating to divorce, such as suspended repudiation and arbitration in cases of injury.

Nor is there evidence of *qāḍī*s resorting to the legal opinions (*fatwā*) of *muftī*s in matters of divorce. Again, in contrast hereto, we find *qāḍī*s in other parts of Libya relying on the *fatwā*s of Mālikī *muftī*s in matters of divorce (forced renunciation of dower, triple repudiation) and other matters—such as the obtaining of a medical opinion on a question of virginity from a non-Muslim doctor. In Algeria under French rule it was usual to obtain from a *muftī* or a *faqīh*, for a fee, a *fatwā* that might make it possible to avoid the consequences of triple repudiation on the ground that the husband (who applied for the *fatwā*) pronounced the repudiation while not in full possession of his mental faculties. The *muftī* sometimes directed the husband to compensate the wife with a gift for the unpleasantness caused to her. In northern Nigeria under colonial rule, the *muftī* was often the *qāḍī*'s clerk, who recorded the proceedings; but occasionally he also examined the parties or the witnesses to elucidate some matters in their statements from a *sharʿī* point of view.[39]

In some isolated cases the *qāḍī* was asked for an opinion in the matter at issue and then gave an "answer" (*jawāb*) and not a judgment. Thus in one case he was asked *ex parte* whether money borrowed in foreign currency might be repaid in local currency, and he said that such a conversion was irregular (*fāsid*) since it was tantamount to charging interest (*ribā*) and that the loan should be repaid in the same currency and in the same amount. In another case, the *qāḍī* gave an opinion in the presence of the two parties. The owner of some camels and a camel driver hired by him for an annual payment—it seems to have been a partnership (*shirka*)—disagreed as to which of them had to pay the government poll tax on the camels. The *qāḍī*, in a *jawāb*, held that in the special circumstances of the

37. A:E102, p. 345 no. 589 12 July 54. For more details see above, p. 146.

38. d'Emilia, pp. 40–42, 50.

39. d'Emilia, pp. 33–34, 38 n. 3, p. 39; Charnay, pp. 39–40; Schacht, *Report*, p. 6.

case the driver should pay. We may have to do here with a remnant, carried over into the *sharīʿa* court, of a customary institution.[40] In other cases there were unilateral applications to the court in matters of divorce or succession that, though similar in style to applications for opinions, seem to have led to ordinary legal proceedings ending with a judgment or order.[41]

There is evidence—though not a great deal—of *fuqahāʾ* participating in proceedings relating to matters of personal status and in acts of the court. They attest that a widow or nonvirgin (*thayyib*) is "free (*khāliya*) from *sharʿī* impediments (*mawāniʿ*) [to marriage] and marriage ties" (i.e., is unmarried), in order to enable her to get married.[42] A woman wishing to redeem herself by *khulʿ* renounces all her dower in the presence of her brother and a *faqīh*. A *faqīh* draws up (*kātib al-ḥurūf*) the *jawāb*, the "answer" or letter of divorce sent to the wife from the husband's abode, and certifies its contents. The *qāḍī* uses the services of a *faqīh* to test the credibility (*tazkiya*) of witnesses brought by a deceased person's daughter applying for a succession order. Although in all these cases it would have been possible to enlist persons without a *sharʿī* training, it seems that the recourse to *fuqahāʾ* is intended to use their legal standing to enhance the *sharʿī* validity of the proceeding in which they took part. They are agents of *sharʿī* indoctrination in that they point out the legal norm and teach ordinary people, inured to custom, to act in accordance with religious law. Typical in this context is the above case in which the wife's brother and a *faqīh* were witnesses to *khulʿ* proceedings; this arrangement was a compromise between the requirements of custom and those of the *sharīʿa*: the brother was to represent the family interest according to custom, while the *faqīh* was to ensure respect for the supremacy of the *sharīʿa*.

The participation of *fuqahāʾ* in proceedings is attested also as regards the Western Desert. A religious functionary or "holy man" is witness to an agreement between the parents of the spouses as to the dower, reads the *Fātiḥa*, and performs or witnesses the marriage. Sometimes religious functionaries from the Murābiṭūn tribe are invited to witness marriages, in

40. KM63DP:EP, K4a n.d. (see Layish & Davis, p. 124); and KM38–43:EA, K4a: no. 6 5 Aug. 32, respectively. Cf. Layish, *Judaean Desert*.

41. E.g., KM63DP:EP, K3: no. 1 9 April 44, no. 2 20 Dec. 44, no. 3 13 March 45; KD59–73, K44: p. 209 no. 502 1 Nov. 64.

42. E.g., AMR42–44, A3: p. 84 no. 84 13 Sep. 43, A5: p. 85 no. 85 13 Sep. 43. Cf. Colucci, *Cirenaica*, col. 39.

the expectation that they will bring blessing (*baraka*). Holy men to whom supernatural powers are attributed grant their patronage to a wife who "throws herself" before them; they persuade the husband to divorce her and her father to return the dower to the husband. The authority of members of the Sanūsī order is invoked to settle disputes between tribes. A tribal amicable settlement (*ṣulḥ ʿashāʾirī*) between Beduin in the Judean Desert is sometimes concluded in the presence of an urban *qāḍī* or *muftī*, probably in order that his religious authority may give added effect to that customary agreement.[43]

To what extent can the inclination of the *qāḍī*s to compromise with custom be attributed to their Sanūsī background? Davis says that many *qāḍī*s of *sharīʿa* courts are Sanūsīs or were trained at Sanūsī educational institutions (in some cases at the Sanūsī university of Jaghbūb). Since Kufra and Ajdābiyya were at some time or other seats of the Sanūsī administration, he estimates that the *qāḍī*s' "unorthodoxy" (by which he means their deviation from the normative *sharīʿa* in the direction of custom) "was deliberate rather than accidental—not an effect of ignorance." He tends to believe that the *qāḍī*s were "unorthodox" also in matters other than personal status; this in his opinion explains to some extent the support for the Sanūsiyya among the tribesmen, since the real needs of individuals in terms of salvation (which are not satisfied within the framework of the orthodox *sharīʿa*) are authoritatively supplied by the Sanūsī doctrine.[44]

Davis' estimate is apparently confirmed both by the identity of the *qāḍī*s and by the Sanūsī doctrine. The names of some of the *qāḍī*s link them to the Sanūsī order. The author's findings are based on decisions of the courts of two localities that have played an important role in Sanūsī history; and it is possible that some of the *qāḍī*s were indeed trained at Sanūsī institutions. Evans-Pritchard says that all Sanūsī *shaykh*s have been trained in theology, law, and exegetics. The Grand Sanūsī, the founder of the Sanūsī order, had a group of *ʿulamāʾ* beside him unsurpassed in learning outside Cairo; the community of Jaghbūb clustered round the religious university, which had a library of 8,000 volumes on Islamic law

43. AP:E2, p. 180 no. 186 24 Dec. 47; B2:KM38-43:T41-43, K7: p. 94 no. 250 3 March 43; AP:E3, p. 354 no. 606 2 Aug. 54; Obermeyer, p. 122; Mohsen, *Conflict*, pp. 73-74, 84, 99ff., 118; Layish, *Challenges*, p. 217.

44. Davis, *Islam*.

and on mystics, philosophy, history, qurʾānic exegetics, etc.; here the Grand Sanūsī trained the future leaders of the order and the *shaykh*s of the *zāwiya*s. The Sanūsī *shaykh*s used their moral-spiritual authority to disseminate the Sanūsī doctrine among the tribes while compromising with Beduin custom.[45]

Ziadeh, who examined the teachings of the Grand Sanūsī on the basis of his books, notes that the Ṣūfī orders left a deep imprint on him during his formative period. Many observers have perceived that the *maṣlaḥa* doctrine is derived from the humanistic element in Sufism.[46] The Grand Sanūsī's legal teachings are of course of especial interest. He belonged to the Mālikī school but, according to Ziadeh, had no inhibitions about deviating from the traditional Mālikī interpretation in some matters of principle. He fully accepted the whole of the Qurʾān and the *sunna* but rejected the *qiyās* and the *ijmāʿ* as sources of law. He held, probably inspired by Ibn Taymiyya, that a jurist is not bound by the *taqlīd*, the established positive law of the Mālikī school, but has some freedom of personal *ijtihād* (reasoning), provided he possesses the necessary intellectual qualifications and the *ijtihād* is anchored in the textual sources. This may be regarded as an appeal, albeit restrained, for the reopening of the gates of *ijtihād*.[47] Shukrī on the other hand holds that the Grand Sanūsī's special contribution to legal methodology is that he sought to synthesize the four orthodox schools of law (*mazj al-madhāhib*) and to fuse them into a new school—which, though, for fear of orthodox reaction, he refrained from propogating; this new school was to suit his type of *ijtihād*.[48] (Here *ijtihād* should not be interpreted in the classical sense but in the sense of *ijtihād al-madhhab*, which does not require reference to textual sources.) It is thus difficult to suppose that the Grand Sanūsī had a developed legal methodology, which is hardly surprising since he headed a religious revival movement rather than a reformist one. It seems, moreover, that even the sporadic legal principles attributed to him left no imprint on the decisions of the Cyrenaican *qāḍī*s. No use is made of *maṣlaḥa*, to say nothing of *ijtihād* in the classical sense, or even of *ijtihād al-madhhab*. As far as reference is made to *sharʿī* sources, they do not belong to Sanūsī but to conventional Mālikī literature. Among

45. Evans-Pritchard, pp. 17, 83, 99–100.
46. Ziadeh, pp. 73ff. Cf. Smith, pp. 62–63.
47. Ziadeh, pp. 78–83, 87, 94, 128.
48. Shukrī, pp. 41, 44.

the reasons for this may be the thinning of the ranks of Sanūsī *ʿulamāʾ* by the suppression of the order under Italian rule, the closing of its *zāwiya*s and teaching centers, and finally its outlawing by Qadhdhāfī. Evans-Pritchard says that since 1911 most Sanūsī *shaykh*s have had little education, sometimes as little as the Beduin themselves.[49] It thus seems that the *qāḍī*s' specific attitude toward custom—and particularly their willingness to compromise with it quite simply, without sophistication—should be attributed to their cultural background and educational equipment.

4. CONCLUSION

Findings from the Cyrenaican *sijill*s reveal that relations between *sharīʿa* and custom are passing through a period of transition corresponding to the transition from a nomadic tribal society to full sedentariness. On the one hand, custom still enjoys almost absolute supremacy in many fields, outside the control of the *sharīʿa* and at times in express contradiction to it; insofar as the *sharīʿa* is followed, it is not by its own right but to the extent that is upheld by custom.[50] On the other hand, there are more and more manifestations of the impact of the *sharīʿa* on tribal society—from slight concessions to it, via peaceful coexistence and even intense interaction (though not on an equal footing) between the two legal norms, to the liquidation of custom in the *sharīʿa* court, either through absorption into the *sharīʿa* or through total displacement by it. Still, the final result is completion of the Islamization of tribal society. Increasing recourse to the courts—mainly prompted by practical considerations and day-to-day exigencies—by Beduin in process of sedentarization is a catalyst in this development.

The *qāḍī*s play a vital role in the Islamization of the Beduin, though in widely different styles and with varying degrees of awareness of the significance of their judicial practice. The willingness of the *qāḍī*s to accept customary practice insofar as it has the consent of the parties, and to endorse it also where it is inconsistent with the *sharʿī* norm or even conflicts with an express *sharʿī* provision, is in fact an efficient, if simple and unsophisticated, mechanism for the absorption of custom into the

49. Evans-Pritchard, p. 83.
50. Cf. Schacht, *Report*, pp. 1, 3.

sharīʿa. The *qāḍī*s' unawareness of the repercussions of their approach does not detract from the importance of its results in bringing Beduin nearer to normative Islam. Besides that approach are instances of *qāḍī*s' wrestling with custom with a view to adapting it to the *sharīʿa* by compromising or even by absorbing it completely into the *sharīʿa*. Some seek to bridge the gap between the two legal norms by couching custom in *sharʿī* terms; others go a long way to meet custom while preserving the nominal supremacy of the *sharīʿa*—this, too, being a simple and efficient mechanism to promote Islamization.

The Mālikī school, probably because of the tribal ambience of Medina, where it developed and took shape, is more inclined than any other orthodox school to compromise with custom. Anderson found that even in the most orthodox centers of northern Nigeria the pure Mālikī doctrine compromised with indigenous customary law, although this fact was commonly veiled in dignified silence and seldom expressly recognized. In Islamic legal theory, custom does not enjoy the status of a source of law but is merely an auxiliary source. In actual fact, however, it has always had, in the Mālikī school, the status of a source of law that, in times when the *sharīʿa* was incapable of meeting the requirements of society, preserved the vitality of the law. Some Mālikī scholars hold that custom is binding where it does not conflict with a textual provision (*naṣṣ*), or even that it is preferable to a textual provision. The eclecticism of the Mālikī school found sophisticated expression in the Middle Ages in the practice (*ʿamal*) of the *sharīʿa* courts, which in the view of some European Orientalists became a source of positive law in its own right. To adopt custom into the *sharīʿa*, the *qāḍī* was prepared to anchor it in an isolated, anomalous (*shādhdh*) legal opinion, as distinct from the dominant (*mashhūr*) opinion, which rejected it. In fact many customary institutions were absorbed into the *sharīʿa* by means of that judicial practice.[51]

As against this, the Cyrenaican *sijill*s do not suggest the existence in the *qāḍī*s' decisions of a sophisticated, systematic approach aimed at adopting custom into the *sharīʿa*. Thus, for instance, there is no conscious attempt to apply the principle of *maṣlaḥa* (the public interest). This principle has

51. Anderson, *Conflict*, p. 443; Milliot, pp. 156–69, 167–78; Berque, pp. 427–28; Schacht, *Introduction*, pp. 29, 61–62; Coulson, *History*, pp. 145ff.; Bousquet, *Islamic & customary law*, p. 60; Layish, *Challenges*, pp. 220–21; Layish & Shmueli, p. 45. Cf. Rosen, p. 235 and the reference in n. 13.

always been used by *fuqahāʾ* and *qāḍīs* as an efficient mechanism to bridge the gap between an ideal *sharīʿa* and a day-to-day practice dominated by custom.[52] Though the *qāḍīs*' decisions show indications of openness to social consideratons, this has not ripened into a systematic application of the *maṣlaḥa* principle, even if one may perhaps see here an unconscious attempt to adapt the *sharīʿa* to social reality or, in other words, to bring it nearer to custom. In this sense, one may say that the interaction between *sharīʿa* and custom continued in the courts, on a modest scale, under the auspices of the *qāḍīs*. In northern Nigeria, where the Mālikī school also is dominant, Schacht found that the *ʿamal* theory was not recognized. At the same time, in matters of evidence, there were concessions by the *sharīʿa* to the practice rooted in the principle of necessity (*ḍarūra*). Anderson recommends adapting the *sharīʿa* in northern Nigeria to modern requirements, either by drawing inspiration for reforms from schools other than the Mālikī (*takhayyur*), as has been done in the Middle East, or by reviving the Mālikī *ʿamal* mechanism, which enables the incorporation of customary practices into the *sharīʿa*.[53]

There is no significant evidence in the Cyrenaican *sijill*s of any attempt by the *qāḍīs* to enlist the help of the *fuqahāʾ*, charged with adapting the *sharīʿa* to changing social conditions by means of religious-legal opinions (*fatwā*); recourse to religious-legal literature is also rare and not significant. The *qāḍīs*' decisions are generally characterized by a formalistic, not value-related approach even within the context of traditional Islamic law. Alongside compromises with custom are instances of its rejection *in limine* and enforcement of the *sharīʿa*, especially in matters embodying the essence of the ethical-religious and social philosophy of Islam. *Sharʿī* indoctrination is also practiced in the courts in matters not under their jurisdiction. This indoctrination finds expression in the reading of the *Fātiḥa* and qurʾānic verses, and sometimes in the enlistment of sanctions based on saint worship in support of *sharʿī* sanctions (syncretism). The enforcement of the *sharʿī* norm on a Muslim population attuned to customary law may be promoted by the fact that in the period of Italian rule in Cyrenaica preference was given to the *sharīʿa* over custom because the colonial regime found it more convenient to control the institutionalized

52. Coulson, *History*, p. 144 and the source indicated there; Schacht, *Introduction*, p. 61; Layish, *Women*, pp. 332ff.; Layish, *Saudi Arabia*, pp. 285ff.

53. Schacht, *Nigeria*, pp. 137, 139; Anderson, *Nigeria*, p. 29.

and well-defined *sharīʿa* than customs varying from place to place,[54] although in certain matters neither norm was ethically in agreement with the European norm. The fact that the Italian regime did not relegate the *sharīʿa* to the status of "native law and custom" made it easier for the *sharīʿa* to compete with custom. Since independence, the *sharīʿa*, representing the Muslim sovereign, has had a clear advantage over custom; this found expression in the revival of Islamic law in the 1970s. It is difficult to assess the efficiency of the *qāḍīs*' efforts to enforce the *sharʿī* norm, but we may assume that where the gap between it and day-to-day practice is too wide, the *sharʿī* norm will be rejected—because reality is stronger than any law, even religious law.[55]

The social background and personal juristic equipment of the *qāḍīs* in districts remote from the administrative centers probably account for their decisions being simple and unsophisticated even where sophistication is required in order to assimilate custom to the *sharīʿa* or to adjust the *sharīʿa* to social reality. Still, this does not detract from the *qāḍīs*' contribution to the narrowing of the gap between *sharīʿa* and custom. On the contrary, there is sometimes an advantage in their unawareness of the full significance of the contradictions between *sharīʿa* and custom, and complex problems that perhaps would not have found a solution at a high juristic level are solved incidentally in the *qāḍī*'s court. In this sense, we may say that the *qāḍī* is, unconsciously, the standard bearer and hero of Islamization, owing to his very presence at the center of operations.[56]

54. Cf. Schacht, *Report*, p. 4; Fyzee, pp. 53ff.
55. Cf. Bousquet, *Islamic & customary law*, p. 60.
56. Cf. Layish & Shmueli, pp. 31–32.

Glossary of Arabic Legal and Technical Terms

(Page numbers in italics indicate principal reference)

ʿāda (pl. *ʿawāʾid*); *ʿādat al-qabīla*, custom; tribal law 19, 49, 171, 175-76, 179; see also *ʿulf*; custom

ʿāhir ghayr maḍbūṭa, adulterous and depraved 21, 120, 167

ajāza, "allows," term here used by *qāḍī* to confirm amicable settlements 2, 9, 36, 131, 132, 135, 151, 190

ʿamal, judicial practice of medieval *sharīʿa* courts xix 206, 207

ʿanat, hardship, often referring to sexual temptation 25-26, 78, 91, 137

ʿaqd, marriage tie 104, 146

athāth, household effects 33, 57, 119, 166

ʿatīq, liberated slave 16, 87; see also slavery

ʿayb, shame 25, 49, 175

basmala, term referring to the formula *bism allāh al-raḥmān al-raḥīm* (in the name of Allāh the merciful and compassionate) 198

al-battata, divorce formula suggesting finality (irrevocable repudiation) 99, 107, 155; see also *ṭalāq bātt*

baynūna kubrā, intermediate period during which a trebly divorced woman is not allowed to remarry her ex-husband *99*, 106, 154; see also divorce, consequences of, legal

baynūna ṣughrā, waiting period after first or second minor irrevocable divorce during which the woman is not allowed to marry someone

* The arabic *al-*, being a definite article, has been disregarded in alphabetization.

other than her ex-husband *98*, 137, 146, 152; see also divorce, consequences of, legal

bayt al-shanāʿa, procedure for proving impotence by means of witnesses 23

bayt al-ṭāʿa, "house of obedience," a legally enforceable judgment of obedience 46

bayyina, evidence through witnesses 129, 138

bināʾ, consummation of marriage 139, 160; see also *dukhūl*

darāʾib, tribal customs 179

ḍarar, injury, prejudice, legal cruelty 24–26, 45, 58, 77, 78, 80, 83–87, *92–94*, 99, 122, 123, 143–47, 187, 200

ḍarūra, principle of necessity 207

dhimma, financial liability 48, 67, 132, 164

dukhūl, consummation of marriage 20, 23–24, 83, 89, 98, 100–101, 110, 111, 118–20, 139, 141, 159–60, 165, 196, 197

fasād, immorality, here referring to adultery 167, 196

fāsid, irregular 201

faskh, dissolution of marriage by legal proceedings 80, 100

al-Fātiḥa (*Ṣūrat*), opening chapter of Qurʾān (public reading); see Index

fatwā, religious-legal opinion of *muftī* 14, 41, 109, 133, 184, 201, 207

fiqh, the science of Islamic law 14

firāq, dissolution of marriage 19, 25, 27, 47, 49, 58, 131, 145, 155

fiṭām; *infiṭām*, weaning 51, 115, 163

fitna, sexual temptation 92, 144

fuqahāʾ (sing. *faqīh*), specialists in science of Islamic law 11, 14, 17, 22, 33, 41, 107–9, 175, 184, 201–3, 206–7; see *fiqh*

ghayb; *ghayba*; *ghiyāb*, absence (of husband as ground for divorce) 25, 26, 49, 81, 87, 88, 138, 139, 175

ḥaḍāna, custody of minor children 14–15, 51–52, 81, 87, 115–17, 132, 163–64, 181; see also custody

ḥadd (pl. *ḥudūd*), qurʾānic punishment prescribed for certain specific offenses 11

ḥadīth, formal tradition deriving from the Prophet 43, 66, 84, 195, 198

ḥajj, pilgrimage to holy places of Islam in Ḥijāz 5

ḥaly, jewelry 30, 119

ḥaml nāʾim, "sleeping embryo," extended period of pregnancy, unlimited in time, in which the embryo does not develop 6, 112, 161, 187

ḥarām oath, oath of abstention from wife, in the view of most jurists equivalent to triple divorce 100, 107–8, 155
ḥīlā (pl. *ḥiyal*), legal device 192
ḥujja, evidence, proof; certificate 156, 166, 192
ḥuqūq zawjiyya, conjugal rights 29, 132, 167

ibrāʾ — see *mubāraʾa*
ʿidda, woman's waiting period after termination of marriage, usually lasting three menstruations 30, 40, 43, 53, 67, 82–83, 97, 98, 99, *100*–105, 109–15, 125, 129, 136–37, 139, 140, 149–52, 158–63, 177, 180, 181, 193, 196, 197
idhn, permission 104
ʿiffa, chastity 144
iftidāʾ, redemption 45–46
ihmāl, "neglect," here referring to maintenance delayed during marriage 50, 108; see also *nafaqa*
ījāb, offer 131
ijmāʿ, "consensus," one of the four "sources of law" 204
ijtihād, "exertion," reasoning; also the classical mechanism for formation of positive law based on the four "sources of law" 11, 204
— *al-madhhab*, exertion within one school of law 204
īlāʾ, dissolution of marriage by oath of husband to abstain from marital relations 28, 81, 99, 108
ilzām, coertion 8
iqrār, acknowledgment 156, 158
ʿirḍ, honor 21
ʿishra, conjugal relations 19, 25, 179; see also *muʿāshara*
iṣlāḥ, reconciliation 19; see also *ṣulḥ*
ʿiṣma, matrimonial authority of husband over wife 29, 129, 139, 149, 150, 152, 160
istibrāʾ, required waiting period for woman who has had illicit intercourse 160
ʿiwaḍ, compensation 43

jabr, coercive power of guardian to marry off ward 14, 40, 44, 174
jawāb, "response" — letter 32, 38–39, *40–42*, 127, 179, 184, 202
— *fatwā* 184, 201
jihād, holy war 12

kafāʾa, principle requiring husband to be wife's equal in specified fields such as lineage and financial standing 99

kafāla, guarantee 72, 136, 174

kaffāra, religious expiation 28

kafīl, guarantor 30, 72; see guaranteeship

khādima, maidservant 32

khalāṣ, divorce 27

khalwa, privacy of husband and wife technically enabling them to have undisturbed marital relations 98, 101, 110

khasāra, husband's losses incurred in consequence of marriage 52, 58

khiyār al-ʿayb, defect extant at time of contract, making it rescindable 22

khulʿ, "divestiture," divorce by agreement by which wife redeems herself from marriage for a consideration 9, 14, 27-28, 32-33, 41, *43*, 45-47, *54-60*, 65-76, 77, 81, 94, 99, 100, 102, 113-16, 126, 128, 130-32, 137, 158, 169, 174, 176, 177-79, 181, 182, 187, 191, 192, 200, 202; see also divorce, by consent

kināya, implicit (declaration) 27, 43, 97

kiswa, clothing 24, 26, *50*, *57*, 67, 88, 112, 114

kulfa, maintenance 112, 113, 130; see also *nafaqa*

liʿān, dissolution of marriage through process of mutual imprecation (in case of unproven charges of adultery against wife) 81, 85, 99, 119

maʾdhūn, authorized *sharʿī* marriage notary 7, 41, 110, 135, 188

maḥḍar, court protocol 2

mahr, 121, 152-53; see also *ṣadāq*

maḥram, degree of kinship forbidden for marriage 67

maṣārīf al-marʾa, expenses incurred on husband in consequence of marriage 52-53

mashhūr, dominant legal opinion 206; see also *ʿamal*

maskan ʿadl, "fair" (legal) dwelling 197

maṣlaḥa, public interest 1, 11, 124, 160, 194, 195, 204, 206-7

masʾūl, "responsible person" (judge) 7

maʿtūq, liberated slave 16; see also *ʿatīq*

maʾūna; *muʾna*, board, food 88, 112, 130

mawāniʿ, *sharʿī*, impediments to marriage 202

mazj al-madhāhib, synthesis of the four orthodox schools of law 204

muʿāshara, conjugal relations 19, 24, 25, 34, 105, 152, 179; see also *ʿishra*

mubāraʾa or *ibrāʾ*, divorce by consent with mutual waiving of any financial obligations 43–45, 49; see also divorce, by consent, "renunciation divorce"

mufattish, "inspector" (judge) 7

muftī, specialist in religious law, giving authoritative legal opinions xxi,11, 13, 14, 95, 109, 133, 184, 185, 201, 203

mughāḍiba, "angry" wife 34

muḥallil mina'l-ṭalāq, a man who marries a trebly divorced woman by intermediate marriage so as to render her lawfully permitted to her former husband 28; see also *taḥlīl*

mukhbirūn, specialists or experts to assess amount of maintenance 166

mutʿa, — temporary marriage 99

— indemnity payable to wife in case of divorce before consummation 111, 119

nafaqa, maintenance 26, 43, 137

— *lil-ʿayyil*, infant maintenance 115

— *ḥaḍāna*, maintenance during the period of custody 116

— *al-ḥaml*, pregnancy maintenance 112

— *al-ʿidda*, waiting-period maintenance 43, 50; see divorce, consequences of, financial

— *ihmāl*, maintenance delayed ("neglect") during marriage 29, 50, 108, 129, 163

nāfidh (*nafādh*), legal act instantly operative 8, 133

nā'ib, deputy 37, 39–40, 61, 64, 69, 126, 179; see also *wakīl*

— *al-qāḍī* 6, 108

nāshiza; *nushūz*, rebellious wife; rebelliousness 54, 93, 187, 197; see also obedience

naṣṣ, textual provision of Qur'ān or *sunna* 206

niyya, intent 23, 27, 31, 97–100, 107–9, 125, 149, 155, 156, 181, 184

nizāʿ wa-shiqāq, dispute and discord, *sharʿī* grounds for dissolution 94, 147, 156

qabḍ, taking possession 73, 118

qabūl, acceptance 131

qāḍī, Muslim religious judge of *sharīʿa* court; see Index: *qāḍī*s

qarāba, blood relationship 19, 24, 93

qiyās, "analogy," tool applied to Qur'ān and *sunna*, one of the four "sources of law" 204 *quṣṣa*; *quṣṣat al-marʾa*, "wife's lock of hair," expression describing customary promissory note drawn up to guard against the unexpected 71–73, 75, 105, 133, 136

rabība, ward 61, 70, 168; see also guardianship
raḍāʿ, suckling 51, 115, 163
raḍwa, propitiation, gift to wife when reinstated after revocable repudiation, or when second wife is taken 103
ribā, interest 201
rushd, maturity of mind 137

ṣadāq, dower 4, 104, 149, 152, 153, 159; see also divorce, consequences of, financial; dower
— *muʾajjal*; *muʾakhkhar*, deferred, payable at termination of marriage 48, 56, 118, 129, 164
— *muʿajjal*; *muqaddam*, prompt, payable immediately upon (and according to custom during) marriage 48, 56
shadhdh, anomalous legal opinion 206; see also *ʿamal*
sharaf, honor 144
ṣarīḥ, explicit (declaration) 27, 97
shahāda, testimony; the Muslim profession of faith 197
— *naql*, transfer of testimony concerning a factual situation 2
sharīʿat al-mujtamaʿ, Qadhdhāfī's perception of the *sharīʿa* 13–14
sharīf, descendant of Muḥammad 188
shiqāq, discord, dispute 19, 47, 94, 136; see also *nizāʿ wa-shiqāq*
shirka, partnership 201
sīdī, honorific before the name of Muslim saints 189
sijill, records of *sharīʿa* court; see Index: *sijill*s
ṣulḥ, amicable settlement 33–36, 47, 54, 63, 123, 124, 131, 132, 136, 151, 174, 188, 190, 198, 203
— *ʿashāʾirī*, tribal amicable settlement 203
sunna, the legally binding precedents as a "source of law" 11, 13, 204

tafwīḍ, delegation of power of attorney 36, 74, 135
— *al-ṭalāq*, "delegated repudiation," delegation to wife of power to divorce herself *35–37*, 126, 140, 180; see also divorce, unilateral
taḥlīl, device of intermediate marriage legally enabling trebly divorced wife to be permitted to ex-husband 99, 100, 155, 157, 181; see also circumvention of matrimonial laws

takhayyur, adoption in legislation of legal elements from other schools of law 10, 207

ṭalāq, dissolution of marriage without resort to legal proceedings 19, 24–34, 41, 45, 56, 58, 62, 64, 68, 78–81, 86, 97, 100, 121–22, 125, 128–34, 139, 151, 153, 158, 173, 180; see also divorce, unilateral

— *ʿalā māl*, divorce in return for property 43

— *bāʾin*, irrevocable divorce, becomes operative immediately with all attendant legal effects 98, 146, 151, 154; see divorce, consequences of, legal

— *bātt*, definitive or irrevocable divorce 107, 151, 155

— *al-bidʿa*, disapproved forms of divorce: triple repudiation or single irrevocable repudiation 109, 181, 195

— *rajʿī*, revocable divorce, operative only after expiry of waiting period *97*, 101, 103–5, 140, *148–51*, 152–53

— *al-sunna*, approved forms of divorce: one single revocable divorce or three successive pronouncements during three consecutive periods of legal purity 109, 181, 195

taʿlīq al-ṭalāq, suspended repudiation 180; see divorce, unilateral

taqiyya, simulation, defense mechanism of persecuted religious communities under compulsion or threat 3

taqlīd, "imitation," unquestioned adherence to an orthodox school of law 204

taʿrīf, identification procedure 138

ṭarīqa, dervish order 189

taslīm, delivery 46

taṭlīq al-ḥākim, judicial divorce (in Mālikī school) where *qāḍī* exercises husband's power to divorce 58, 80–81, 92, 146

tazkiya, credibility test 127, 156, 202

thayyib, nonvirgin 203

ʿulamāʾ (sing. *ʿālim*), religious scholars of Islam 11, 13, 124, 185, 203, 205; see also *fuqahāʾ*

ʿumda, shaykh elected by village notables 75

ʿurf, custom 13, 171, 175; see also *ʿāda*; custom

wakīl, proxy 37, 38–40, 61, 64, 65, 69, 70, 72, 74, 78, 89, 105, 126, 137, 138, 146, 153, 179, 195; see also *nāʾib*; proxy

walī, holy man, saint (in popular Islam) 189

— *mujbir*, guardian authorized to marry off ward compulsorily 133; see *jabr*

walīmat al-faraḥ, wedding festivities 52

waqf, religious endowment; see Index: *waqf*

yamīn al-istiẓhār, "oath of disclosure," part of procedure granting dissolution in husband's absence 138–39, 142, 197

zāhida, "abstinent" wife, initiator of divorce and bearing financial liability 9, 21

zakāt, alms tax 12

zaʿlāna, an ill-tempered woman 189

ẓālim, wrongdoer, transgressor, meaning sinner in the religio-ethical sense and offender in the customary legal sense 36, 53, 72, 174

zāwiya, center of worship of Ṣūfī order 5, 16–17, 204, 205

zifāf, the nuptial procession 132

ẓihār, form of customary divorce where husband swears that wife is forbidden to him, comparing her to a kinswoman of prohibited degree 28, 81, 107–108, 173

zinā, adultery 21; see women

Bibliography

ARCHIVAL SOURCES

Presented according to the provisional arrangement of the files in John Davis' collection, Eliot College, University of Kent at Canterbury, with a key to the abbreviations (in alphabetical order) used in the Notes.

Sharīʿa Court of Ajdābiyya

A:E102 (-104)	Ajdābiyya, Envelope 102 (-104)
AMR42-44 (50)	Ajdābiyya, [Marriage] Register, 1942-44 (50)
AP:E1 (-4)	Ajdābiyya, Puzzles, Envelope 1 (-4)

Sharīʿa Court of Kufra

B2:KM38-43:T41-43	Box 2: Kufra, Marriages 1938-43: *Ṭalāq* 1942-43
T43	*Ṭalāq* 1943
EA	Envelope A
KAMD	Kufra and Ajdābiyya Marriage Documents
KD59-73	Kufra, Divorce, 1959-71, 1973
KDP	Kufra, Divorce, Puzzles
KM38-43:EA	Kufra, Marriages, 1938-43, Envelope A
KM63DP:EP	Kufra, Marriages, 1963, Duplicates, Puzzles: Envelope Puzzles.
KM71-76:E[A]5	Kufra, Marriages, 1971-76, Envelope [A] 5

SECONDARY SOURCES

Listed in alphabetical order of the abbreviations used in the Notes. The prefix *al* in Arabic (and *ha* in Hebrew) has been disregarded in the alphabetical arrangement.

ʿAbd Allāh — ʿAbd ʿAlī Salmān ʿAbd Allāh. *al-Mujtamaʿ al-rīfī fīʾl-ʿirāq*. Baghdād, 1980.

ʿAbduh — Muḥammad ʿAbduh. *Taqrīr fī iṣlāḥ al-maḥākim al-sharʿiyya*. Cairo, 1317/1900.

Abou El-Haj	Rifaat Abou-El-Haj. "An agenda for research in history: The history of Libya between the sixteenth and nineteenth centuries." *IJMES*, vol. 15, no. 3 (1983): 305–19.
Anderson, *Africa*	J. N. D. Anderson. *Islamic law in Africa*, 2d ed. London, 1970.
Anderson, *Conflict*	———. "Conflict of laws in northern Nigeria: A new start." *ICLR* 8 (1959): 442–56.
Anderson, *Future*	———. "The future of Islamic law in British Commonwealth territories in Africa." *JAL*, vol. 27, no. 4 (1962): 617–31.
Anderson, *Nigeria*	———."Law and custom in Muslim areas in Africa: Recent developments in Nigeria." *Civilisations*, vol. 7, no. 1 (1957): 17–29.
Anderson, *Reform*	———. *Law reform in the Muslim world*. London, 1976.
Anderson, L.	Lisa Anderson. "Nineteenth century reform in Ottoman Libya." *IJMES*, vol. 16, no. 3 (1984): 325–48.
Ansell & al-Arif	M. O. Ansell and I. M. al-Arif, eds. *The Libyan revolution: A sourcebook of legal and historical documents*. vol. 1: *1 September 1969–30 August 1970*. Harrow, 1972.
al-ʿĀrif	ʿĀrif al-ʿĀrif. *al-Qaḍāʾ baynaʾl-badw*. Jerusalem, 1933.
Behnke	R. H. Behnke, Jr. *The herders of Cyrenaica: Ecology, economy, and kinship among the Bedouin of Eastern Libya*. Illinois Studies in Anthropology, no. 12. Illinois, 1980.
Berque	J. Berque. *EI*², s.v. "ʿAmal," pp. 427–29.
Bousquet, *Coutumes kabiles*	G.-H. Bousquet. *Justice française et coutumes kabiles*. Algiers, 1950.
Bousquet, *Islamic & customary law*	———. "Islamic law and customary law in French North Africa." *JCLIL*, vol. 32, pts. 3–4 (1950): 57–65.
Bousquet, *Précis*	———. *Précis de droit musulman principalement malékite et algérien*, 2d ed. Algiers, 1950.
Charnay	J.-P. Charnay. *La vie musulmane en Algérie d'après la jurisprudence de la première moitié du xx*^e^ *siècle*. Paris, 1965.

Cicchitti	A. Cicchitti. "Il problema religioso nella legislazione coloniale italiana." *RC* 21 (1926): 474–96.
Colucci, *Cirenaica*	M. Colucci. "Il Diritto consuetudinario della Cirenaica." *RGMEOGC*, vol. 1, nos. 1–2 (1932): cols. 38–50.
Colucci, *Tribù*	———. "Il Diritto consuetudinario delle tribù della Cirenaica." *RC* 22 (1927): 24–37.
Coulson, *Commercial law*	N. J. Coulson. *Commercial law in the Gulf States.* London, 1984.
Coulson, *Conflicts*	———. *Conflicts and tensions in Islamic jurisprudence.* Chicago, 1969.
Coulson, *History*	———. *A history of Islamic law.* Islamic Surveys 2. Edinburgh, 1964.
Coulson, *Succession*	———. *Succession in the Muslim family.* Cambridge, 1971.
Davis, *Islam*	J. Davis. "Islam and the history of the Libyan state." Manuscript.
Davis, *Koufra*	———. "La structure sociale de Koufra." *AAN* 22 (1983): 545–64.
Davis, *Note*	———. "A note on some Libyan archives in Canterbury." *BBRISMES*, vol. 9, no. 1 (1982): 75–79.
Davis, *Politics*	———. *Libyan politics: Tribe and revolution.* London, 1987.
d'Emilia	A. d'Emilia. "La giurisprudenza del Tribunale superiore sciaraitico della Libia in materia di fidanzamento, matrimonio e divorzio (1929–1941)." *RSO* 21 (1946): 15–50.
Doumani	B. B. Doumani. "The Islamic court records of Palestine." *BRR*, no. 2 (1985–86): 3–29.
Dozy	R. Dozy. *Supplément aux dictionnaires arabes*, vol. 1, 2d ed. Leiden and Paris, 1927.
*EI*²	*Encyclopaedia of Islam*, 2d ed. Leiden and London, 1960—.
Evans-Pritchard	E. E. Evans-Pritchard. *The Sanusi of Cyrenaica.* Oxford, 1949.
Farīq al-Muzhir	Farīq al-Muzhir Āl Firʿawn. *al-Qaḍāʾ al-ʿashāʾirī.* Baghdad, 1941.
Fluehr-Lobban	Carolyn Fluehr-Lobban. *Islamic law and society in the Sudan.* London, 1987.

Fyzee — A. A. A. Fyzee. *Outlines of Muhammadan law*, 3d ed. Oxford, 1964.

Gellner — E. Gellner. *Muslim society*. Cambridge, 1981.

Goitein & Ben Shemesh — S. D. Goitein and A. Ben Shemesh. *ha-Mishpaṭ ha-muslimi bi-medinat yisraʾel*. Jerusalem, 1957.

Harris — Lillian C. Harris. *Libya: Qadhafi's revolution and modern state*. London and Sydney, 1986.

Hava — J. G. Hava. *al-Farāʾiḍ al-durriyya fīʾl-lughatayn al-ʿarabiyya waʾl-inklīziyya: Arabic-English Dictionary*. Beirut, 1951.

Hill — Enid Hill. *Mahkama! Studies in the Egyptian legal system*. London, 1979.

Kressel — G. M. Kressel. "Sororicide/filiacide: Homicide for family honor." *CA* 22 (1981): 141–58.

Lane — E. W. Lane. *An Arabic-English lexicon*. London, 1863–93.

Layish, *Challenges* — A. Layish. "Challenges to customary law and arbitration: The impact of Islamic law upon settled Bedouin in the Judaean Desert." *TAUSL* 5 (1980–82): 206–21.

Layish, *Contribution* — ———. "The contribution of the modernists to the secularization of Islamic law." *MES*, vol. 14, no. 3 (1978): 263–77.

Layish, *Druze* — ———. *Marriage, divorce and succession in the Druze family*. Leiden, 1982.

Layish, *Islamization* — ———. "The Islamization of the Bedouin family in the Judean Desert as reflected in the *sijill* of the *sharīʿa* court." In *The changing Bedouin*, edited by E. Marx and A. Shmueli, 39-58. New Brunswick, N.J., 1984.

Layish, *Judaean Desert* — ———. "Beduin of the Judaean Desert: Islamization of tribal society. A study based on legal documents of arbitrators and *sharīʿa* courts." In preparation.

Layish, *Maḥkama* — ———. *EI*², s.v. "Maḥkama," 4ii–ix, xiii, fasc. 99–100, pp. 25–38, 40–42.

Layish, *Mālikī waqf* — ———. "The Mālikī family *waqf* according to wills and *waqfiyyāt*." *BSOAS*, vol. 46, pt. 1 (1983): 1–32.

Layish, *Saudi Arabia* ———. "Saudi Arabian legal reform as a mechanism to moderate Wahhābī doctrine." *JAOS*, vol. 107, no. 2 (1987): 279–92.

Layish, *Shariʿa u-minhag* ———. "Shariʿa u-minhag ba-mishpaḥa ha-muslimit bi-yisraʾel." *MḤ*, vol. 23, no. 4 (1974): 377–409.

Layish, *Sijill* ———. "The *sijill* of Jaffa and Nazareth *sharīʿa* courts as a source for the political and social history of Ottoman Palestine." In *Studies on Palestine during the Ottoman Period*, edited by M. Maʿoz, 525–32. Jerusalem, 1975

Layish, *Taqiyya* ———. "*Taqiyya* among the Druzes." *AAS*, vol. 19, no. 3 (1985): 245–81.

Layish, *Women* ———. *Women and Islamic law in a non-Muslim state*. Jerusalem and New York, 1975.

Layish & Davis A. Layish and J. Davis. *Libyan society: A selection of documents from the* sijills *of the* sharīʿa *courts of Ajdābiyya and Kufra*. Jerusalem, 1988.

Layish & Shmueli A. Layish and A. Shmueli. "Custom and *sharīʿa* in the Bedouin family according to legal documents from the Judaean Desert." *BSOAS*, vol. 42, pt. 1 (1979): 29–45.

Linant, *Khulʿ* Y. Linant de Bellefonds. "Le '*khulʿ*' sans compensation en droit ḥanafite." *SI* 31 (1970): 185-95.

Linant, *Traité* ———. *Traité de droit musulman comparé*, vol. 2. Paris, 1965.

Mandaville, *Jerusalem* J. E. Mandaville. "The Jerusalem *sharīʿa* court records: A supplement and complement to the central Ottoman archives." In *Studies on Palestine during the Ottoman period*, edited by M. Maʿoz, 517–24. Jerusalem, 1975.

Mandaville, *Syria & Jordan* ———. "The Ottoman court records of Syria and Jordan." *JAOS*, vol. 86, no. 3 (1966): 311-19.

Mayer, *Criminal law* Ann E. Mayer. "Reinstating Islamic criminal law in Libya." In *Politics of law in the Arab world*, edited by D. Dwyer. Forthcoming.

Mayer, *Interest* ———. "The regulation of interest charges and risk contracts: Some problems of recent Libyan legislation." *ICLQ* 28 (1979): 541-59.

Mayer, *Livre vert* ———. "Le droit musulman en Libye à l'âge du 'Livre vert.'" *MM*, special issue on Libya 1978–81, no. 93 (1981): 5–22.

Mayer, *Marriage* ———. "Developments in the law of marriage and divorce in Libya since the 1969 revolution." *JAL*, vol. 22, no. 1 (1978): 30-49.

Mayer, *Resurgence* ———. "Islamic resurgence or new prophethood: The role of Islam in Qadhdhāfī's ideology." In *Islamic resurgence in the Arab world*, edited by Ali Dessouki, 196–220. London, 1982.

Mayer, *Sexual mores* ———. "Libyan legislation in defense of Arabo-Islamic sexual mores." *AJCL*, vol. 28, no. 2 (1980): 287-313.

Milliot L. Milliot. *Introduction à l'étude du droit musulman*. Paris, 1953.

Mohsen, *Conflict* Safia K. Mohsen. *Conflict and law among Awlad ʿAli of the Western Desert*. National Center for Social and Criminological Research. Cairo, 1975.

Mohsen, *Women* ———. "Aspects of the legal status of women among Awlad ʿAli." In *People and cultures of the Middle East*, vol. 1, edited by Louise E. Sweet, 220–33. New York, 1970.

Nelsen H. D. Nelsen, ed. *Libya, A country study*, 3d ed. Area Handbook Series. Washington, D.C., 1979.

Obermeyer G. J. Obermeyer. "Structure and authority in a Bedouin tribe: The ʿAishaibat of the Western Desert of Egypt." Ph.D. diss., Indiana University, 1968. University Microfilms # 69–10572.

Oweidi Ahmad Saleh Suleiman Oweidi. "Bedouin justice in Jordan." Ph.D. diss., Cambridge University, 1982.

Pesle O. Pesle. *La femme musulmane dans le droit: La religion et les mœurs*. Rabat, 1946.

Peters, *Aspects* E. L. Peters. "Aspects of the family among the Bedouin of Cyrenaica." In *Comparative family systems*, edited by M. F. Nimkoff, 121–46. Boston, Mass., 1965.

Peters, *Bridewealth* ———. "Aspects of Bedouin bridewealth among camel herders in Cyrenaica." In *The meaning of*

	marriage payments, edited by J. L. Comaroff, 125–60. London and New York, 1980.
Peters, *Proliferation*	———. "The proliferation of segments in the lineage of the Bedouin of Cyrenaica." In *People and cultures of the Middle East*, vol. 1, edited by Louise E. Sweet, 363–98. New York, 1970.
Qasem	A. M. Qasem. "A judicial experiment in Libya: Unification of civil and shariat courts." *ICLQ* 3 (1954): 134–37.
Rosen	L. Rosen. "Equity and discretion in a modern Islamic legal system." *LSR*, vol. 15, no. 2 (1980–81): 217–45.
Schacht, *Introduction*	J. Schacht. *An introduction to Islamic law*, 2d ed. Oxford, 1966.
Schacht, *Nigeria*	J. Schacht. "Islam in northern Nigeria." *SI* 8 (1957): 123–46.
Schacht, *Papers*	———. Joseph Schacht's Papers. Bodleian Library, Oxford. Files: "Islamic law in practice" and "East Africa."
Schacht, *Report*	———. "Report on the position of Muhammadan law in northern Nigeria." Colonial Social Science Research Council Committee on Law and Land Tenure (50) 1 28209/233/50 DC52926/1, Oxford, 19 September 1950. In Schacht, Papers. File: "Islamic law in practice."
Schacht & Layish	———. [A. Layish]. *EI*², s.v. "Maḥkama," 4i, fasc. 99–100, pp. 22–25.
Shaham	R. Shaham. "The Muslim family in Egypt 1900–1955: Continuity and change. A study based on the *sijill*s of the *sharīʿa* courts." Ph.D. diss., Hebrew University, Jerusalem. In preparation.
Shinar	P. Shinar. *Islam maghrébin contemporain: Bibliographie annotée*, Paris, 1983.
Shukrī	Muḥammad Fuʾād Shukrī. *al-Sanūsiyya dīn wa-dawla*. [Cairo], 1948.
Shuqayr	Naʿʿūm Shuqayr. *Taʾrīkh sīnāʾ*. Cairo, 1916.
Simon	Rachel Simon. "The Ottoman involvement in Libya during the war with Italy (1911–1919)," Ph.D. diss.,

	Hebrew University, Jerusalem, 1983.
Smith	W. C. Smith. *Islam in modern history*. New York, 1963.
Stern	Gertrude Stern. *Marriage in early Islam*. London, 1939.
Stewart, *Cases*	F. H. Stewart. *Cases in Sinai Bedouin law*. Wiesbaden. Forthcoming.
Stewart, *Texts*	———. *Texts in Sinai Bedouin law*. Pt. 1, *The texts in English translation*. Wiesbaden, 1988.
Stewart, *Tribe and law*	———. *A Bedouin tribe and its law*. Forthcoming.
Tucker	Judith E. Tucker. *Women in nineteenth-century Egypt*. Cambridge, 1985.
Wehr	H. Wehr. *A dictionary of modern written Arabic*, 3d ed. Edited by J. Milton Cowan. Beirut and London, 1974.
Ziadeh	N. A. Ziadeh. *Sanūsīyah: A study of a revivalist movement in Islam*. Leiden, 1968.

PERIODICALS

Listed in alphabetical order of the abbreviations used.

AAN	*Annuaire de l'Afrique du Nord*
AAS	*Asian and African Studies (Israel)*
AJCL	*The American Journal of Comparative Law*
BBRISMES	*Bulletin of the British Society for Middle Eastern Studies*
BRR	*Birzeit Research Review*
BSOAS	*Bulletin of the School of Oriental and African Studies*
CA	*Current Anthropology*
ICLQ	*International and Comparative Law Quarterly*
ICLR	*International and Comparative Law Review*
IJMES	*International Journal of Middle East Studies*
JAL	*Journal of African Law*
JAOS	*Journal of the American Oriental Society*
JCLIL	*Journal of Comparative Legislation and International Law*
LSR	*Law & Society Review*
MES	*Middle Eastern Studies*
MḤ	*ha-Mizraḥ he-Ḥadash* (The New East)

MM	*Maghreb Machrek*
MSH	*al-Muḥāmāt al-Sharʿiyya* (a monthly law journal published in Cairo)
RC	*Rivista Coloniale*
RGMEOGC	*Revista Giuridica del Medio ed Estremo Oriente e Giustizia Coloniale*
RSO	*Revista degli Studi Orientali*
SI	*Studia Islamica*
TAUSL	*Tel Aviv University Studies in Law*

Index

(Page numbers in italics indicate principle references. Unless indicated as appearing in the Index, all references to Arabic legal and technical terms appear in the Glossary)

* The Arabic *al-*, being a definite article, has been disregarded in alphabetization.